In Search of a Forgotten Architect: Stefan Sebök 1901–1941

Lilly Dubowitz

Architectural Association

In Search of a Forgotten Architect:
Stefan Sebök 1901–1942
Lilly Dubowitz

With essays by Éva Forgács
and Richard Anderson

AA Managing Editor: Thomas Weaver
AA Publications Editor: Pamela Johnston
Editorial Assistants: Mollie Claypool, Clare Barrett
AA Art Director: Zak Kyes
Design: Zak Group

Printed in Oberhausen by Printmanagement Plitt

ISBN 978-1-907896-21-7

AA Publications
36 Bedford Square
London
WC1B 3ES
T: +44 (0)20 7887 4021
F: +44 (0)20 7414 0783
publications@aaschool.ac.uk
www.aaschool.ac.uk/publications

This book is dedicated to the memory of Stefan Sebök,
a victim of two tyrannies, who never reached his full potential

Portrait of Stefan Sebök in Berlin, *c* 1928

István (Stefan) Sebök was a Hungarian-born architect who worked with Walter Gropius in Dessau and Berlin between 1927 and 1931. Reproductions of his drawings for theatres and other buildings appear in many postwar books on the Bauhaus, usually misattributed to Gropius, with hardly any mention of his name, background or the contribution he made to the innovative design work being carried out at the time. Exacerbating this amnesia, Sebök was forgotten not only by the architectural world, but also to a great extent by his family. He was my uncle – my father's youngest brother – but until relatively recently I was aware of very little beyond his family background, which of course is also mine.

Stefan was born in 1901 in Szolnok, Hungary, a medium-sized town approximately 100km east of Budapest which came to prominence with the building of the railways in the mid-nineteenth century. Stefan's father, my grandfather, Nándor Sebök, was a prosperous textile merchant and local councillor whose fashion warehouse, founded in 1888, occupied a key position in part of the town hall building in Szolnok's main square and featured prominently on many postcards of the town dating from the turn of the century. According to a newspaper article of 1928, his company was considered extremely innovative, both in its stock and in the way it was run; the article also comments on Nándor's great integrity as a businessman, particularly during the postwar inflationary period.

Stefan's mother, Matilda Reichenberg, was born in the Transylvanian town of Nagyvárad (now known as Oradea and part of Romania). Nagyvárad was also prosperous from the mid-nineteenth century on, and this wealth is still apparent today in its stunning, but unfortunately extremely poorly maintained art nouveau buildings. Besides Stefan, Matilda had two other boys – Gyula (my father) and Sándor – and two girls – Boriska and Serena. During the war she became a Red Cross nurse and received various decorations for her activities. From the few surviving letters to her children, from the descriptions of my family and from my own memories of my grandmother she was a matriarch who held a tight rein on her household.

Education was always a priority and before my grandfather's financial stability was shattered by bankruptcy (the result of his patriotic investment in what turned out to be volatile Hungarian war bonds) he followed the custom of other well-to-do families in sending his children to Austria or Germany for their further education. My father studied textile engineering in Reutlingen, while three of his siblings enrolled in courses in Dresden – two studied art while Stefan began his training as an architect. The only other thing I knew about Stefan was that after Dresden he went to work with Gropius at the Bauhaus school in Dessau and later lived and worked in Moscow. I had no idea what he did there, and from the mid-1930s he seems to have completely disappeared off the map.

Above and overleaf: Stefan Sebök's student sketches of his hometown Szolnok, Hungary, 1923–24

Sebök family, 1905, with Stefan Sebök on the far left

Nagy Naptára

Above and overleaf:
Stefan Sebök, portraits of his father and mother (1924) and self-portrait (1917)

Family folklore has it that I met Stefan once, but as I was only 13-months-old at the time I obviously have no recollection of it. Nor can I rely on any memories of him from the rest of the family – when I was a child no one close to me ever seemed to talk about my uncle. In retrospect, though, this silence was understandable. In the fervently anti-Soviet climate of pre Second World War Hungary, people would have been too intimidated to mention any relative who lived in a communist country. Casting aside these fears, my father went to visit his brother in Moscow in 1937 while my mother and I joined my aunt and cousin at the Austrian lakes for our summer holiday. Although quite young, I remember the trip well, largely because of the vivid memories I still have of the present my father brought back for me – a remarkable nest of Russian dolls, which were then practically unknown in Hungary.

After the war, however, the situation changed dramatically. Hungary became part of the Eastern Bloc and an ally of the Soviet Union. It became acceptable – fashionable even – to have a relative living in Moscow. My mother asked a friend of my father's who often went to Moscow as a trade commissioner to look up Stefan's apartment. On finding the address he was told by a caretaker that Sebök and his family had left the building on the day the war broke out and had not been seen since. Curious about what had become of them, my mother and my aunt started to speak about Stefan and pull out faded old family photographs. A wide-eyed little boy seen alongside his brothers and sisters and parents was pointed out to me, in a photograph from 1905. Other pictures taken in Hungary showed him as an older child, while the pictures of Stefan as a grown-up had been posted to us from Germany. Our last photograph of him, dated 1932 and sent from Moscow, showed a confident young man sitting at a desk in front of an architectural drawing of a building I couldn't identify. The back of the photograph was inscribed, 'taken on our wedding anniversary in 1932'.

Four years after the end of the war, aged 18, I emigrated to Australia and like most survivors of the war I was encouraged to put the past behind me and try not to resuscitate old ghosts. For the next few years I more or less forgot about Stefan. In 1958 I returned to Europe and soon got married and started a family. It was not until 1976, while we were living in London, that I took the family to Hungary for the first time to introduce them to some of their roots. There I met up with my only surviving relative, and among many family stories and reminiscences she casually mentioned the Sebök–Gropius connection, showing me a catalogue featuring a building she thought Stefan had designed. She promised to see if there might be some more material among her papers, but died a couple of years after our visit without uncovering anything else.

Partly inspired by my own son's architectural studies I continued to buy and research books on the Bauhaus looking for any mention of Sebök's drawings or even just of his name. Nothing much turned up until 1995, when my husband was invited to a conference in Leipzig

Walter Gropius, Totaltheater, 1927, interior sketch view by Stefan Sebök

and decided to take a small detour to Dessau, armed with my family photographs. He showed them to the archivist there, who said that Stefan (or Istvan in Hungarian) Sebök was unknown to them, but further enquiries would be made. My husband then spent the rest of the day browsing through the archives and exhibitions. Leafing through a catalogue titled *Bauhaus Utopien* (1988), his eye was drawn to an image of a spiralling, conical structure, reminiscent of a project our son did as a student. He decided to buy the book for him. When flicking through the catalogue again on the train back to Leipzig he noticed a caption underneath the spiralling illustration that read: 'Durchkonstruiert von Stefan Sebök'. He had not only found an attributed work but, equally interesting, a short biography.[1] According to this, Stefan Sebök was born in Hungary in 1904 but lived abroad from 1919. He obtained his degree (*Diplom-Ingenieur*) from the Technische Hochschule (TU) in Dresden and his final diploma project was for a 'Tanztheater für Dresden'. From 1928 he was employed in Walter Gropius's architectural office in Dessau, where he participated in the design of the Totaltheater (Total Theatre) for Erwin Piscator and other competition projects. His work with Moholy-Nagy was also mentioned. In 1930 he moved to the Soviet Union where he worked with El Lissitzky and Moisei Ginzburg.

When I contacted Dessau to find out the location of the various works listed in the catalogue they suggested that most of them had ended up in the Gropius archives in the Busch-Reisinger Museum at Harvard. These, they thought, consisted of just a few drawings for the Totaltheater. They also referred me to another catalogue, *Wechselwirkungen*[2] (1986), which offered a slightly more detailed biography and list of works, many of which were illustrated. According to this second biography, Sebök studied art history in Vienna and gave a lecture at the Kupferstichkabinett on the Viennese baroque. It added that he probably died in the Hungarian Resistance movement at the end of the war.

Although I was aware that some of the biographical detail in both catalogues was incorrect it was at least a starting point on a trail. The first opportunity I had to visit the Busch-Reisinger archives at Harvard was in 2001. I was accompanied on this and many future trips by my husband, who supplied moral support and acted as a kind of photo archivist. The 'few drawings' there turned out to be over 100 full-scale architectural renderings of which around 70 had Sebök's signature. They were interleaved with other variations, obviously by the same hand, which had been crossed through and labelled 'superseded'. Many of the drawings related to the Totaltheater, designed in 1927 for the 'epic theatre' director, Erwin Piscator, who had run the Volksbühne in Berlin since 1924. Piscator was famed for his productions employing vast crowds, with actors mingling with the audience and mixing live performance with projected images and animated cartoons. Because he pitched his productions at a populist scale he wanted the building's design to accommodate large numbers of people. This, in turn, precipitated the elimination of the

1
Stefan Kraus, *Bauhaus Utopien: Arbeiten auf Papier* (Berlin: Hatje Cantz, 1988), p 350.

2
Hubertus Gassner, *Wechsel Wirkungen: Ungarische Avantgarde in der Weimarer Republik* (Marburg: Jonas Verlag, 1986), p 585.

Stefan Sebök in Dessau, *c* 1927, photo Gyula Pap

proscenium arch, forcing actors and audience closer together. I learned more about the theatre's background and history from Emilie Norris, deputy curator of the Busch-Reisinger Museum and keeper of the Gropius archives, who had written her 1992 Harvard MA thesis on the project.[3] According to her, Piscator's aim was to promote the communist cause through theatre, and his plays dealt with great economic and political themes. To lend the drama the authority of a documentary, images and captions were projected as a backdrop to the live performance. Existing theatre buildings, such as the Volksbühne proved very cumbersome to adapt to this kind of performance, and so in 1926 he started to think of his own purpose-built theatre – a 'theatre machine', as he put it, which would be equipped with the most modern lighting techniques and incorporate movable stages and projection facilities.

Norris notes that Gropius, unlike Piscator, considered himself apolitical and had little personal experience of theatre design: he was most likely attracted to the project because it offered an opportunity to use architecture and technology to shape the experience of theatre audiences and incorporate the latest techniques in lighting and projection. Norris has also analysed how the design was influenced by philosophical movements in Berlin and Dessau at the time, as well as by other theatre, art and architectural proposals: 'While Moholy had a general influence in light, colour and shape, two of his younger associates from Hungary, Farkas Molnar and Stefan Sebök, were important to the actual theatre project in very direct ways. In 1924 Molnar had designed a "U-Theater" with multiple and moving stages extending into the audience; these designs were incorporated into Carl Fieger's preliminary drawings for the project. The other, Stefan Sebök, did the large majority of the architectural drawings. Ise Gropius noted in her diary that Fieger's preliminary design had been unsatisfactory and Gropius gave the task to Sebök, with a much more satisfactory result.'

Sebök probably had the greatest influence on the design largely because of the formal similarity between his Tanztheater (Dance Theatre) and the Totaltheater. As Norris explains, 'Sebök's drawing for the Dresden Tanztheater (executed as a student before he ever met Gropius) shows the same assembly of mathematical shapes so that volumes overlap or circumscribe each other in careful alignment.' The design was presented to Piscator in June 1927, although there is no record of exactly which version this was, and Gropius's office continued to experiment with variations on the project over the following few months. The final design, built as a model and with drawings by Sebök, was a constructivist elliptical theatre with a parabolic roof and mechanisms for providing three different stages, all of which could be changed during the performance, as could the seats. But Piscator's theatre was never built. Even before a site had been found, the funding for it evaporated in the financial chaos following the 1929 Black Friday crash. Nevertheless, unbuilt, it remains one of the keystone projects for modern architectural design.

3
Emilie Norris, 'Walter Gropius 1927 Totaltheater Design: A Synthesis of Innovative Ideas', Harvard University MA thesis, 1992.

Stefan Sebök, *c* 1927

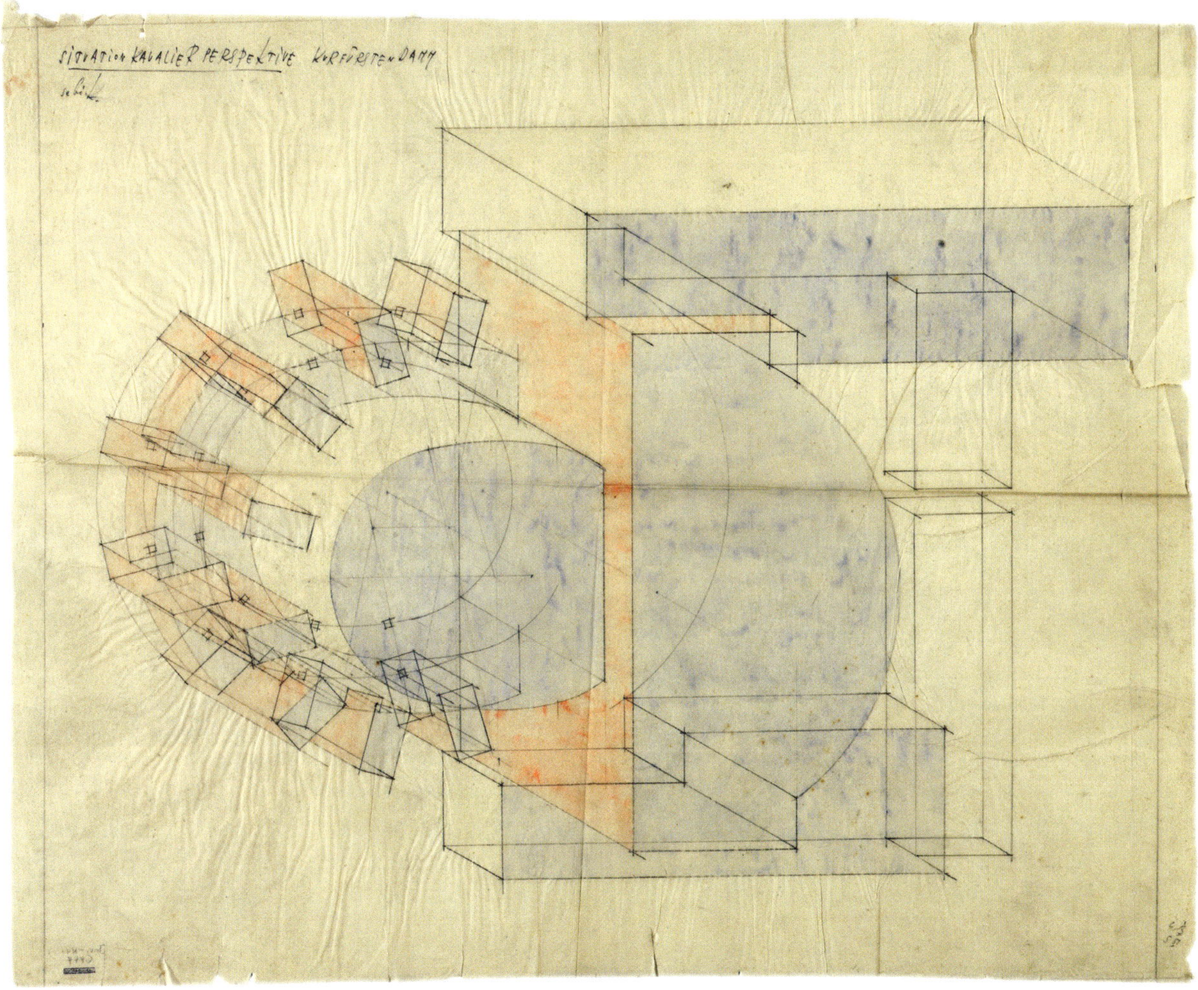

Above and overleaf: Walter Gropius, Totaltheater, 1927, plans, section and perspectival views by Stefan Sebök

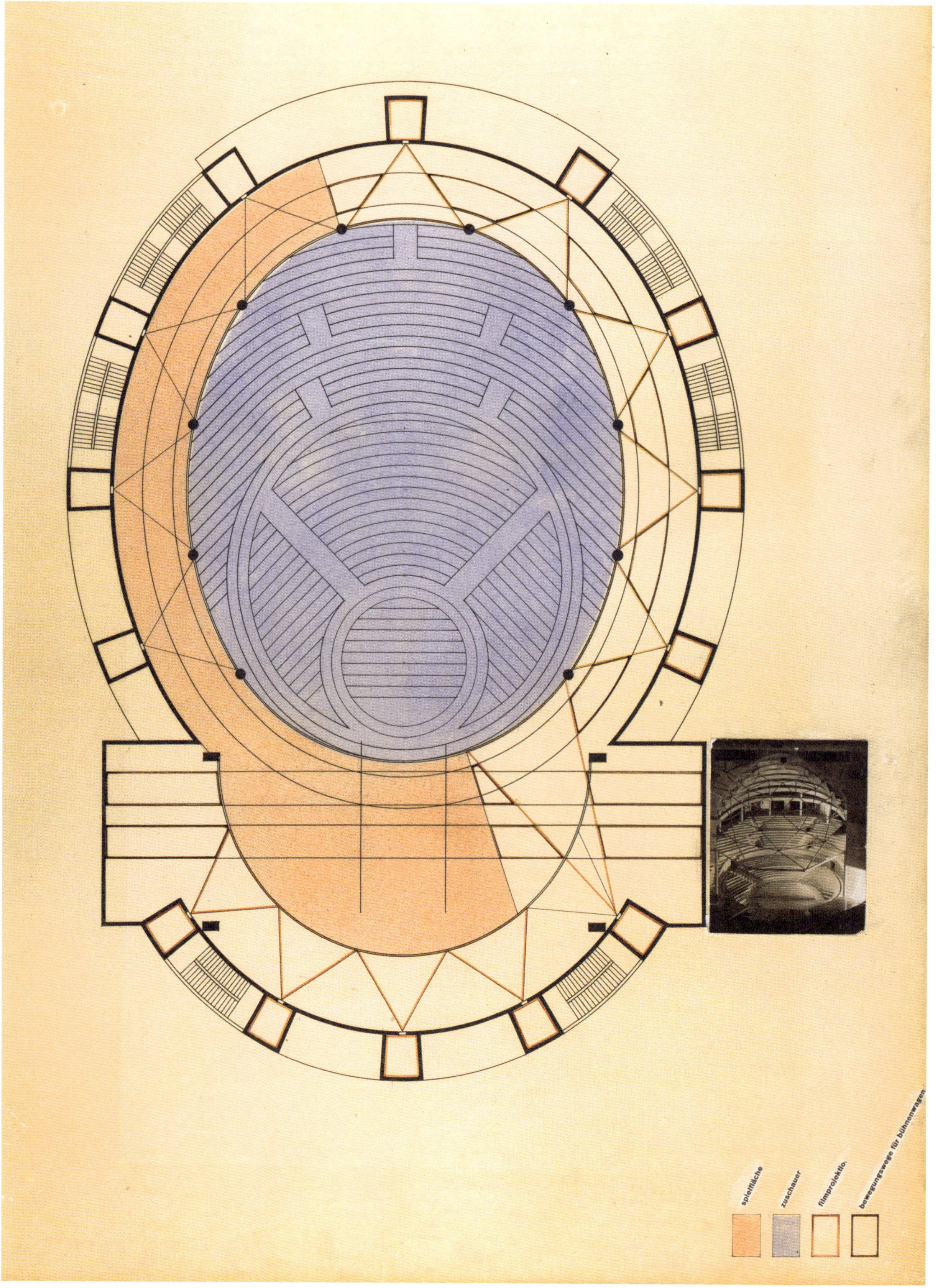
spielfläche
zuschauer
filmprojektio.
bewegungswege für bühnenwagen

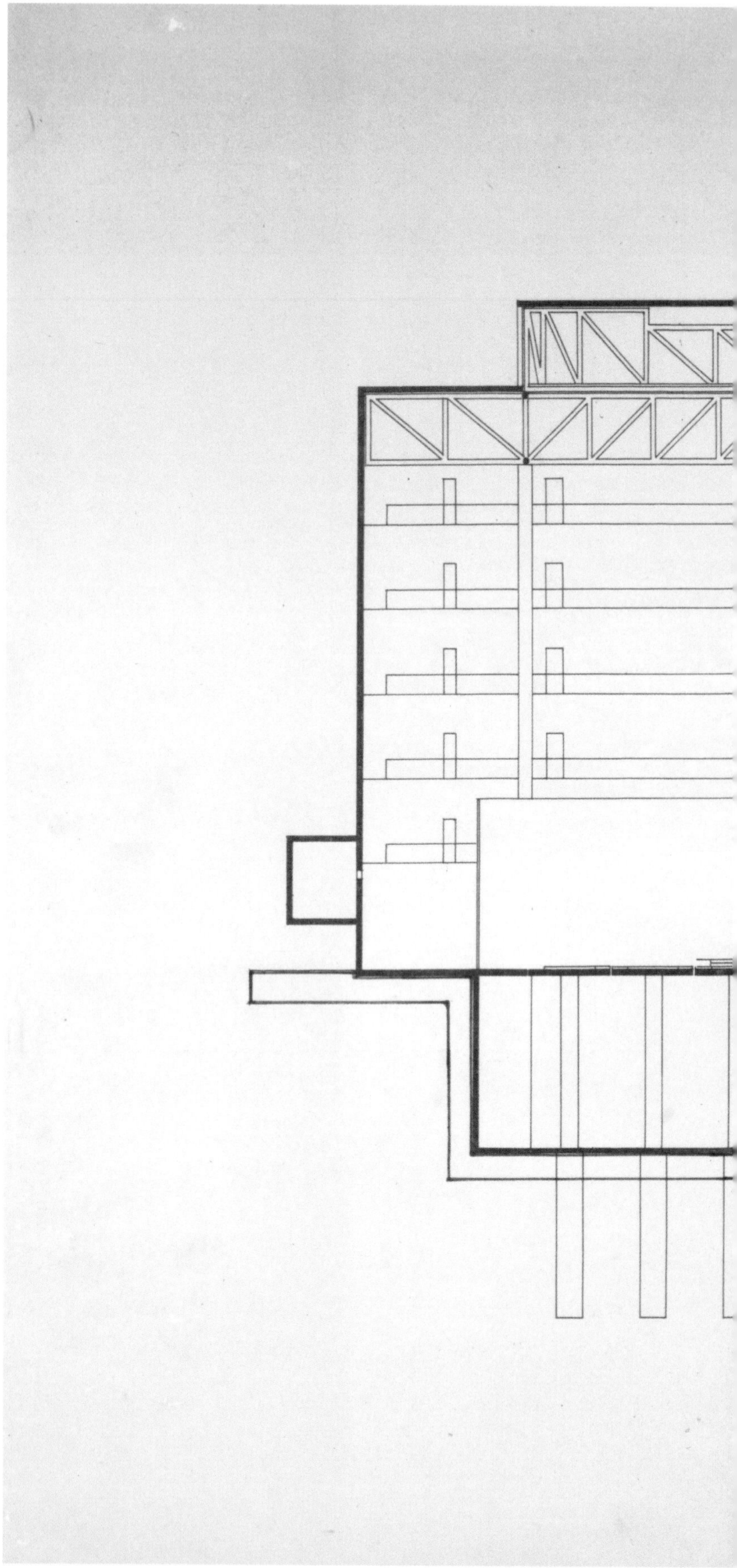

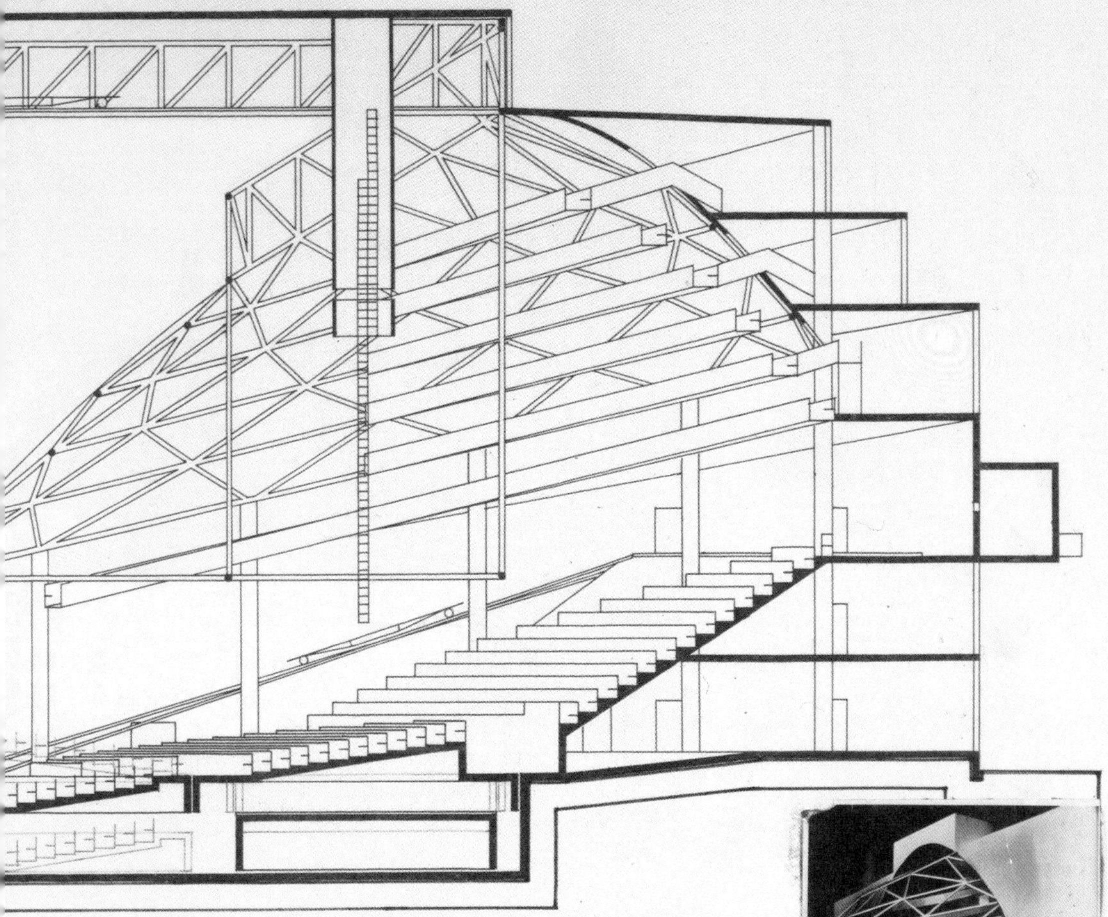

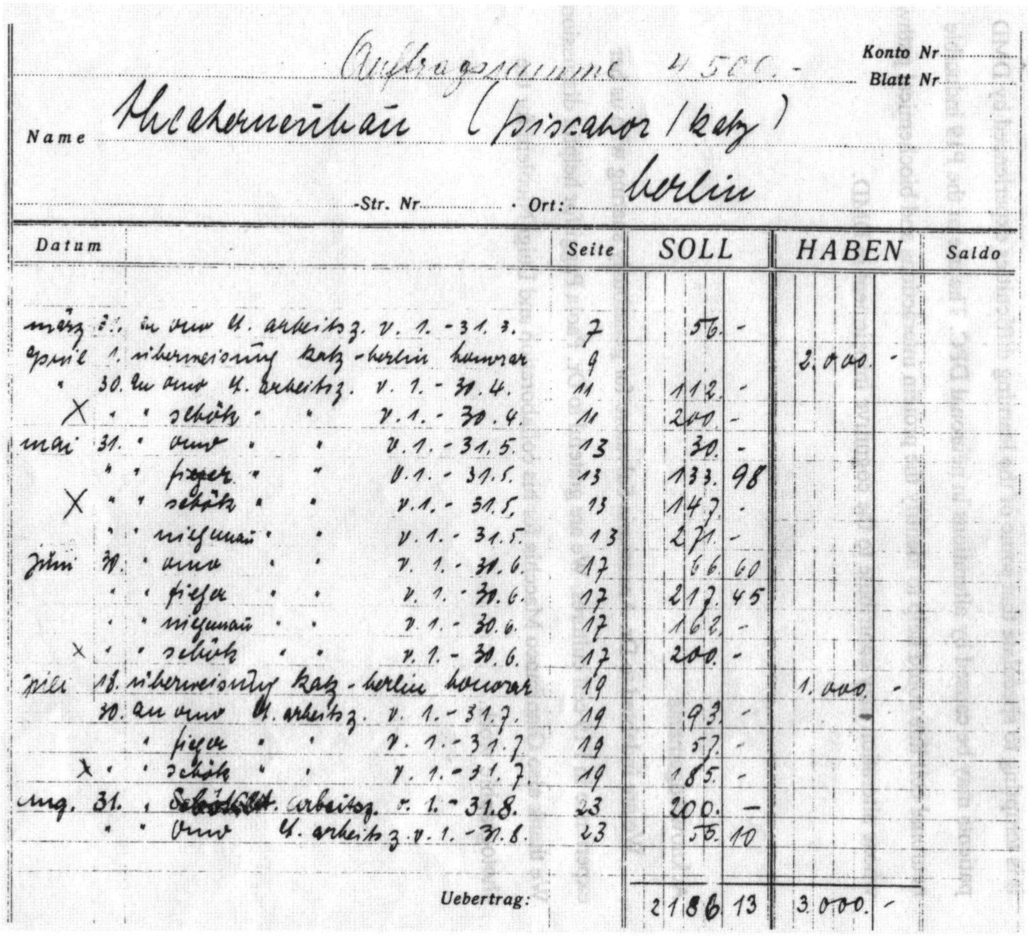

Auftragssumme 4 500.-

Konto Nr.

Blatt Nr.

Name theaterneubau (piscator / katz)

-Str. Nr. · Ort: berlin

Datum		Seite	SOLL	HABEN	Saldo
märz 31.	an arch. u. arbeitsz. v. 1.-31.3.	7	56.-		
april 1.	überweisung katz-berlin honorar	9		2.000.-	
" 30.	an arch. u. arbeitsz. v. 1.-30.4.	11	112.-		
X " "	sebök " " v. 1.-30.4.	11	200.-		
mai 31.	" arch. " " v. 1.-31.5.	13	30.-		
" "	fieger " " v. 1.-31.5.	13	133.98		
X " "	sebök " " v. 1.-31.5.	13	147.-		
" "	niegemann " " v. 1.-31.5.	13	271.-		
juni 30.	" arch. " " v. 1.-31.6.	17	66.60		
" "	fieger " " v. 1.-30.6.	17	217.45		
" "	niegemann " " v. 1.-30.6.	17	162.-		
x " "	sebök " " v. 1.-30.6.	17	200.-		
juli 18.	überweisung katz-berlin honorar	19		1.000.-	
30.	an arch. u. arbeitsz. v. 1.-31.7.	19	93.-		
"	fieger " " v. 1.-31.7.	19	57.-		
X " "	sebök " " v. 1.-31.7.	19	185.-		
aug. 31.	" ~~sebök~~ arbeitsz. v. 1.-31.8.	23	200.-		
" "	arch. u. arbeitsz. v. 1.-31.8.	23	55.10		
	Uebertrag:		2186.13	3.000.-	

Payroll slip for Stefan Sebök from the office of Walter Gropius

As with a number of other highly significant, though unrealised, modernist design proposals (notably Vladimir Tatlin's Monument to the Third International or Le Corbusier's Dom-ino frame), the Totaltheater has manifested itself more recently through a virtual reconstruction – the architect Javier Navarro de Zuvillaga built a detailed digital model of the building for the 2004 'Absent Architectures of the Twentieth Century' exhibition in Madrid. In making the model Navarro, like Norris, commented on the fact that in spite of the large number of drawings of the theatre, the plans lacked consistency or any descriptive text. To make his reconstruction he therefore relied on three sets of plans, but found contradictory information between one drawing and another – 'the project was an amalgamation on the one hand of Piscator's requirements and on the other of the theatrical projects previously created by Farkas Molnar, Andreas Weininger and Stefan Sebök... The drawings by Sebök in particular have such an emphasis on the diagrammatic and kinetic aspects that we cannot help but conclude that his conception resembled Moholy-Nagy's Light-Space Modulator, an apparatus that could manipulate light and space with an emphasis on overlapping planes and forming and re-forming with light, an end in itself, thus ultimately drama had little to do with it.'[4]

When you get face to face with the Totaltheater drawings you can very quickly see, as both Norris and Navarro discovered, that their sheer number obscures the fact that collectively it is still very difficult to accurately discern the details of the building. This is also complicated by the sequence in which the plans are presented – an ordering of drawings originally established by the Gropius office and maintained by the Busch-Reisinger Museum. Later, when I asked the Bauhaus archive in Berlin where I could find more documentation on the project, or descriptive text, the answer was always that there wasn't any. This, it turned out, was only partially true, as there are some descriptions in an unpublished manuscript by Gropius called the 'Universales Ei Theater' (Universal Egg Theatre) – evidently the name of the project before Moholy-Nagy's term, 'Total Theatre', came to be adopted.[5] In this text Gropius describes the building as being constructed from concrete, glass, steel and other metals.

While still at Harvard, I came across more archival material that extended beyond the Totaltheater and covered other architectural projects by Sebök. These included a number of drawings for a community housing proposal – the Dr Aschrott Wohlfahrtshaus – as well as a school in Schwarzerden that was the brainchild of a Dr Volger, a physician especially interested in incorporating aspects of health into building design.[6] Accordingly, the orientation and form of the school take into account the direction of the sun and sources of maximum light, as described in a brief accompanying the drawings. Interestingly, in contrast to the Totaltheater, there is a lot of documentation on how this project was supposed to be built. The archive has the initial architectural drawings as plans and also a final, fabulous perspective drawing. Like nearly all the buildings that Sebök was involved in, it too was never built.

4
Javier Navarro de Zuvillaga, 'Walter Gropius: Teatro Total de Walter Gropius' in *Arquitecturas ausentes del siglo XX* (Madrid: Rueda, 2004).

5
Nachlass Walter Gropius, Bauhaus-Archiv, Berlin, II/26.

6
Winfried Nerdinger, *Der Architekt Walter Gropius* (Berlin: Mann, 1996), p 148.

Walter Gropius, competition entry for a school in Schwarzerden-Rhön, 1930
Above: Cover of project description. Right and overleaf: Elevation and perspectival views by Stefan Sebök

During this first visit to the Busch-Reisinger Museum I also met its director, Peter Nisbet, who took the line that Sebök was a draughtsman who would have had no involvement in the overall design of the structures that he drew. Although Nisbet was aware of the similarities between Sebök's Tanztheater diploma project and Gropius's Totaltheater, his explanation was that Sebök had probably worked as an intern with Gropius during his student days and absorbed ideas from him into his school projects. Later that year, however, my next visit along the archival trail, to the Bauhaus in Berlin, proved this theory most unlikely. During a subsequent visit to the Bauhaus I also found among the Ise Gropius diaries detailed records of Sebök's first encounter with Walter Gropius.[7] The entry for 1 April 1927 reads: 'Today an apparently very talented young architect came to see Gropius. Although his contract with Mendelsohn was nearly finalised, on seeing the Bauhaus he was so entranced with it that he would very much like to work here. As he is very involved with the problems of theatre design and as this is very topical in the office right now, Gropius wants to take him on.' Why theatre design was topical is also well documented in the diaries. An earlier entry on 12 March 1927 reads: 'discussion with Erwin Piscator from the Volksbühne who is planning a new theatre. The finance should be available for it. Mendelsohn and Hartig are bidding for it but this is not certain and one has the feeling that Piscator would prefer to hand it over to Gropius.' The next relevant entry is on 27 March 1927: 'Piscator gave a definitive offer for his project.' It would appear that apart from his attraction to the Bauhaus, young Sebök had got wind of Piscator's change of intention and wasted no time in trying to follow the theatre project from Mendelsohn to Gropius. Ise Gropius also notes, on 27 May 1927, that after 'the initial plan with Fieger [another Gropius associate] failed to satisfy the rather difficult brief, Gropius worked with Sebök today on the theatre project, at last a good solution was found to the apparently nearly insoluble problem.'

Following up a lead in the *Wechselwirkungen* catalogue about a letter from Sebök to Gropius, I visited the Harvard University library where Gropius's own correspondence is housed. Unexpectedly, this search drew a complete blank. There were many letters to Gropius and copies of some he had written, but not a single one relating to Sebök or to anybody in Russia. While in Boston I telephoned Eva Forgács, an art historian recommended to me by the Bauhaus in Dessau, to see whether she knew where this correspondence might be found. She thought, as did the Harvard librarian, that the letters relating to Russia were never passed on by Gropius. It was difficult to determine whether this was because of the 1950s McCarthyite purges against anyone with communist sympathies or for other personal reasons. Gropius may well have destroyed them long before he reached the United States. In one of his biographies he mentions how difficult it is to go through life and discard all the things that one has treasured and kept over the years. Forgács suggested that Sebök might have gone to Moscow with Hannes Meyer.

7
Ise Gropius, Bauhaus-Archiv, Berlin, Inv Nos BA1998/54, 1998/55.

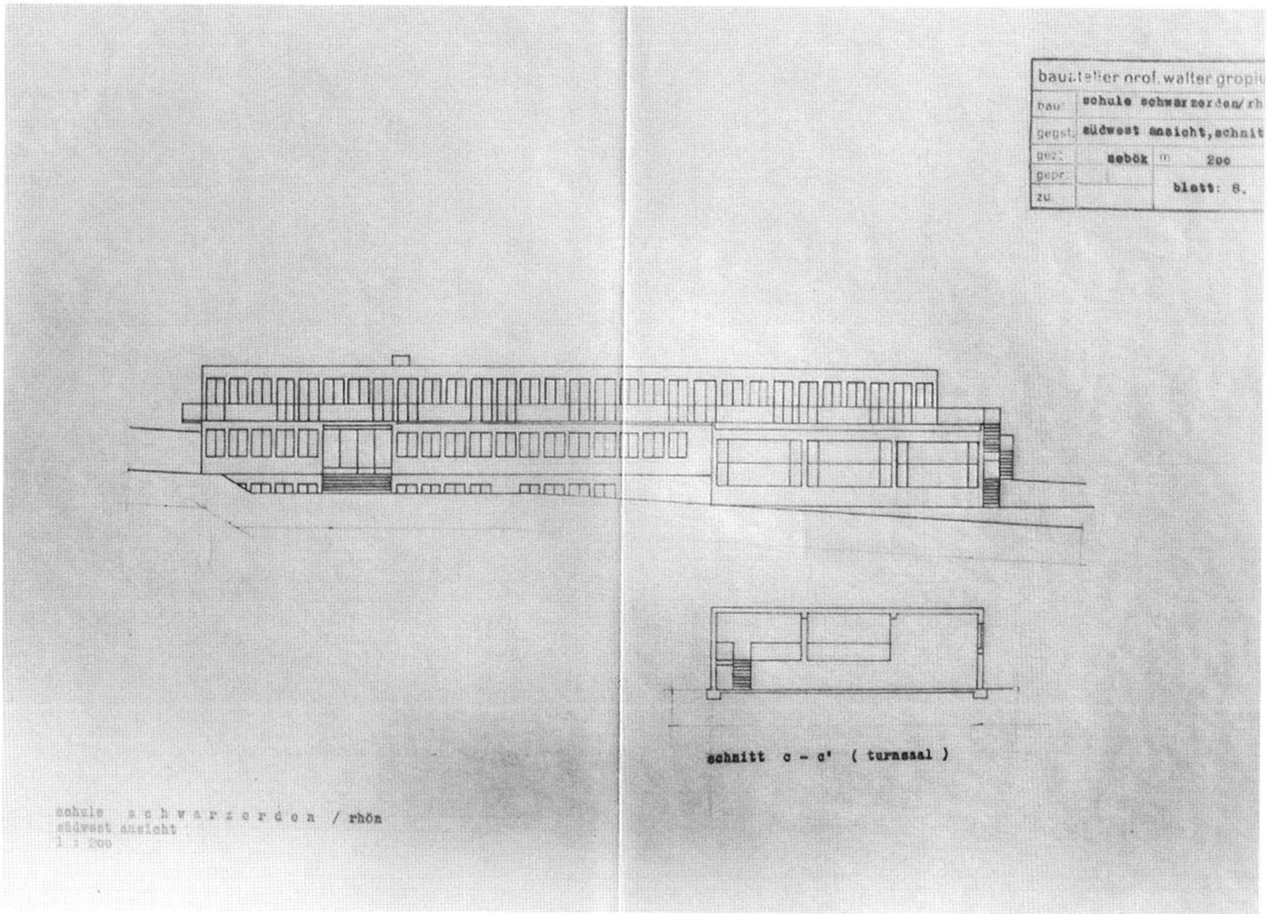
bau:atelier prof. walter gropiu
bau: schule schwarzerden/rh
gegst. südwest ansicht, schnit
gez: sebök m 200
gepr.
zu.
blatt: 8.
schnitt c – c' (turnsaal)
schule s c h w a r z e r d e n / rhön
südwest ansicht
1 : 200

Walter Gropius, competition entry for Aschrott Community Centre (top) and scheme for Karlsruhe-Dammerstock (bottom)
Sketch and perspective views by Stefan Sebök

When Gropius left for Berlin, Meyer took over as director of the Bauhaus, but was forced to leave in 1930 because of his leftist views. Shortly afterwards he went to Moscow with a group of young architects, the so-called Red Brigade. Forgács recalled a book featuring essays by the art historian Magdalena Droste and others and seemed to remember seeing Sebök in a group photograph in this book. She also thought there were more documents related to this Red Brigade in the Getty library in Los Angeles.

This assumption, unfortunately, produced no new leads – the following year, when I visited the Getty Research Institute with Forgács, there was nothing about Sebök in their archives; nor could we find him in any of the pictures. Forgács did, however, make a recommendation that later led to one of the most important turning points in my search: she suggested that on my next trip to Hungary I should try to meet László Moholy-Nagy's nephew, Levente Nagy, who might be able to offer more help. After a number of calls and letters, I met up with Levente in July 2001 in an old art nouveau cafe in Budapest. At that time he was over 70, yet still very active and really impressive. He had also amassed a comprehensive personal collection of his uncle's writings and books. Though he had very little knowledge of Sebök he was still able to offer some interesting suggestions. Crucial among these was his idea that Sebök, who had apparently disappeared without trace in Russia, might have suffered a similar fate to his own uncle, Akos – László Moholy-Nagy's brother and a wartime correspondent in Japan for the Soviet news agency TAAS. On his return to the USSR Akos was arrested as a spy and executed. Levente suggested that I should contact his cousin, Erwin Nagy, who had unearthed all the KGB files on his father's trial and execution, which not only told him about the false charges, but also gave him information on his family about which he was completely unaware (as part of their interrogation prisoners had to give a detailed account of their whole family history). It was through this lead, and a visit to the KGB archives, that I was later able to discover not only Sebök's eventual fate and details of his work in the Soviet Union but also many other aspects of his life.

Before then, however, and on returning from Boston home to London, I immediately contacted the Bauhaus archive in Berlin to find out more about the material they held in their collection. The then director, Peter Hahn, was extremely helpful and suggested I come over for a visit. At the same time he forwarded two rather interesting documents. The first of these was a recent letter from Hubert Hoffmann, a Bauhaus contemporary of Sebök's, to the Hungarian art historian Eva Bajkay, in reply to some enquiries. Bajkay had been working on the *Bauhaus Utopia* exhibition catalogue and had wanted to know more about the drawings that Hoffmann had passed on to the Bauhaus and about the person (Sebök, as it turned out) who produced them. She writes that she tried to get some information from the Bauhaus but at the time they were completely unaware of who Sebök was or where he came from.

Above: Walter Gropius, vocational school, Berlin-Kopernick, interior view by Stefan Sebök
Right: Stefan Sebök, single-storey house, 1925

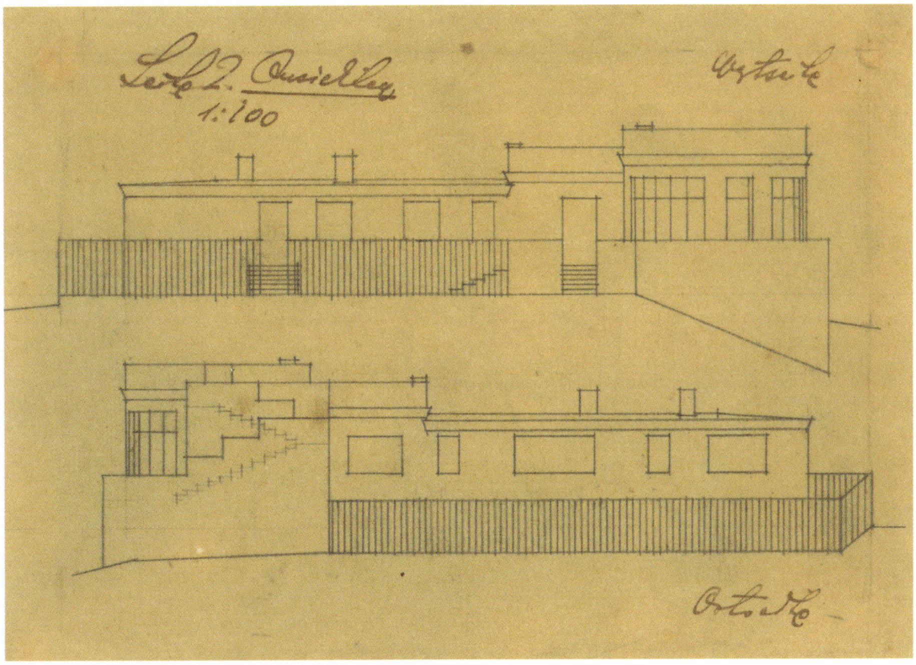
1:100

Cover of *Dokumentum*, with Stefan Sebök's article on Gret Palucca, 1926

PALUCCA

(Új tánc)

A táncot szemünkkel érzékeljük. Leírások a táncról csak megközelítő képet adhatnak. De megkísérlem néhány példának szavakba való átültetését. A példák anyaga a Palucca-csoportnak december 5-én a drezdai állami színházban lefolyt matinéjából való.

Ezt a színpadot táncra alkalmassá az tette, hogy le tudtak mondani színpadi lehetőségeiről: teljes mélyében és hosszában kiürítették. Szürkés színek és üresség.

Zene. Induló, menetelő tempóban. A tér megtisztul: egy szürke csoport precizül körüllépi a teret; tapogatódzva meghódítja háromdimenzióját.

Expanzív, lenyügöző gesztusok feloldják a testeket a térben, egyelőre még feszültség nélkül

Végül: a feszültség megszületik. Magyar ritmusú zene, motorikus akkordokkal. Palucca megadja a főmotivumot: egy erőteljesen kiugró mozdulatot. Feszültséggel telten előretör. Az erő viharosan belenyúl a térbe, egyre újabb irányokba, egyre újuló szenvedéllyel.

Hasonlat: emberentúli erők harca Buonarotti alakjaiban: a test mintha magábafogadná a dinamizmust, mintha kiszolgáltatná magát neki. Féktelen feszültségű mozdulatokat formál, nincs — még tökéletes — gesztusa se, fenséges bábunak látszik, melyet a túlvilágról mozgatnak, a legszélsőbb fizikai határokig pontosan működik.

Más példa: Dobtánc.

Vörös.

A zene csak lazán kötődik a tánchoz, csak hallható együttrezgés. Itt feloldhatlan optikai-akusztikai egységgé fejlődött. Menetelő ritmus, mely a vér lüktetésévé válik. Emelkedik, önmagát duplázza. Düh. Extázis. Felfokozott kifejezés. Önmagunk vidám elengedése, messze minden fülledt exotikumtól.

S Palucca legnagyobb értéke: a lendület. Feszültség és erő, mit nem hajít kifelé, de tudatosan felfog s leigáz. Játszva lenyügözött technika. Erőteljes ritmusok dallamos kötöttségben.

A szín is kifejezetten együttleng a tánccal. Palucca minden táncnak felfedezi a színét, aranysárgán fénylőt, ezüstösen hatalmasat, vöröset a dobhoz, kék menetelőt. Piros-kék mozdulat a lendületben. Szereti az egyszerű töretlen színeket melyek megfelelnek tánca örömteljességének. A szürkét is szereti, ellentétben a fojtott örömtelen színekkel.

Művészetének döntő törvényei, melyek itt is kiütköznek: a világosság, a tisztaság, a külső forma rendje. Technikája a legmagasabb fokon áll. A lendületben a részlet mozgása is precíz. A pillanatfelvétel matematikailag pontos vonalvezetést mutat.

Egy csoport megsokszorosítja a mozgást, eljátsza ennek skáláját: mindig áttekinthető szerkezet marad.

A formák tisztasága megadja az új tánc irányát: nem érzelmek illusztrációja, nem irodalmi ábrázolás. Palucca számára a tánc komoly játék, magánéletének is nélkülözhetetlen tartalma. **Öncéllá vált, a céloktól megszabadított életerő közvetlen formábaállása.**

Sebők István

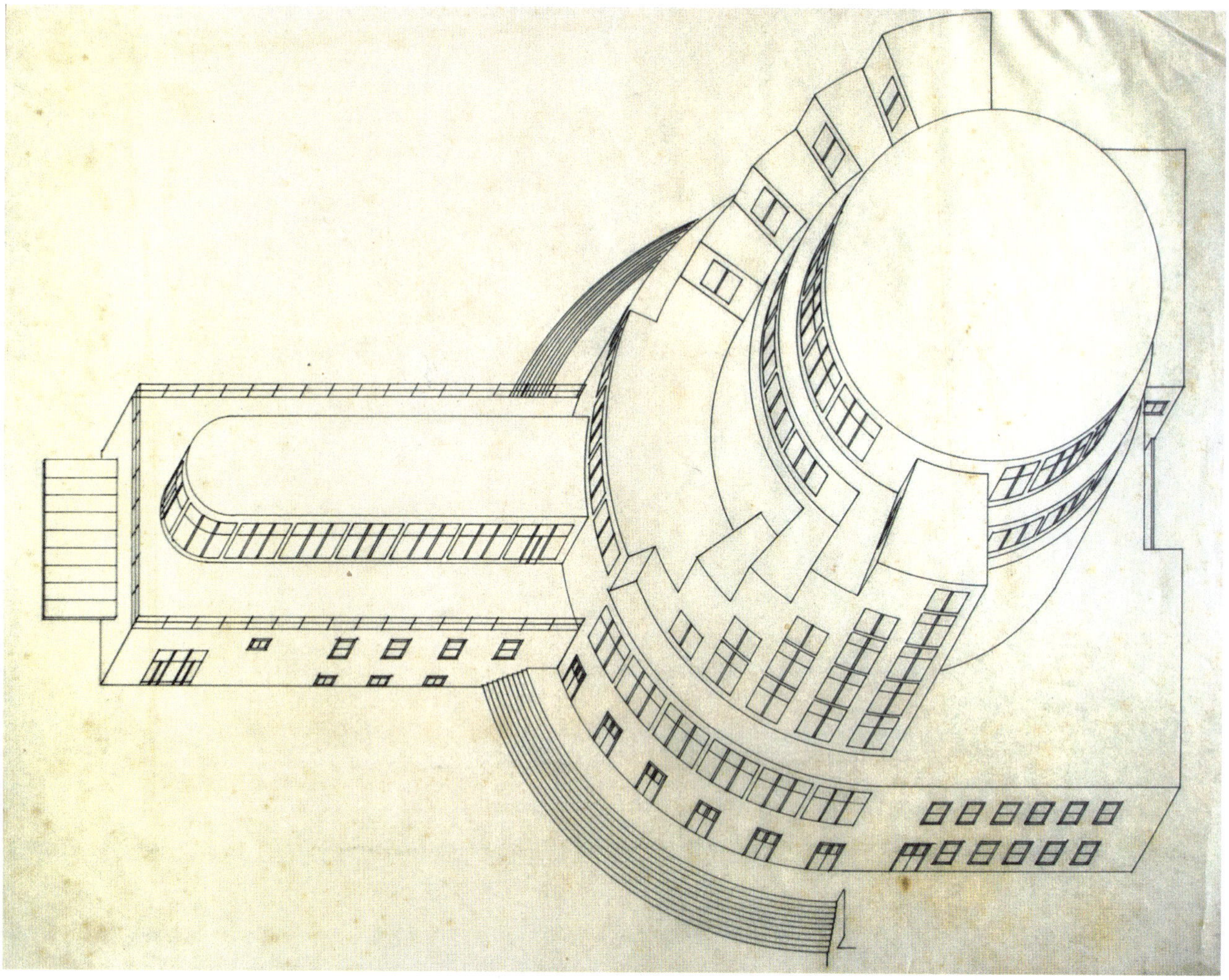

Above and overleaf: Stefan Sebök, Tanztheater diploma project, 1926–27

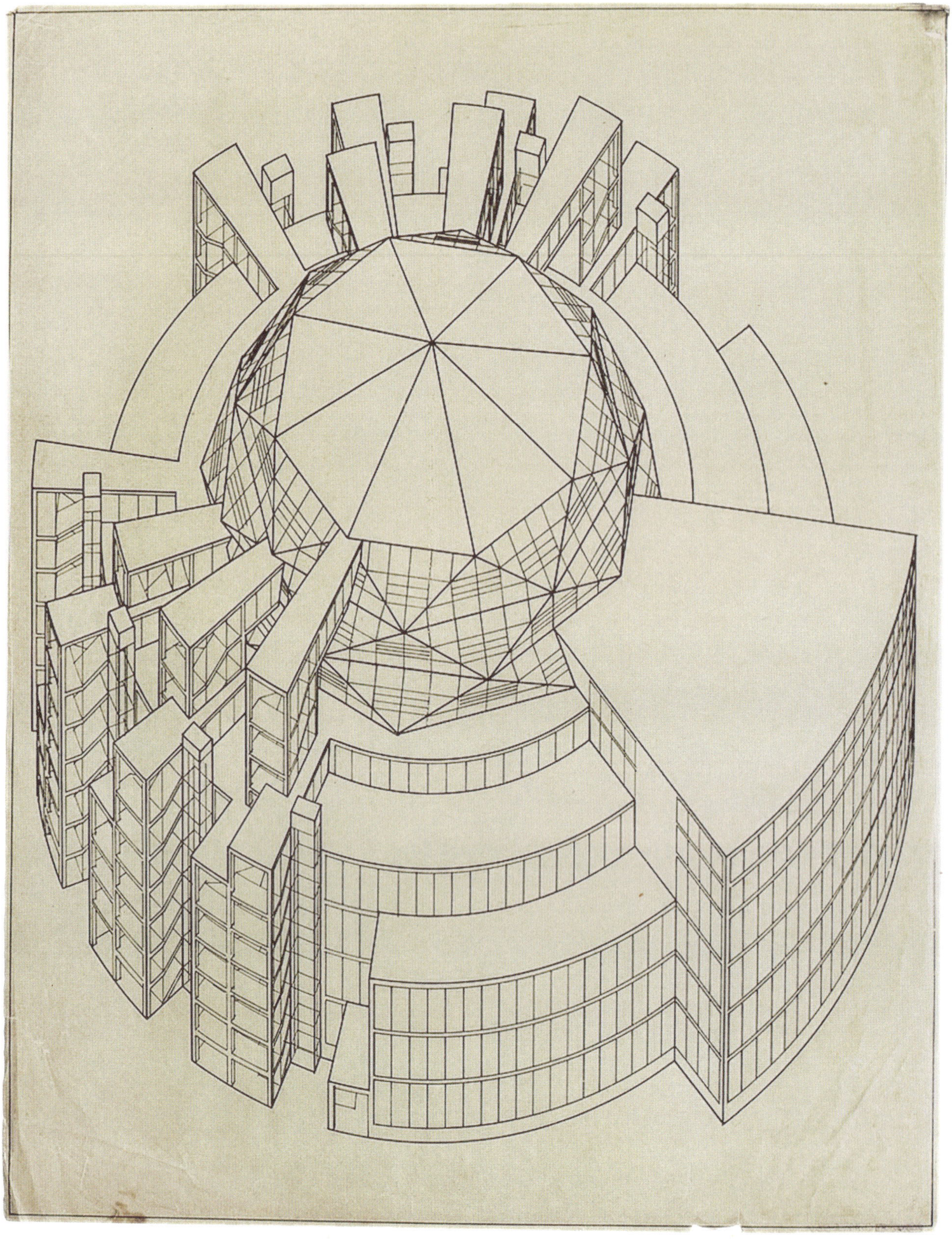

In his reply Hoffmann describes himself as Sebök's closest friend and relates how he had come into possession of a suitcase and three packages that Sebök had left with Gropius when he departed for Russia. On leaving for the United States, Gropius thought it best to pass these effects on to Hoffmann for safe-keeping until Sebök could reclaim them. Hoffmann's letter gives a brief biography and description of Sebök, suggesting that despite his leftist leanings he was never a member of the party 'as he didn't like collectivism'. He also comments on his extraordinary three-dimensional constructive abilities, his talents as a 'debater' and his absolute intellectual honesty. This was the first personal description I had managed to find of Sebök, even if it was written by a man who was then 81-years-old and whose memories of the 1920s, as he himself admitted, were somewhat clouded by the subsequent stormy events of the twentieth century. Despite this admission, the biographical details he supplied for Sebök have been quoted as factual in all subsequent publications referencing him.

Hahn also sent me an article about 'István Sebök' by the art historian Karin Wilhelm which had appeared in November 1988 in *Casabella*, the Italian architecture and design magazine. In this scholarly and extremely well-illustrated article (which strangely seems never to have been fully absorbed by either the archives in Dresden, Dessau or Berlin or by historians of the period), she details Sebök's importance in the evolution of modern theatre design and describes him not as an architect but as an engineer. I wrote to Wilhelm, and taking up Hahn's invitation, we both visited the Bauhaus archive in Berlin in November 2001. There we found a large number of architectural drawings, including Sebök's original proposal for his Tanztheater project in Dresden. These were produced sometime around 1926, the year before he joined Gropius's office.

Among the Sebök drawings at the Bauhaus were six very beautiful colour renderings and some further drawings of details done in pen on trace. Although originally it was thought they all belonged to one project, it seemed they actually offered two different variations. In the first one, the theatre appears in the round, with the roof presented as an articulated glass dome reminiscent of the Jena planetarium. A section illustrates the seating, which was mainly in the roof space – the idea being for the audience to look down on the performers. The second version of the project has a phalanx, presumably for ancillary facilities. Like Emilie Norris's own research, Wilhelm's article suggested that the Tanztheater design was probably influenced by the Hungarian architect Farkas Molnar's 1923 U-Theater. Looking at the drawings, while the exterior of Sebök's scheme bears similarities to Molnar's design, the inside contains a round stage rather than a rectangular proscenium. A couple of years later Sebök again reworked the project, probably in response to an offer to take part in an exhibition on theatre design in Magdeburg, into another proposal, the Problemtheater, which was shown in Switzerland and a number of other places (he is listed as a contributor to both exhibition catalogues).[8]

8
Hermann Ginzel, 'Das Problemtheater' in *Die Tribüne, Halbmonatsschrift der Städtischen Bühnen Köln*, 1929–30, p 543.

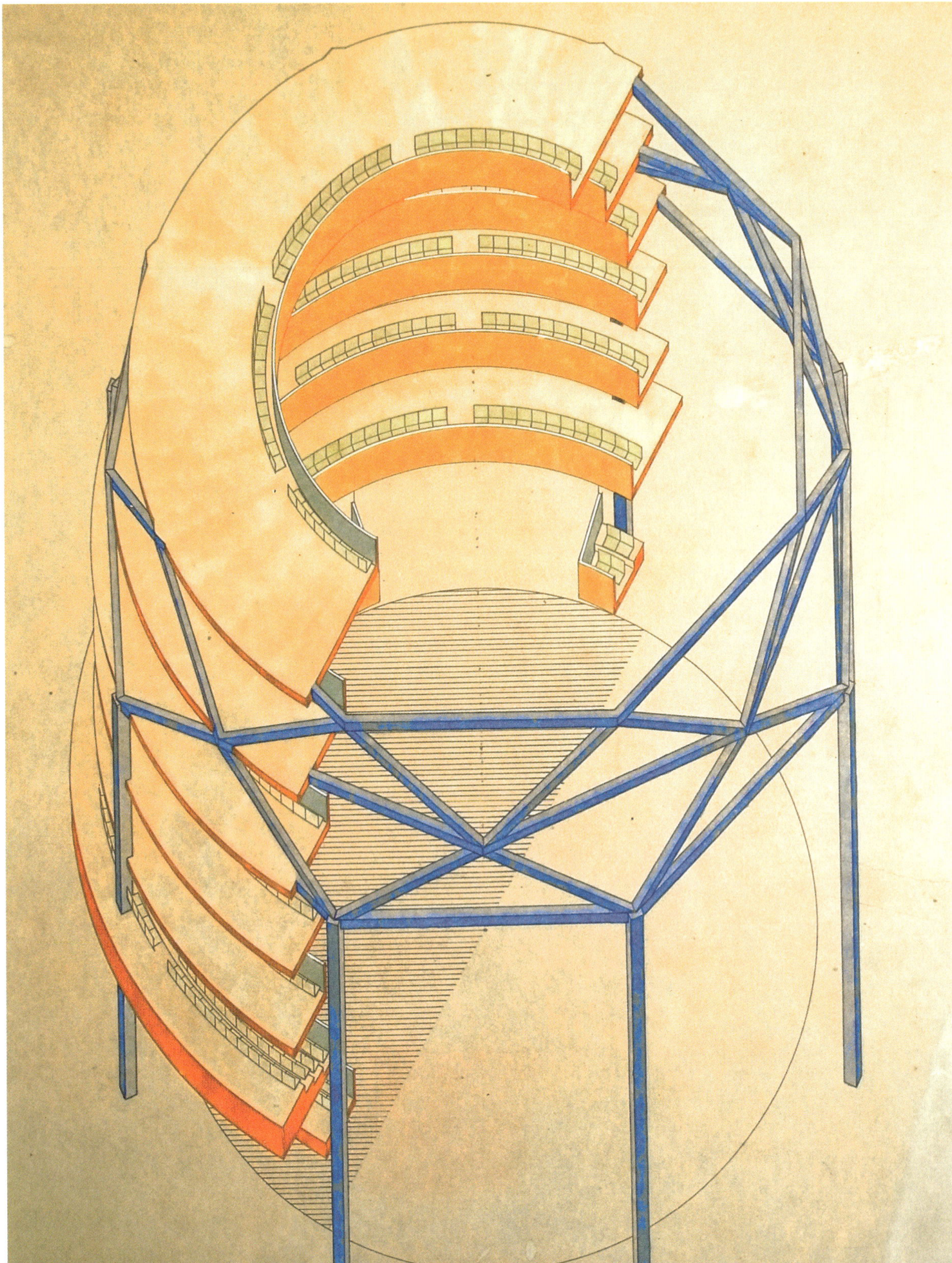

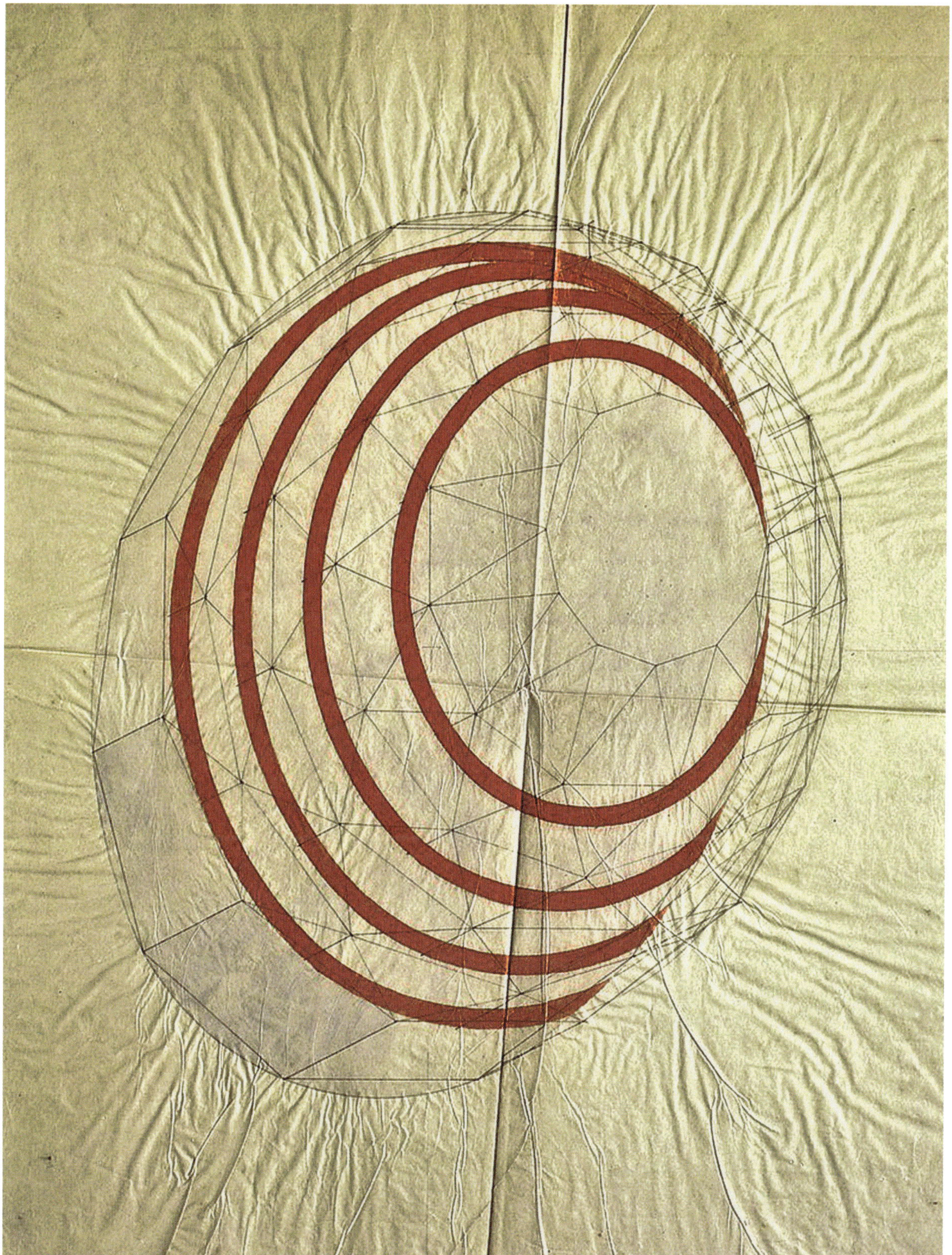

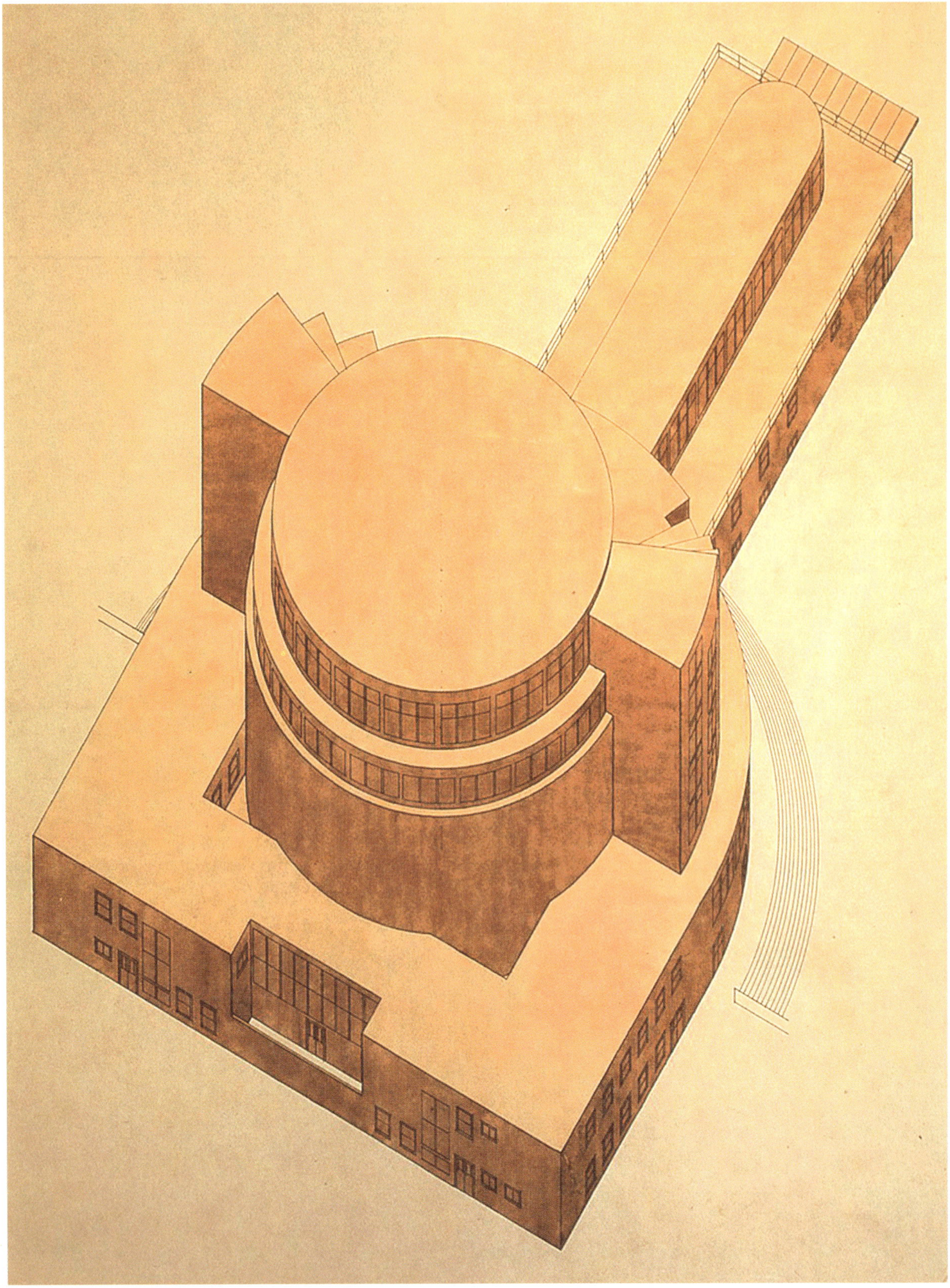

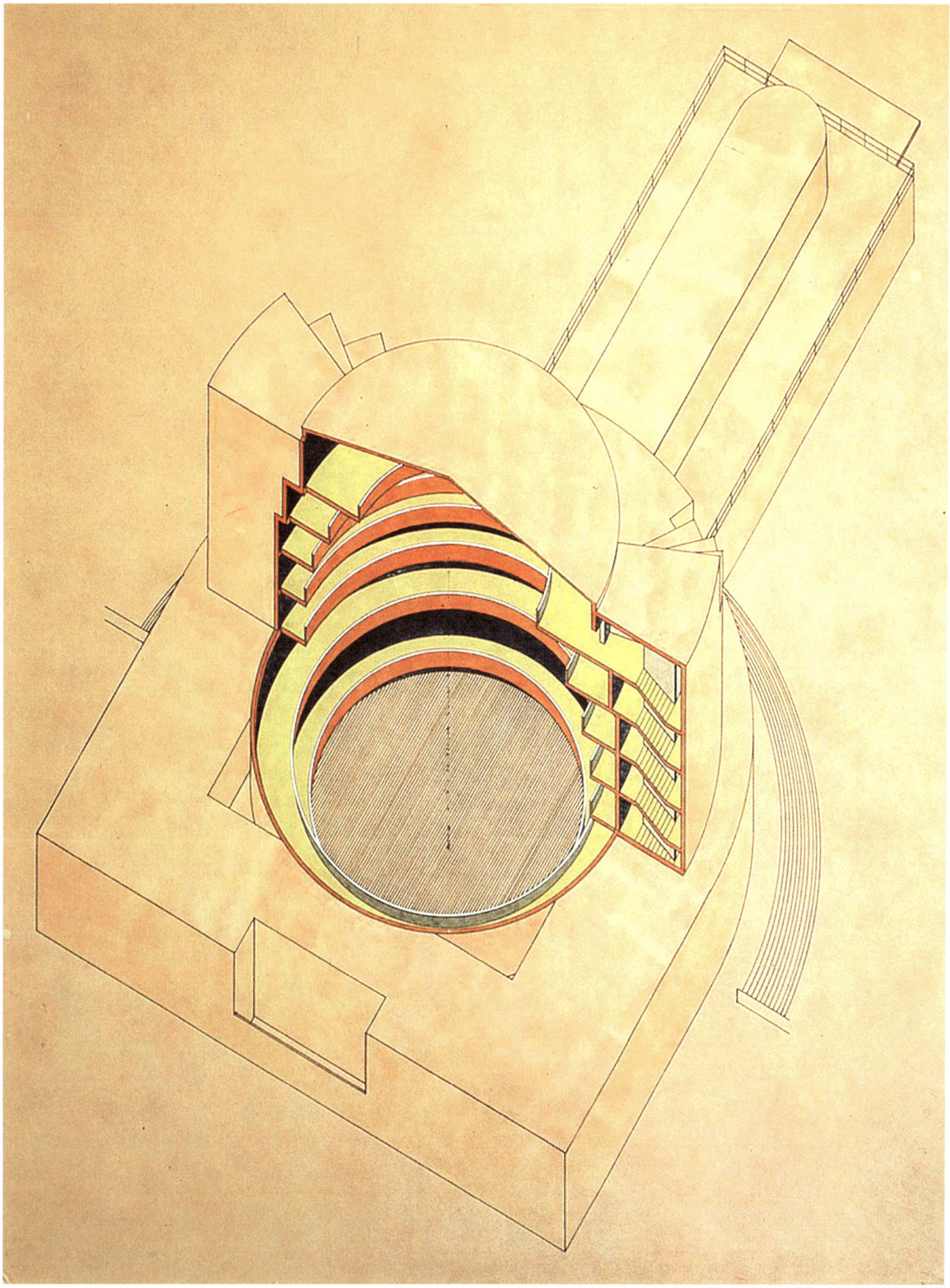

Stefan Sebök, Tanztheater diploma project variation, 1928
Right: Interior view displayed at the 'Problemtheater' exhibition in Cologne, from *Die Tribüne*

In the new version he tries to synthesise the two designs, combining an articulated glass roof and a phalanx. The exhibition was reviewed in *Die Tribune* by Hermann Ginzel, with Sebök's project highly praised. But although a drawing of his Tanztheater was illustrated in the review it shows only a view of the stage, so it is difficult to see which variation might finally have been exhibited.

In addition to the Tanztheater drawings the Bauhaus also had a large number of sketches, some bearing a Dresden Technische Hochschule stamp, showing that this work was examination material originating from his student days. The hand drawings ranged from studies of plants and nudes to portraits and sketches of buildings. The most poignant for me were two sketches of my grandparents and one which was probably of my mother. For Wilhelm, who had always regarded Sebök as an engineer, the breadth of this subject matter was particularly surprising, as it suggested that Sebök's training was more in accord with a classical education in art and architecture than it was with engineering.

During this visit Karin Wilhelm and I were also able to study another document uncovered in the Gropius correspondence file – a letter Sebök wrote to Gropius while he was living in Moscow.[9] The letter consisted of two parts. There are four pages that he wrote on 4 January 1936 and tried to send to Gropius via Moholy-Nagy, but the address was apparently incorrect and the letter was returned. Adding a further two pages, he re-sent it some months later via Farkas Molnar, who was then living in Budapest, and this time was successful. [10] The first part refers to some past difference of opinion on the direction that Soviet architecture was taking. It would appear that Gropius had voiced concerns and possibly considered Sebök naïve. In response, Sebök seems to have taken offence and suspended all contact for a couple of years. Now, in 1936, Sebök concedes that his views might have been simplistic, but at the same time he writes at considerable length in defence of Soviet society and on the progress, as he saw it, of Russian architecture. He is particularly fulsome in his praise of Ginzburg.

This letter gave me the first feeling for Sebök's voice, as well as some indications of what he might have been doing in the Soviet Union. One can sense his excitement at having joined the famous constructivist architects Ginzburg, the Vesnin brothers and El Lissitzky. It followed a somewhat dull period spent in the architectural department of the Soviet railways, where he was disenchanted with his work, but reluctant to quit as the job guaranteed him a comfortable apartment in a building reserved for the technical staff of the railway department. However, as he writes, by the end of 1935 he had the promise of work with El Lissitzky, which gave him the impetus to leave. Sebök also mentions that in 1932 he had married a woman called Mariya Levina, who was then studying chemistry in Moscow. From the letter it is clear that Gropius already knew Mariya, as Sebök refers to her as the person who helped Gropius translate his manuscript for the Palace of the Soviets project into Russian (later I found this translation, dated 1931, in the Bauhaus archive).[11]

9
Stefan Sebök, 'Letter to Walter Gropius', Briefe mit Personen, Bauhaus-Archiv, Berlin, GS19, Signatur 613.

10
Farkas Molnar, 'Letter to Walter Gropius', Korrespondenznachlass, Gropius Archives, 1937–1969: 497/1, Bauhaus-Archiv, Berlin, 41/435.

11
Walter Gropius, 'Erläuterungen Internationaler Wettbewerb Palast der Sowjets, Moskau, 1931', Walter Gropius Archive, Bauhaus-Archiv, Berlin, GS 20: Mappe 87.

Stefan Sebök, woodcut print made from self-portrait, 1924

Stefan Sebök, self-portraits, 1924

Stefan Sebök, portraits of Marcel Breuer, 1924

Overleaf: Stefan Sebök, letter to Walter Gropius, 1935

Se6öK (1936)

lieber herr g r o p i u s

einen sehr schlechten gewissen habe ich ihnen gegenüber.sie haben auf meine briefe immer sehr herzlich und schnell geantwortet und mir immer mut gemacht wieder 'mal zu schreiben.ich aus beispiellosen leichtsinnigkeit habe fertiggebracht auf ihren letzten brief,welche sie mir nach ihre leningrader vorträge (24.1o.33.) geschrieben haben nicht zu antworten.ich war damals sehr-sehr verstimmt eben wegen ihre stimmung.anstatt dass ich versucht hätte damals mich in ihre verfassung sich vorzustellen,habe mich einfach der wirkung ihre zeile ausgesetzt und mir die primitive endfolgerung gemacht:bei herrn gr-s die stimmung nicht positiv - d.h.alles ist aus...

erst nach eine weile zeit kam ich meiner eigener kurzsichtigkeit dahinter.wenn ich zu ihnen nicht so eine tiefe menschliche und schöpferische beziehung früher jahre hindurch in mir gepürt hätte,dann könnte es eventuell passieren (auch als eine aussergewöhnlichkeit),dass ein brief auf einem ein s c h w e i g e n aufbringt.aber in unserem falle,so ein verhalten -zart ausgedrückt- ein masslose primitivheit.

sie sehen lieber herr gropius,dass ich mein fehler -wenn auch tüchtig verspätet- eingesehen habe und eben,wie dieser brief zeigt versuche ich es gutzumachen.

anfang war der dumme reaktion ihre zeilen,welche mich zu schweigen brachte,später das schlechte gewissen liess mir nicht zu einen brief anzufangen.noch später -d.h.etwa vor anderthalb jahren- wusste ich einfach nicht,wo sie sind.unlängst erst durch zufall,durch ellen ge-dt,die in berlin mit herrn dr.vo-er zusammenkam erfuhr ich,dass sie im hannover sind und die adresse von herrn moholy.

vor ein paar tagen habe ich mit prof.ginsburg gesprochen und er war sehr erstaunt,dass ich nichts ausführliches über sie erzählen könnte.er hat mir richtiggehend vorwurf gemacht,dass ich fertiggebracht habe solange ihnen nicht schreiben.(sein empörung würde wohl noch grösser,wenn er wüsste,dass eigentlich ich bin der schuldige mit briefantwort).er bat mich ihnen ein gruss zu bestellen lassen und er würde sich sehr freuen,wenn sie 'mal ihm schreiben würden.

obwohl sie nach meinen letzten brief (6 maschienengeschriebene seiten) bei dessen lesen "technisch auf schwierigkeiten stiessen", werde ich diesmal wieder ausführlicher sein um etwas nachzuholen. .

um den faden von 1933 zu fassen habe nochmals durchgelesen die kopie meine 6 seitige "lektüre" und ihren antwort darauf.sie haben recht,dass ich denke über die sachen,wie z.bp."eine vergnügungsreise" "viel zu einfach".überhaupt mein brief von damals kommt mir heute nach zwei und ein halb jahren in vielen stellen viel zu naiv vor.(vielleicht ist das ein beweis davon,dass man älter wird!).

wie damals schon geschrieben,über ihre leningräder vorträge war in die zeitungen,leider,nur eine kurze notiz und so könnte es passieren,dass sogar solche leute,wie ginsburg über euere verweilen in der nähe nicht wussten.

was ihr damalige sowjetpalast entwurf betrifft kann ich sa-
gen,dass ich nicht blos gesehen,sondern damals der ausstellungsleitung
es "vorgestellt" habe.die bestellte projekte (die ausländische und einige sowjetische) wurden ausgestellt mit angabe der autoren,da diejeni-
ge gingen äusser konkurrenz.die leute als sie ihr projekt ausgepackt haben,haben sie gleich getauft auf "le corbusier".die ausstellung war
noch nicht geöffnet,aber das schild mit der fremden name hing.auf meine energische eingreifen haben sie dann die richtige beschriftung ge-
macht.dass ihr entwurf mir ausserordentlich gefiel,glaube brauche ich
nicht ihnen besonders zu bestätigen.die aufmachung durch die dustmann-
sche farbige darstellungen (oder habe geirrt - es stammten die von je-
manden anderen?) hat ausserordentlich viel gewonnen.ich weiss (bin davon oft selbst zeuge gewesen),dass leute,die mit der "säulenlosigkeit"
der architektur auch nicht übereinstimmen,doch von der art der aufmachung
welche letzten endes keine nur blose oberflächliche formalität ist,wa-
ren herzlichst begeistert."ja,die sache hat s e i n e k u l t u r !"
so hat man doch ungewollt ausdruck einer achtung gegeben ein können gegenüber,welche selbst noch nicht haben.

ich hab'in jenen brief über die organisierung von architektonische meisteratelier's geschrieben.auch liess ich einige seufzen los
bezüglich der "säulenhaftigkeit" der architektur.lieber herr gropius,
das zwischenzeit hat vieles gebracht.bei mir eine gewisse verständniss
davon,warum hier solche "säulen"-strömung entstehen könnte.bei der grossen öffentlichkeit ein vorbehalt,ja vorsichtigkeit gegenüber diese "säulen"-verkünder.damals,als sie im leningrad waren,war eben die kritisches-
te periode.damals fing es an die kampagne gegen die grenzenlose verein-
fachung,verschematisierung,welche bei schlechten bauausführung richtig-
gehende "schachtel-architektur" brachte.uns,die ausländische beispiele
von "moderne architektur" gesehen haben ist immer klar gewesen,dass die
entscheidende bei unsere architektur ist eben dass,wie die projekte in
die wirklichkeit ausgeführt werden? eine karrikatur kann entstehen von
eine gute architektonische gedanke,wenn es in schlechte umgebung,schlecht
ausgeführt wird.jene kampagne liess einige gegenbeispiele zu entstehen.
so z.bp.hier ist ein sehr autoritätsvoller akademiker scholtowskij,wer
ausgezeichnet kennt die renaissance baukünstler und kann er die auch
gut kopieren.er machte einige bauten in diesem sinne.es dauerte nicht
lange,als die reaktio zu merken war.gewiss bedeutet dies nicht eine um-
drehung auf 18o grad.bedeutet nur das,dass die ganze öffentlichkeit,wel-
che mit architekturfragen sich beschäftigt genau achtet eben auf fragen
der bauausführung,neuzeitliche baumaterialien und bauprozess,auf falsche
deutung der generallinie"kampf gegen vereinfachungs tendenzen,gegen ver-
ständnisslose kopierung klassische formen,gegen vernachlässigung der
wichtigkeit der grundrisslösung".ich weiss nicht,lieber herr gropius
wieweit sie interessiert,was hier alles im architektur geschieht und
wieweit sie über die hiesige architektur-ereignisse unterrichtet sind.
deshalb will ich ihnen über diese teme ohne speziell ihre bitte nicht
schreiben,da will ich sie,wenn auch der interwall 2 1/2 jahr geworden
ist mit "schwere lektüren" zu verschonen.jedoch als eine kleine kost-
probe über architekturneuigkeiten,will ich ihnen einige sätze von ginsburg übersetzen,welche im neujahrsnummer der "architektur zeitung"(das

ist eine art 5-tages zeitung,kolossal verbreitet,volkstümlich gehalten) unter ausführungen von bekannten sowjetarchitekten erschienen unter titel "dem neuen jahr entgegen". "die architekten müssen ernsthaft darüber nachdenken,wie ihre projekte g e b a u t werden.im projektierungs prozess soll schon der architekt eine klare vorstellung haben von methoden der verwirklichung sein architektur projekt.er soll verstehen das spezifikum der industriellen bauherstellung um mit das nachher umgehen zu können.ein von meine grösste bauten im jahre 1936 wird sein eine 12 geschossige gebäude in tagil (neue sozialistische stadt),welche so wird projektiert,dass seine teile industriemässig hergestellt werden und mit trockenmontage in 2-3 monaten zusammengestellt werden" diese arbeitsprogramm,welche in sich nicht fantastisch gross,sondern ganz konkret und real ist,heute bedeutet einen grossen schritt vorwärts.ich glaube,lieber herr gropius,dass sie selbst bestätigen werden,dass man hier in der letzten zeit sehr-sehr vorwärtsgekommen ist,was architektur betrifft.

selbstverständlich viele werden geben,die nicht ganz so sprechen.corbusier,may,taut,hannes meyer sind diejenigen,die nach eine gewisse zeit verstimmt geworden sind.aber schütte,schütte-lihotzky, hebebrand,schmidt,kurt meyer,lurcat und noch viele von der bekanntere n leben da und wenn auch anfangs etwas schwer gehabt haben,jetzt schaffen und selbst und die allgemeinheit ist damit zufrieden was sie machen.

lieber herr gropius ich würde ihnen ausserordentlich dankbar,wenn sie in ihren nächsten brief etwas von sich selbst hören lassen würden.es ist schande,aber nichts,garnichts hört man über sie hier! nur dass sie mal eine zeitlang in london waren.dass sie mal in budapest gewesen sind,weiss ich zufälligerweise durch meine mutter,die mir mal eine foto aus einer dortigen zeitung zugeschickt hat.sie spielen daran mit einen kleinen junge.("mit dem sohn eines seinen ungarischen folgerer").die frau gropius schaut sie vergnügend zu. Molnár

in einen ausländischen zeitung habe mal einen kurzen notiz gelesen,dass sie mit einen italienischen architekten einen "massentheater für 4o tausend"projektiert haben.leider nirgendwo,obwohl ich die verschiedenste ausländische architekturzeitungen in die hände bekomme, keine publikation darüber fand.ich würde diesüber speziell grosse freude haben.noch im frühjahr wurde ich aufgefordert zu der sog.allunionistischen architektentagung (wo sehr viele aus ausland speziell herkommen werden) zu eine vortrag über theaterbau,zur frage:problematische im theaterbau einen sondernreferat zu halten.

durch diese theater-tema kam ich wieder in kontakt mit piskator und mit dem filmregisseur dowschenko.

in meinem damaligen brief habe geschrieben,dass ich bei dem eisenbahn gearbeitet habe.ich habe tatsächlich bis herbst 1935 auch dort vegetiert.in den vergangenen jahr-anfang durch die ständig wächselnde unmittelbare leitung (welche unglücklicher weise zu architektur keine verständniss hatte) habe entschlossen von dort aus fort gehen.nur dadurch dass ich von der eisenbahn wohnung bekam (2 zimmer mit allem komfort) kann ich das nicht so einfach durchführen.seit einige zeit ofiziell war ich ohne arbeit.praktisch aber hatte immer 'was zu tun.

habe sogar in meine frühere arbeitsstelle bei der eisenbahn, wo inzwischen eine bessere architektonische leitung ist inofiziell gearbeitet.in der nächste zeit werde ich 2 ofizielle arbeitsstelle haben: in dem architektur-atelier von ginsburg (mit der 2 bruder wesnin zusammen arbeitet er - der dritte der starb,von welche ich damals schrieb, ist doch nicht der wichtigere in der bruder-trio gewesen!).und mit lissitzki zusammen in seinen neu zu gründenden atelier.er hat sehr viel auf einmal zu tun.

mit schrecken konstatiere,dass dieser brief ist länger geworden,wie derjenige,welche ich damals schrieb.

schnell noch von mir zu vollständigkeit.noch im 1932 (irgendwie in unsere korrespondenz wird es nicht erwähnt) maria lewin,die ihnen später bei sowjetpalast projekt mit der übersetzung geholfen hat, ist meine frau geworden.kann mit freude ihnen verraten,dass wir mit diese tatsache s e h r zufrieden sind.sie wird bald ihre universität beendigen und als fiziko-chemikerin einen wissenschaftlichen laufbahn beginnen,auf welche sie grosse veranlagung hat und auf welche hier grosse zukunft wartet.

meine adresse:moskau,nowo-basmannaja 4/6 whg.2o4

wenn sie wollen,sie können mir durch österreich schreiben:

herrn adolf popper,an st.se-k,wien XX,brigittaplatz 18.2.26

laut einen schreiben,in welcher steht,dass "unterzeichneter (d.h. se-k) erklärt sich einverstanden keinerlei ersatzansprüche an herrn prof.gr-s bezügl.seiner,auf dem boden des letzteren untergebrachten sachen zu stellen....usw.(27.7.31.)"habe ich sie mit 1 koffer und 3 packete belastet.wenn diese sachen noch existieren,so werde ich 'was ausdenken von ihnen die fortschaffen zu lassen.

auf meine schuldige seele lastert noch die ungarische übersetzung von einen artikel von ihnen,welche sie im "hamburger fremdenblatt"(28.5.3o.)geschrieben haben über "wohnen im hochhaus".die übersetzung ist fast fertig.bei mir ist auch ausserdem die zeitungsausschnitt. wenn sie die sachen interessieren,so kann ich sie ihnen zuschicken.

glaube über alles geschrieben zu haben.kann ich schluss machen.

lieber herr gropius,seien sie bitte nicht böse,wegen mein unverschämtes (und dummes) schweigen und schreiben sie bald.

mit herzlichen gruss an frau gropius und an sie

ihr

Sebök

6.1.36.

-

(erst diese zeilen zu lesen !)

meinen brief von 6.1.36.an sie habe ich,wie geschrieben versucht durch herrn moholy an sie zu bestellen lassen.die adresse aber, an welche ich schickte war falsch,da mein brief aus amsterdam zurück kam.nun mache den versuch durch molnar farkas sie zu erreichen.hoffentlich,wenn auch der weg komplizierter,wird schneller und sicherer.

einige ergänzungen zu meinen brief:

seit ende jauar arbeite ich mit el lissitzki zusammen.wir machen eine grosse architektur ausstellung zu der architekten tagung.wir sprechen sehr oft auch über sie.l-ki schätzt sie sehr und spricht ebenso, wie ich schon erwähnte,wie ginsburg,mit einen freundschaft über sie.

ich glaube selbst die tatsache,dass lissitzki die ausstellung macht,welche völlig behält den lissitzki karakter der presse und hygiene ausstellungen,welche sie gut kennen,spricht davon,dass mit der modernen in der architektur steht gar nicht so kritisch,wie sie (und sogar ich und noch viele) es früher vorstellten.

eine andere tatsache,dass man inofiziell vorlaufig davon spricht dass man sie einladet zu der moskauer architektentagung ist auch ein zeichen,welche richtig verstanden sein muss.heute werde ich mit absich nicht ausführlicher.wenn ich aber von ihnen 'was höre,und sie nicht dagegen werden,so gewiss gerne,hole alles ein,was ich aus m e i n e fehler versäumt habe.

die architekturtagung wird keine representation,sondern eine konkrete schöpferische arbeits festlegung sein.dazu werden eingeladen 5o international bekannte ausländische architekten.und keinesfalls zu glauben,dass n u r leute von alte konservativen verfassung! man legt xxx grossen wert darauf,dass zu auskrisstalisierung einer meinung (es geht eben diese prozess jetzt vor uns) eben eine vielseitige auseinanderlegung vorangeht.aus diesen gründen wird diese tagung eine ganz besondere interesse haben für alle,die mit architektur i n ni g sich verbunden fühlen.

wenn es bei ihnen damals,jene brief,was sie mir schrieben entstehen könnte (sogar mit recht),so heute sind die ereignisse auf linie der architektur soweit entwickelt,dass es eben nicht mehr treffend für das,was hier geschieht.

mein lieber herr gropius,ich schreibe diesmal wieder solche "einladende" sachen,auf welche sie nachher mir wieder so schreiben, dass ich zu"einfach denke eine vergnügungsreise hierher zu machen". ich muss ergänzen:ich habe die ereignisse von damals gut mir wieder erwogen + die augenblichliche ereignisse hier + die ereignisse um sie selbst herum -leider infolge völlige nichtorientiertheit- nur so beilaufig... und habe mir die schlussfolgerung gemacht,dass dies alles ihnen als material zu überlegung geben ist keinesfalls nicht leichtsinnig in j e n e m f a l l e w e n n sie von hier aus durch die nötige instanzen einen o f f i z i e l l e n e i n l a d u n g bekommen. wenn sie es t a t s ä c h l i c h in ihre hände haben,so bitte sie keinesfalls abzusagen,weil die sache bedeutet es nicht nur dass die organisierungskomitet der architektentagunng die kosten ab grenzen der udssr auf sich nimmt,sondern,und das ist die h a u p t - sache,dass man mit ihren herkommen ernst rechnet.lieber herr gropius, ich betone wieder diesen "wenn". die situation ist heute nähmlich so, dass von ganz anderer seite (also keinesfalls von mir aus !!!) ihre kandidatur um sie zwischen die 50 ausländische architekten-autoritäten ganz ernst vertreten ist.z.zt.ist dies aber ganz und gar inoffiziel. offiziel wird nur im moment sein,als die liste von entsprechende stellen (die sache hat letzten endes eine grosse moraliche-materielle schwere) bestätigung bekommt.dann werde ich auch in der lage sein um sie richtiger zu orientieren,die namen der übrigen eingeladeten anzugeben.

lieber herr gropius,ich möchte hoffen,dass diesmal diese tema glücklicher auslaufen wird,wie vor 3 jahren.letzten endes "tempora mutantur..."

unabhängig von dies ich möchte von ihnen wiederholt bitten das, was ich an der 6-te seite über ihre 40tausend theater geschrieben habe.ausserdem,da wir ausländische architekten aufgefordert worden sind bei der aussprache nach der vorträge aufzutreten,möchte ich unbedingt ergänzend einige neuheiten auf gebiete der ausländische theaterarchitektur (inkl.kino,cirkus und massenmietings stellen) zu geben,über die neueste programmstellungen in beziehung der zuschauersaal und scene und regisseurmässige möglichkeiten der bühne selbst.hier leider weiss man gar nicht davon,was in diesem gebiet z.zt.im ausland gemacht wird.hört man weder von ihnen,noch von moholy,schlemmer,weininger usw. ich wäre ihnen ausserordentlich dankbar,wenn sie mir diesbezüglich helfen würden.selbstverständlich,die beste hilfe wäre,wenn sie selbst nachher hierher kämen und auch auf diese frage selbst eingehen würden. aber solange dies nicht entschieden ist,möchte auf alle fälle ihre hilfe in form von information,wenn es geht,sogar mit bild (dies letzte wenn sie wollen leihweise.eingeschriebene sachen gehen nicht verloren !)

entschuldigung,dass ich mein schon 4 seiten langen brief noch mit weiteren 2 verlängert habe.

nochmals die herzlichste grüsse an sie und an frau gropius.

wenn sie jetzt in hannover sind,auch an ihre liebe frau mutter.

By the time Sebök wrote the second part of the letter, he was working with El Lissitzky, preparing designs for an exhibition for the All Union Congress. He stresses how much the style of El Lissitzky's presentation resembles his famous PRESSA exhibition in Cologne in 1928 and the Hygiene exhibition in Dresden in 1930. The rest of the letter deals with a forthcoming invitation to Gropius as one of the 50 foreign architects chosen to present at the All Union Congress in Moscow. He tries very hard to convince Gropius to accept this invitation. Through these entreaties one gets the feeling that he is not quite as happy about the Soviet situation as his first letter suggested, and that he hoped Gropius's visit might somehow improve things. He also mentions that he is due to give a lecture on modern theatre design to the congress, but says it is hard to get hold of any material reporting on developments outside Russia. He asks Gropius if he could supply him with some information in this field. This letter is the last surviving personal communication from Sebök. The tone is very much that of a junior to a revered senior, but at the same time it does show Sebök as someone who doesn't hesitate to assert his own views.

These visits to the Busch-Reisinger Museum at Harvard University and the Bauhaus archive in Berlin gave me the opportunity to see some of Sebök's projects from his student days in Dresden and his other work associated with the Bauhaus, but they offered only glimpses of what he was like as a person. I was desperate to find out more, both about him and his work, and immediately started to put out more feelers. After the opening gambit of the North American and German archival visits, and the obvious institutional focus for any exploration, the search became like a game of chess, with random movements in different directions, some offering only dead-ends, while others unexpectedly provided new leads.

The first of these was a trip in February 2002 to the Haus der Kunst museum in Munich. The chief curator there, Hubertus Gassner, had been responsible for the 'Wechselwirkungen' exhibition on the Hungarian avant-garde in Kassel in 1985. He also had a long-standing interest in Sebök's work, having come across him through a monument he designed in a 1930 competition to commemorate Taras Shevchenko (Gassner later reconstructed this unbuilt monument as the centrepiece of his show in Munich on the Central European avant-garde – the first postwar recognition of his work). Taras Shevchenko (1814–1861) was a Ukrainian poet who had a major influence on his country's literary and political culture. Born a serf, he was presented by the Soviet authorities 70 years after his death not so much as a vocal proponent of Ukrainian nationalism but as an internationalist and defender of the lower classes. The monument, built in Shevchenko's home city of Kharkov, was just one aspect of this recasting – a strategy designed to suppress any separatist sentiments and promote the greater Soviet collective.

Stefan Sebök, design for a fundraising programme, 1926

Portrait of Stefan Sebök, *c* 1928, photo Lucia Moholy

Commemorative monuments of this kind may have had a clear purpose, but there was still considerable controversy in the USSR about the form they should take. Right at the outset of the Russian revolution, for example, Anatoly Lunacharsky had launched a movement against the trend to honour the heroes of the revolution with overly monumental bronze effigies (a movement best illustrated by Tatlin's spiralling Third International tower and later by the wishes of Lenin's widow, who argued against pompous busts and statues in favour of libraries, hospitals and schools built in her husband's name). Over the decade immediately after Lenin's death in 1924, constructivist writers and artists continued the fight against the conventionally monumental, arguing instead that a better solution could be achieved through films and agitprop posters. Despite the popularity of this approach, only two Russian monuments using film have been previously recorded – El Lissitzky's 1920 Lenin Tribune and a 1924 Gustav Klucis design for a speaker's podium. Responding to a competition brief calling for a Soviet-style memorial in the socialist spirit that would attract and involve the masses, Sebök's own proposal offers a third such example. His design constituted an abstract, modernist tower on an iron base, with a spiral staircase leading up to a platform used for speeches and performances. Suspended above the platform were three large screens for film projections and poster displays. The three-armed design is reminiscent of Moholy-Nagy's *Lichtrequisit einer elektrischen Bühne*, a construction produced just a year later in 1931 and one Sebök was also involved with, and similarly promoted the idea that viewers around the monument could spontaneously choose and request films they wished to see – interactive media design *avant la lettre*.

The presentation of the project itself included illustrations of Shevchenko's activities and facsimiles of quotes by him. It was also accompanied by a text explaining the philosophy behind the memorial. The German version of this text can be found in the archives of the writer Alfred Kurella in the Akademie der Künste in Berlin,[12] but there are no comments in the archives as to what Kurella's exact involvement was with the project. Most probably he helped Sebök write this text for its submission in Russian, as he was not long returned from Moscow, after two years as the chief administrator for literature and art for the People's Commissariat for Popular Education.

Sebök's design for the Shevchenko competition was shown for the first time in Berlin in 1930 at an exhibition of the Soviet constructivist group OKTJABR. Though it was reviewed very favourably in the German-language press in Moscow, notably in the *Moskauer Rundschau*,[13] it failed to win – instead, buoyed by the rising currents of Stalinist socialist realism, a very traditional monumental bronze sculpture by sculptor M G Manizer and architect I G Langbard secured first prize. None of Sebök's original drawings survive but a miniature of the project boards, in the form of a tiny concertinaed *leporello*, was presented by Sebök to Gropius on 1 November 1930.

12
'Shevchenko Monument notes', Kurella Archives, Akademie der Künste, Berlin.

13
'Review of the Shevchenko Monument' in *Moskauer Rundschau*, 18 January 1931.

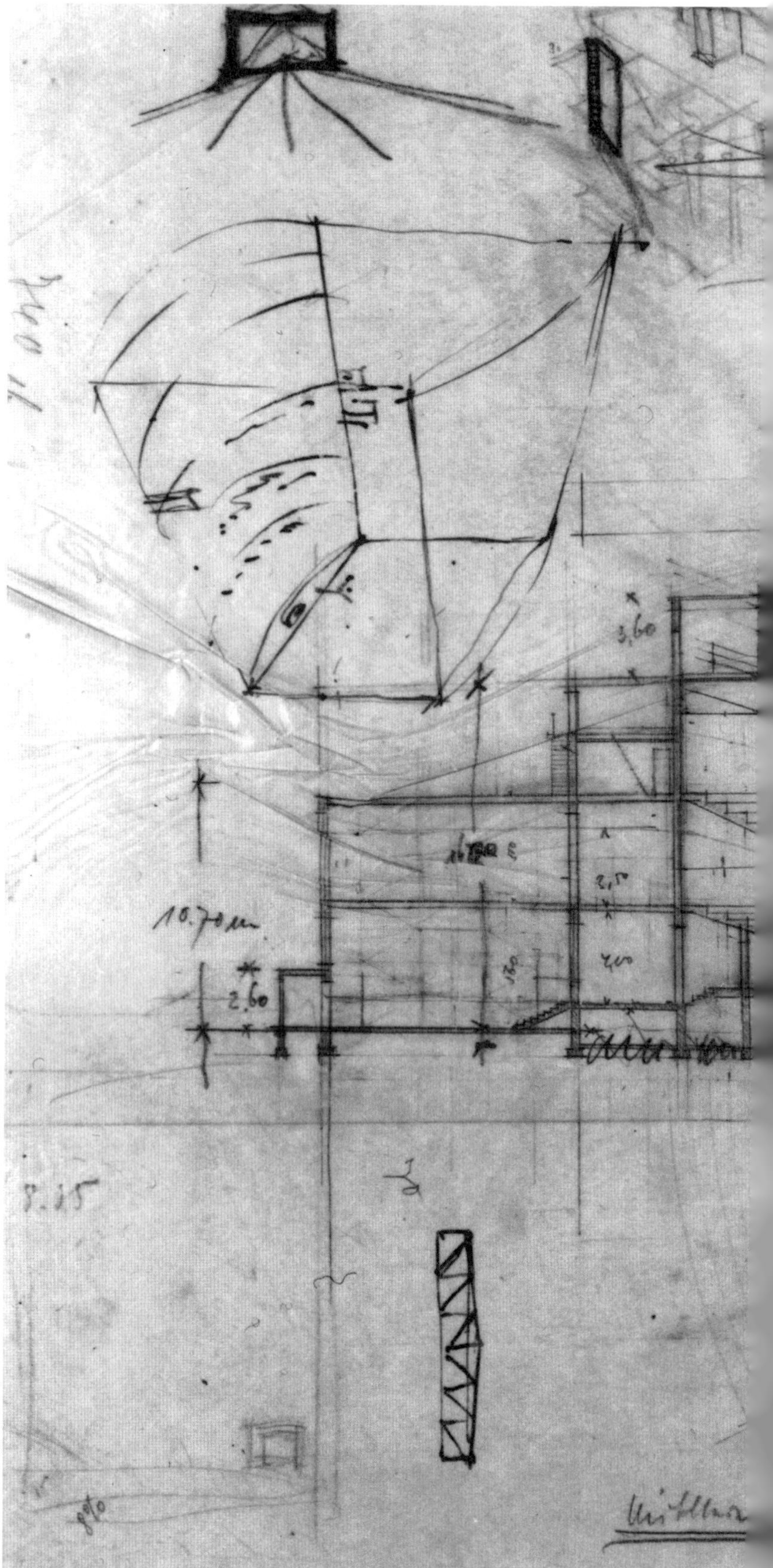
3,60
10.70 m
2,60
8.15

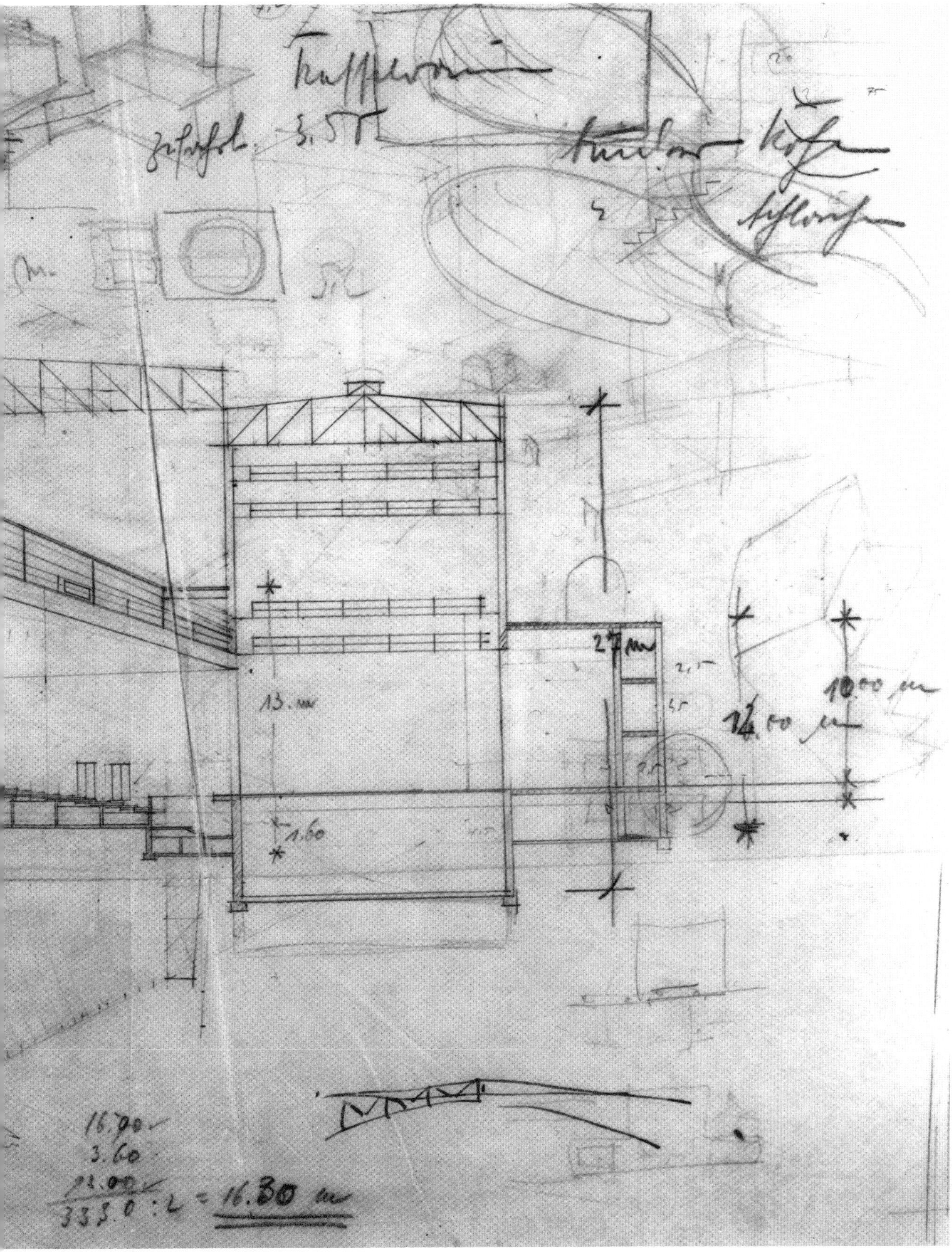

Above and overleaf: Stefan Sebök, Györ theatre competition, 1928–29

jel: 

szinháztervpályázat

györ szab. kir. város

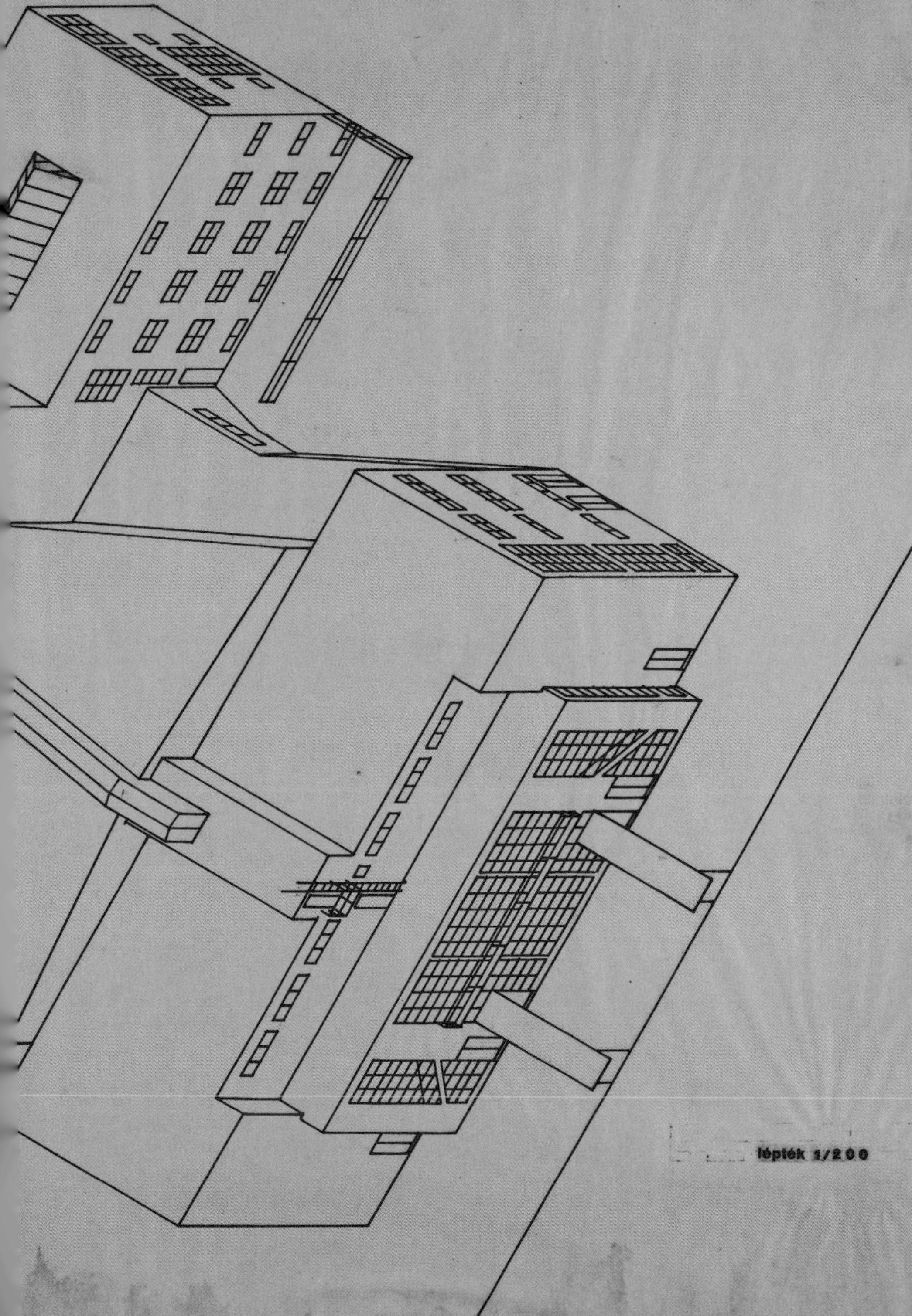

lépték 1/200

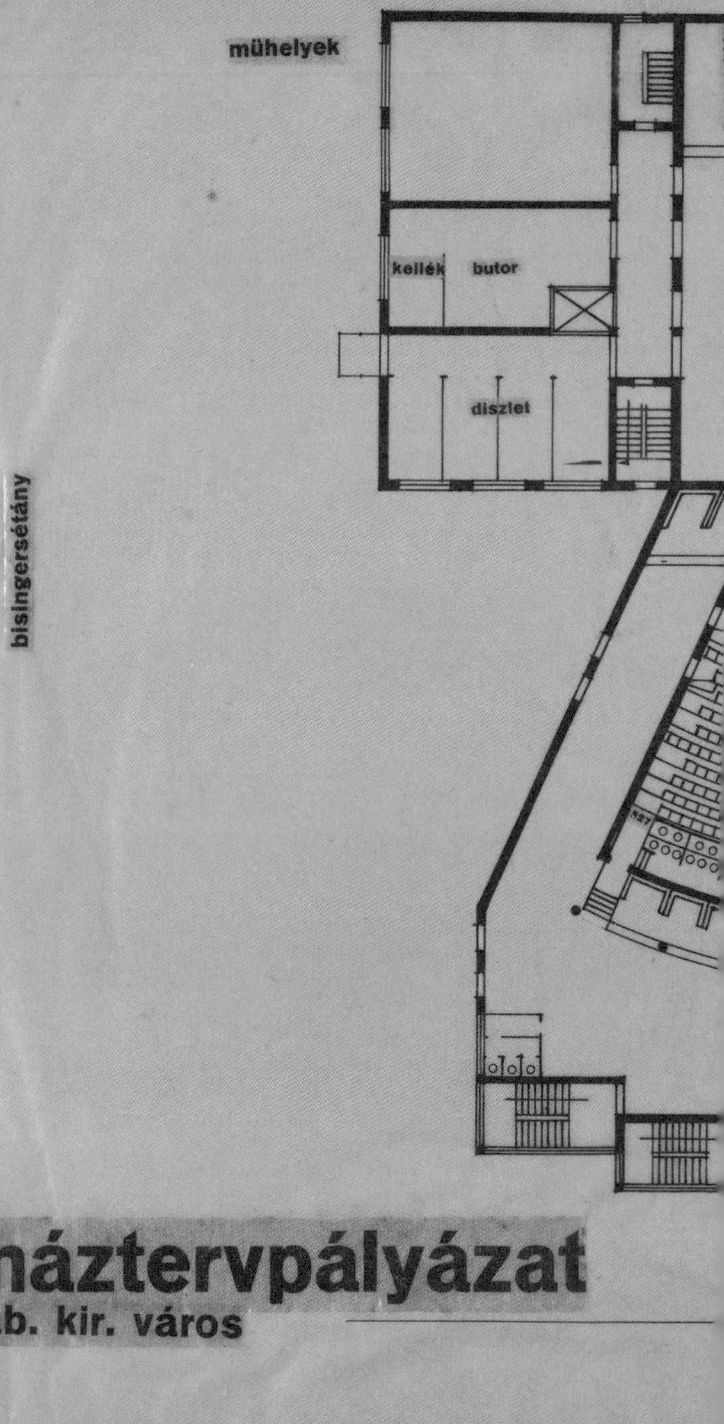

szinháztervpályázat

győr szab. kir. város

DIN A 2

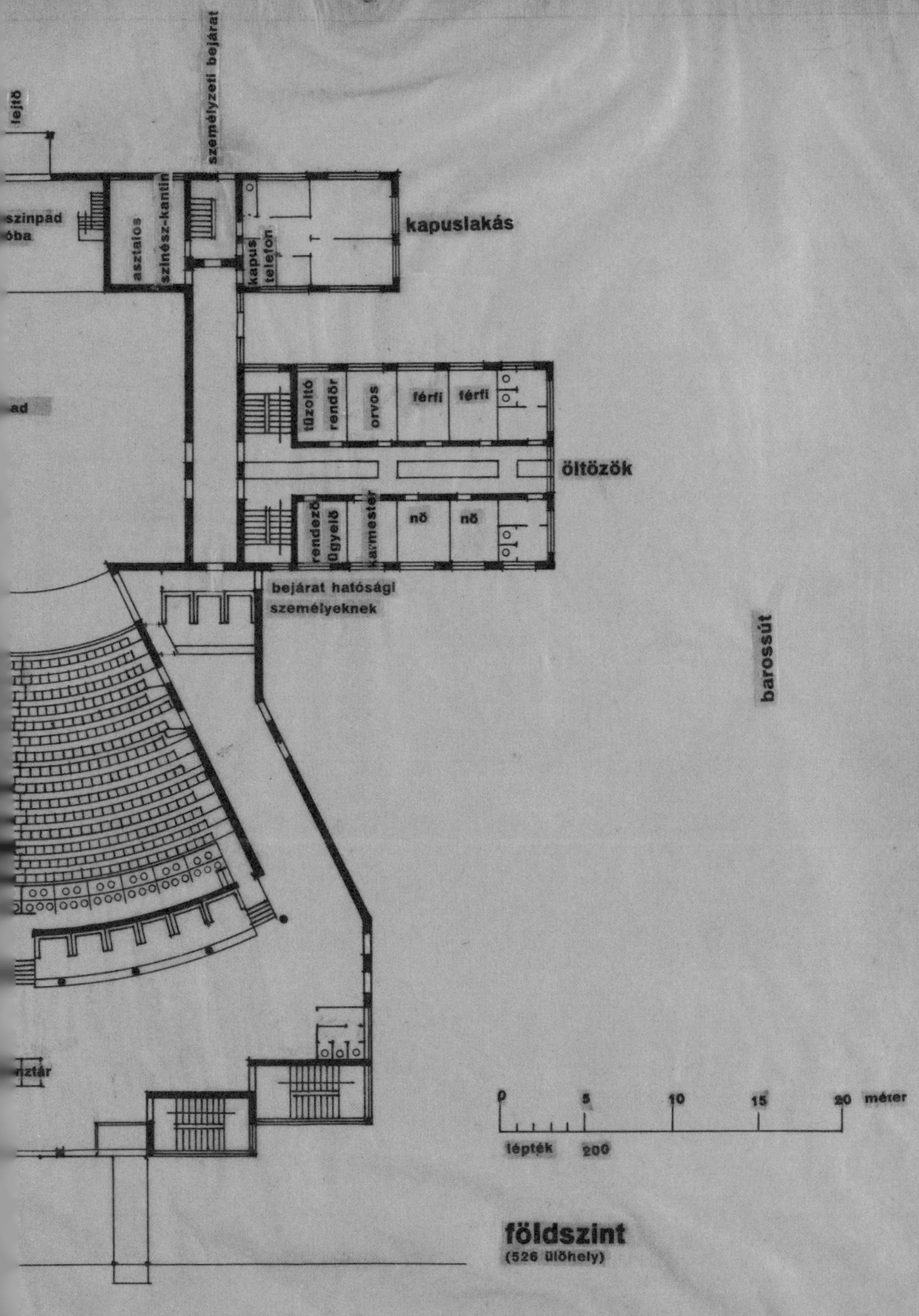
lejtő
személyzeti bejárat
színpad
óba
asztalos
színész-kantin
kapus
telefon
kapuslakás
ad
tűzoltó
rendőr
orvos
férfi
férfi
öltözők
rendező
ügyelő
karmester
nő
nő
bejárat hatósági
személyeknek
barossút
nztár
0
5
10
15
20 méter
lépték
200
földszint
(526 ülőhely)
császárút

2 lap

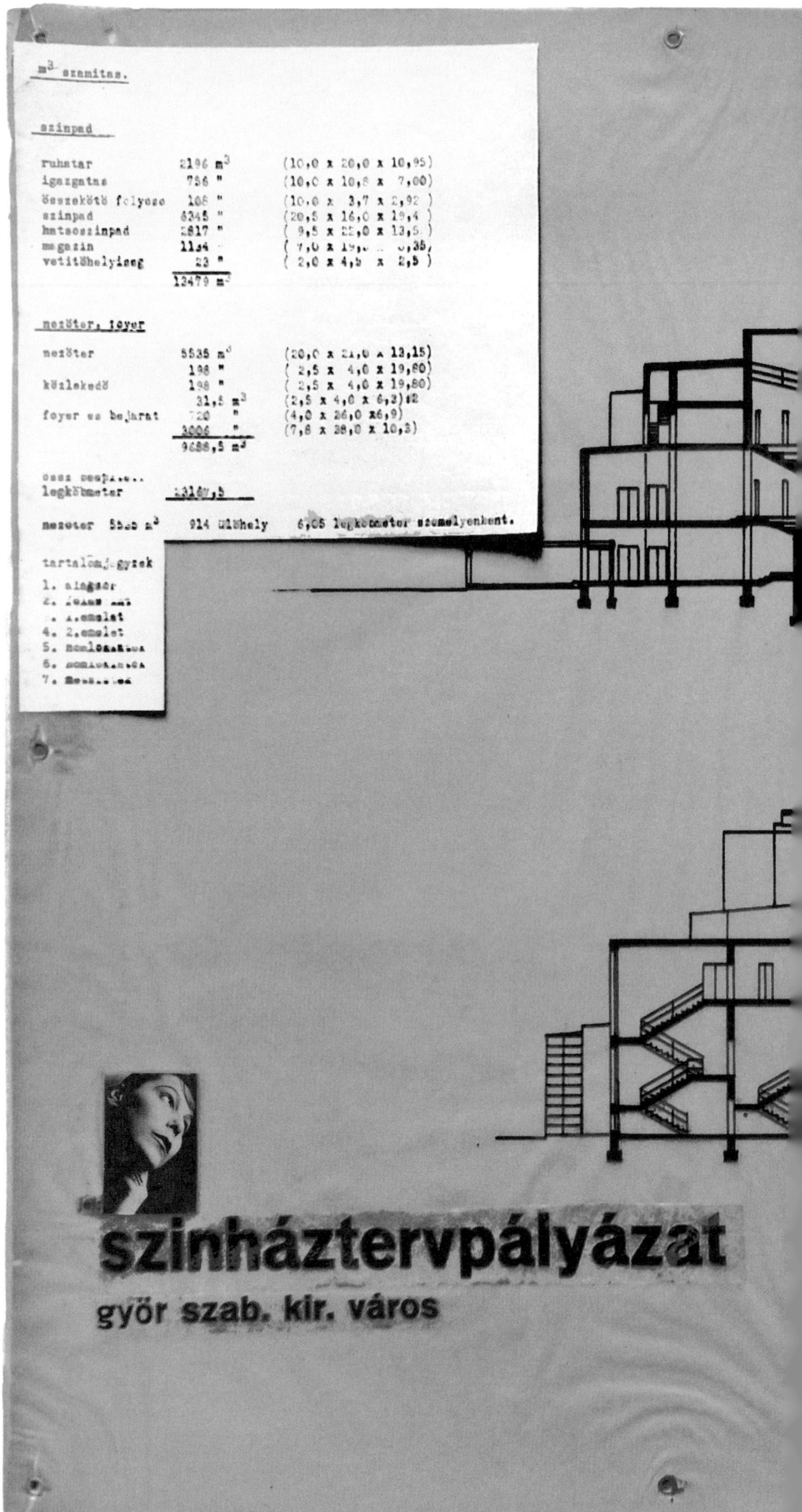
m3 szamitas.
szinpad
ruhatar 2196 m3 (10,0 x 20,0 x 10,95)
igazgatas 756 " (10,0 x 10,8 x 7,00)
összekötö folyoso 108 " (10,0 x 3,7 x 2,92)
szinpad 6345 " (20,5 x 16,0 x 19,4)
hatsoszinpad 2817 " (9,5 x 22,0 x 13,5)
magazin 1134
vetitöhelyiseg 23 " (2,0 x 4,5 x 2,5)
13479 m3
nezöter, foyer
nezöter 5535 m3 (20,0 x 21,0 x 13,15)
198 " (2,5 x 4,0 x 19,80)
közlekedö 198 " (2,5 x 4,0 x 19,80)
31,5 m3 (2,5 x 4,0 x 6,3)x2
foyer es bejarat 720 " (4,0 x 26,0 x6,9)
3006 " (7,8 x 38,0 x 10,3)
9688,5 m3
legköbmeter
914 ülöhely
6,05 legköbmeter szemelyenkent.
tartalomjegyzek
3. 1.emelet
4. 2.emelet
szinháztervpályázat
györ szab. kir. város

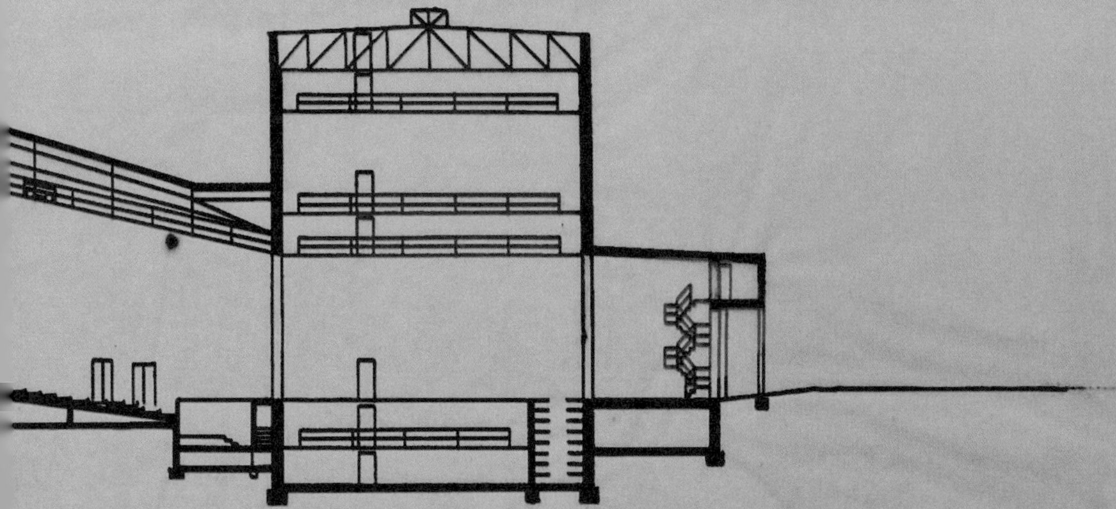

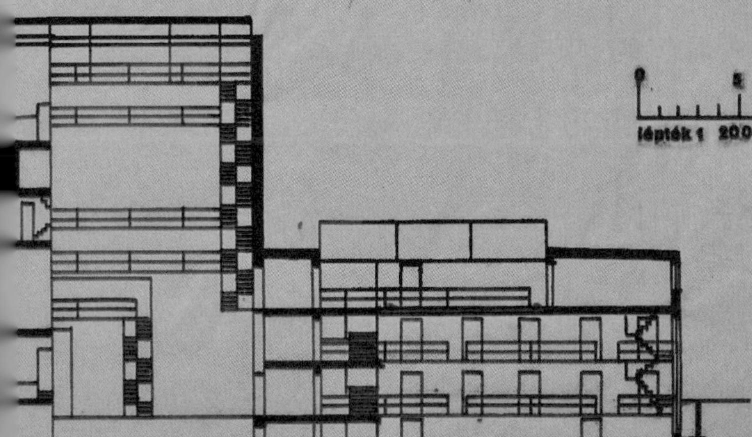

hosszmetszet
keresztmetszet

7 lap

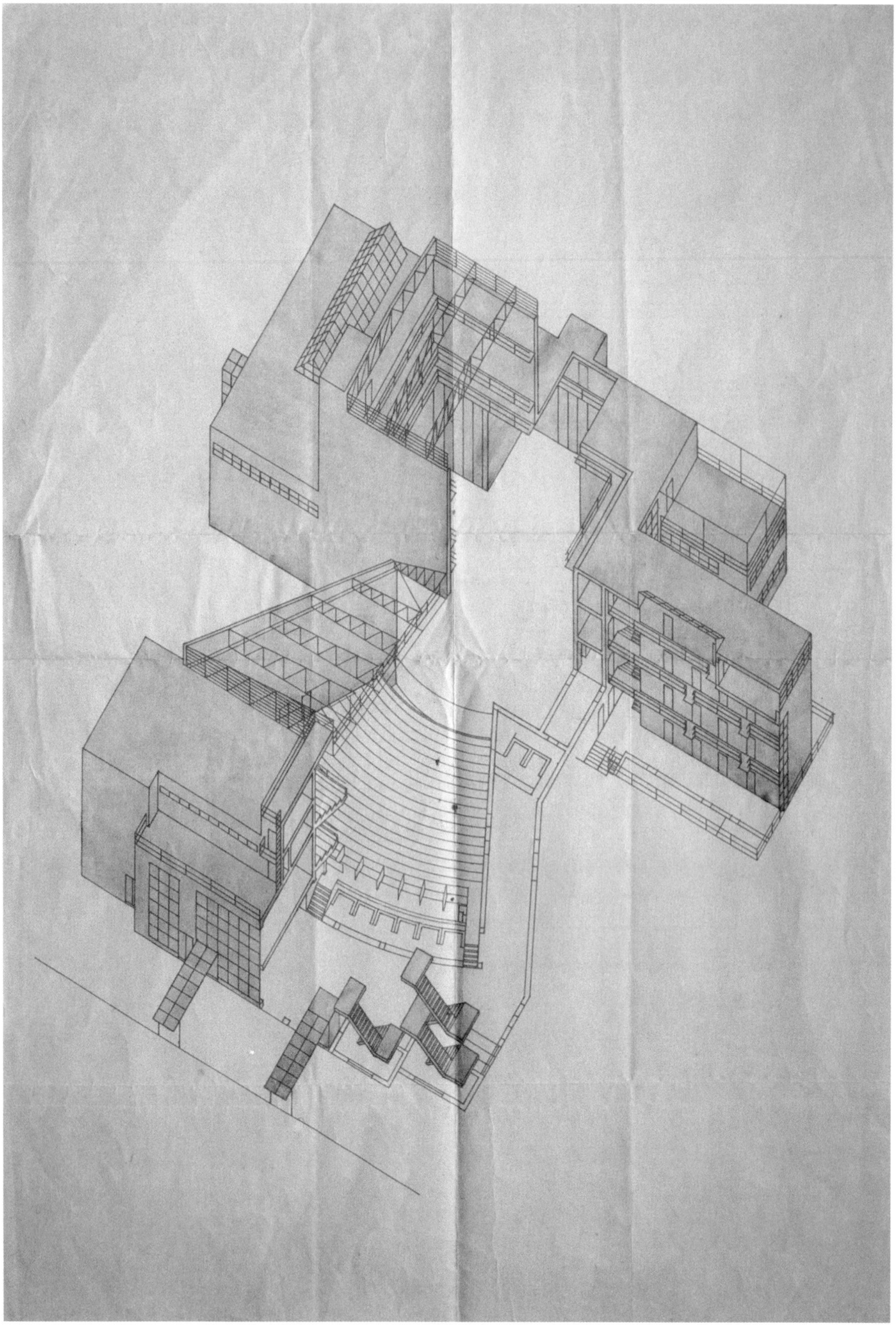

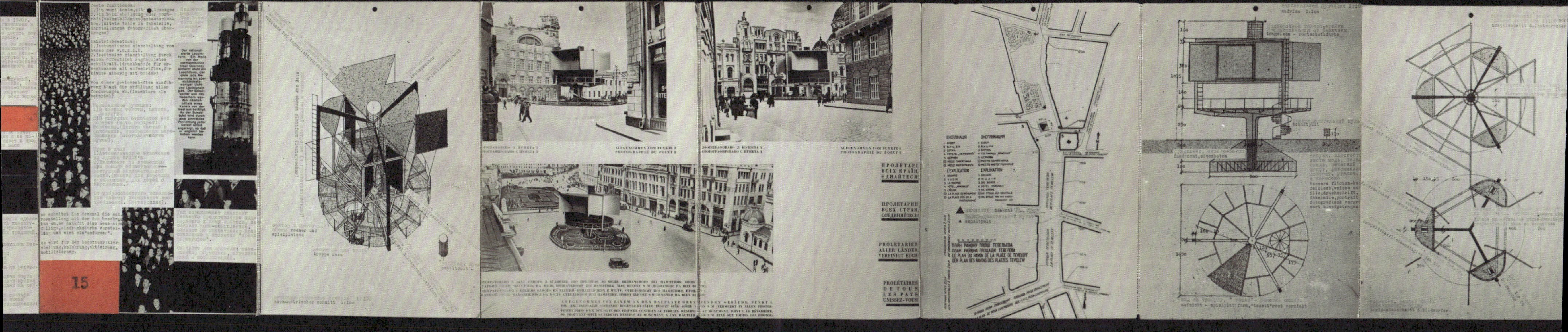
15
AUFGENOMMEN VOM PUNKTE 3
PHOTOGRAPHIE DU POINT 3
AUFGENOMMEN VOM PUNKTE 4
PHOTOGRAPHIE DU POINT 4
ПРОЛЕТАРИИ ВСЕХ СТРАН, СОЕДИНЯЙТЕСЬ!
PROLETARIER ALLER LÄNDER, VEREINIGT EUCH!
PROLÉTAIRES DE TOUS LES PAYS UNISSEZ-VOUS!
ЭКСПЛИКАЦИЯ
EXPLICATION

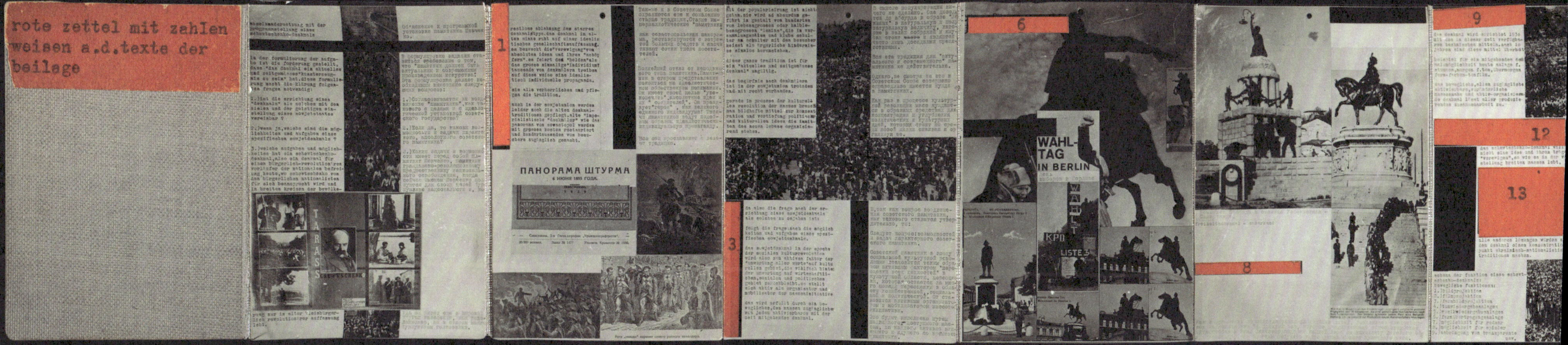
rote zettel mit zahlen weisen a.d.texte der beilage
1
ПАНОРАМА ШТУРМА
3
6
WAHL-TAG IN BERLIN
KPD
8
9
12
13

As much as Gassner's interest in these monumental designs, what I found fascinating was his view that Sebök had not merely played the role of a junior draughtsman in the Gropius office, but had directly influenced the projects produced, in particular the theatre designs. He backed this up by pointing to an interesting sequence of events, beginning with Sebök's Tanztheater diploma project, which showed that he had a certain experience with theatre design before he was recruited by Gropius. There is a comment in one of the letters in the Bauhaus archive that the Totaltheater project had reached a kind of impasse 'until the arrival of a young Hungarian engineer'. While the Totaltheater has a rather different shape and seating arrangement to the Tanztheater, there are some marked similarities in the roof structure and balconies. There are also parallels between Gropius's later Kharkov theatre and Sebök's own projects for the Györ theatre and Shevchenko monument. In one of the photographs and drawings of the model for the Kharkov theatre there is also a tower-like structure similar to one Sebök used as the basis for the Shevchenko monument.

A month after meeting Gassner, I headed off to Hungary. My aim was to visit the local museum in Sebök's birthplace, Szolnok, in the hope that they might have some material, but at the time I found nothing there. In Budapest, a few days later, I also turned up very little that was new, though I did get the chance to meet a number of leading Hungarian art historians – Eva Bajkay, Kristina Passuth and Eva Hokum (Farkas Molnar's daughter) – who were all experts on the Bauhaus, and were able to provide me with valuable snippets about life in the Bauhaus and some of the people Sebök would have been involved with, such as Gropius, Moholy-Nagy and Gyula Pap, the Hungarian painter and photographer. I recognised Pap's name from a photograph of Sebök in the Wechselwirkungen catalogue – a sweet shot of him and his wife, their heads peering out from above their legs – and with the help of these historians I arranged to visit Pap's widow, Lenke Haulis, herself an art historian. She had broken her hip a few days earlier, so my visit had to be short, but she talked about the photograph and related how her late husband had spoken a lot about Stefan and thought highly of him. Just as I was leaving, she mentioned another Hungarian historian called Julia Szabó, who had interviewed her husband some years before and published the piece, which contained a reference to Sebök, in a Hungarian art magazine. After tracking down Szabó's contact details, I managed to reach her on the phone. She was extremely helpful and sent me the transcript of her interview. In it Pap describes how Moholy-Nagy was always very generous and managed to get him various commissions while he was in Berlin. He mentions, amongst others, the commission for the Russian trade fair, and it was in this context that he recalls how many of the people working there at the time were from Hungary. These included the director for the Soviet Pavilion – an architect also named Pap – and its designer, one of his ex-Bauhaus friends who was also his 'neighbour' at the Ittenschule – Stefan Sebök.[14]

14 Julia Szabó, Gyula Pap interview in 'László Moholy-Nagy kiállítása ürügyé', *Ars Hungarica*, 1977, p 147.

prom xport

Stefan Sebök, Soviet pavilion project for the Leipzig Fair, 1931, photo Lucia Moholy

Stefan Sebök, student sketch, 1924

It was not clear whether the term 'neighbour' referred to Sebök's home or place of work. If it meant workplace, it suggests that Sebök was probably working at the Ittenschule in Berlin at that time. Johannes Itten, a Swiss painter, designer, teacher, writer and theorist, taught at the Bauhaus between 1918 and 1922, developing an innovative preliminary course on the basics of material characteristics, composition and colour. Itten, however, was also something of a mystic and his mysticism and hold on the students increasingly alienated him from the other leading figures at the Bauhaus, particularly Gropius and Theo van Doesburg, who were moving the school in a direction that embraced mass production rather than individual artistic expression and craftsmanship. The rift led to Itten's forced resignation and the establishment, four years later, of his own private art school in Berlin, the Ittenschule (1926–1934). According to Peter Hahn, there were no living quarters for teachers or students there, which seemed to suggest that Sebök's neighbourliness was based on his own teaching role. Only later did I discover that the Ittenschule rented out studio spaces in its building and Pap and Sebök found themselves, as tenants, in adjacent spaces.

Before my return to London, I took the train from Budapest to Graz to meet with the widow of Hubert Hoffmann, a custodian of much of Sebök's surviving material, and Hoffmann's stepdaughter, Helga Moriz. It was a fascinating visit. Hoffmann led very much a bachelor's life, right up to the age of 90 when, somewhat surprisingly, he finally got married. I learned how he loved the whole lifestyle of the Bauhaus and all of the theatrical activities that went on there, and tried to relive these for the rest of his life, right into his old age. Even at 90, just before his death, he would still enjoy dressing up and acting out various roles.

Hoffmann was also an incredible hoarder. He kept and duplicated every piece of paper that came his way. His stepdaughter jokingly commented that the house was more or less held up, not by bricks and mortar, but by all the bits of paper stuffed in between the furniture and the ceiling joists. As a result, when he died, the chaos of sorting everything out was quite considerable. As I understood it, he did not actually make a will or bequeath his belongings to the Bauhaus or the Akademie, largely because of the fact that the legacies of all academicians automatically went to the Akademie. Instead his stepdaughter, desperate to be rid of all the material that had accumulated in the house, but believing that it must be of interest to somebody, contacted every museum she could think of, including the Bauhaus archive. Nobody seemed interested. Eventually Matthias Schirren, director of the architectural department of the Akademie der Künste in Berlin, came along, looked through the material and made a selection of things that appealed to him. These included all of the Sebök drawings, some of which she had been keen to keep. However, as Schirren pointed out to her, probably quite correctly, all of this material would eventually disintegrate if left in her home, and only a museum archive would ensure its survival.

While visiting Hoffmann's widow and stepdaughter I was also able to clarify the origins of a book Moholy-Nagy had given to Sebök. A few months earlier, Peter Hahn, the director of the Bauhaus archive, had contacted me to say he had spotted at a Berlin book fair a copy of the important Bauhaus publication, Kandinsky's *Punkt und Linie*, with a handwritten dedication to Sebök on its inside cover. On hearing this I immediately felt I should buy the book, if only because I own so few of Stefan's possessions and some totems of his life and work would be nice to have while I continued my search. And so I contacted the bookseller, who offered a German translation of the inscription: 'Wunden heilen in Frühling' (Wounds heal in springtime). This seemed a bit puzzling, but as I had learned from his letters to Gropius, Sebök appeared to be somewhat sensitive to criticism, and so I assumed that this was probably Moholy-Nagy simply reassuring him about something.

When the book arrived I quickly turned to the first page. Translated from the Hungarian into English the dedication read: 'To Sebök, 21.3.1929, spring day, Moholy-Nagy', which of course makes sense as 21 March is the summer equinox. There was no other inscription in the book which would have corresponded to the German translation, nor was there any separate piece of paper from which this might have originated. I phoned the bookseller but he insisted that his translation was correct. After a bit of probing he also informed me that the book itself originated in Vienna. I had asked Hoffmann's stepdaughter about this when in Graz. She said that after Hoffmann's death a second-hand bookseller was brought in to clear out all the old paperbacks. She thought that this book could easily have been amongst them. The art historian Eva Bajkay later clarified the inscription. When I read the original Hungarian to her she burst out laughing and pointed out that if the name *Seb* was translated from Hungarian it would mean 'wound', and Sebök was simply taken as its plural. The date was translated as 'springtime' and the 'healing' clearly added as a bit of poetic licence on the translator's part. It all just showed what can be lost or gained in translation.

I returned to Berlin in April 2002 to see the archives of the Akademie der Künste and revisit the Bauhaus archive to study the rest of the Sebök material. At the Akademie, the first important item I found was the manuscript for a lecture Sebök had given on the Viennese baroque, apparently at the Kupferstichkabinett in Vienna in 1925. On the first page there is a note saying that the hand-drawn illustrations to this lecture had been lost in the files of the Technische Hochschule,[15] but it was not clear which school this referred to – Vienna or Dresden. The curator of the Viennese Kupferstichkabinett clarified the location, informing me that the lecture must have taken place in Dresden, as the space in Vienna would not have been big enough to host a public talk. But the purpose of the manuscript, an erudite piece of work, was initially a mystery. What was Sebök doing in 1925 writing and lecturing on the baroque?

15
Stefan Sebök, 'Wiener Barock', Akademie der Künste, Berlin, HHof Signatur 102.

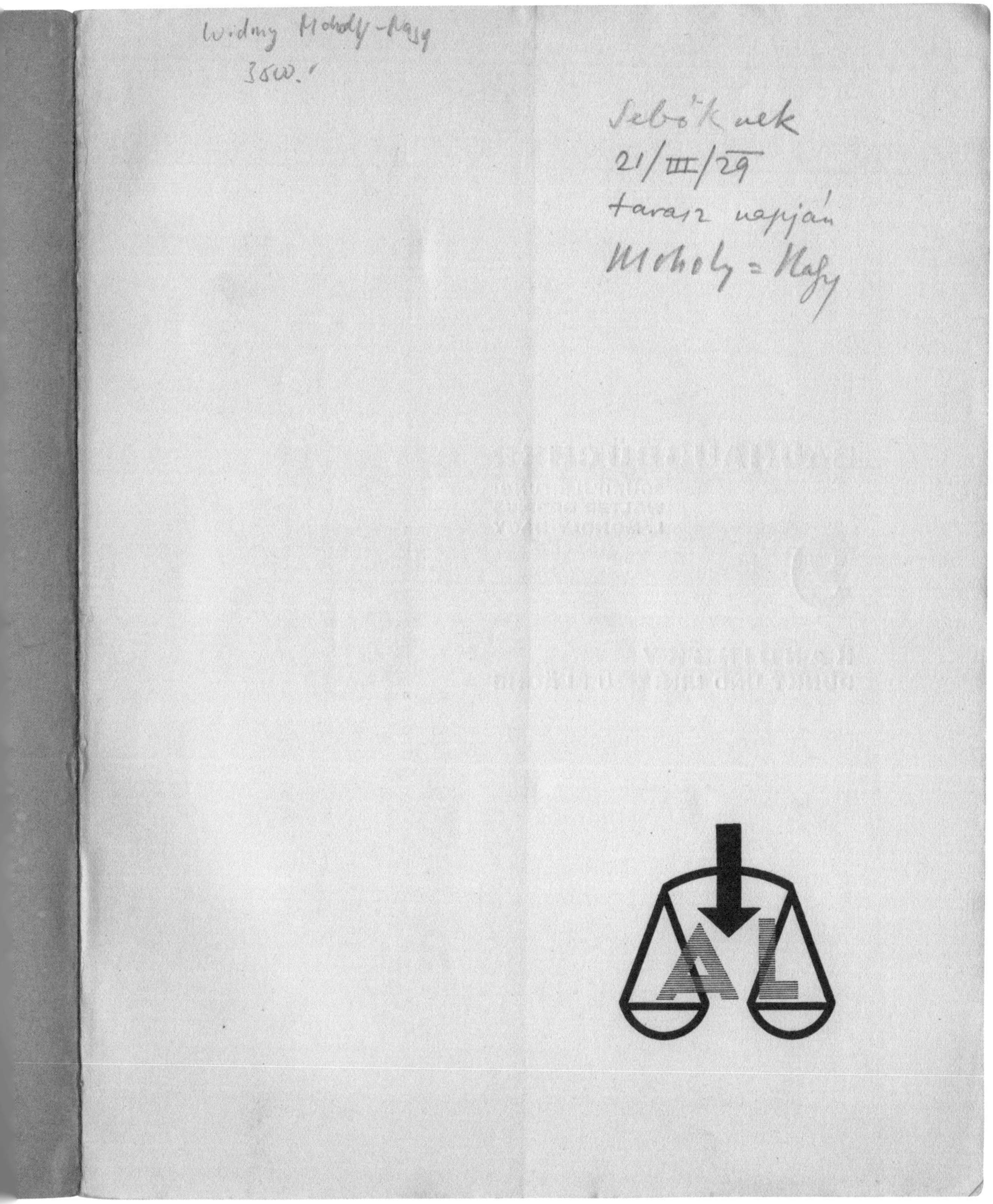

Dedication by László Moholy-Nagy to Stefan Sebök,
inscribed on the front page of Wassily Kandinsky's *Punkt und Linie*, 1929

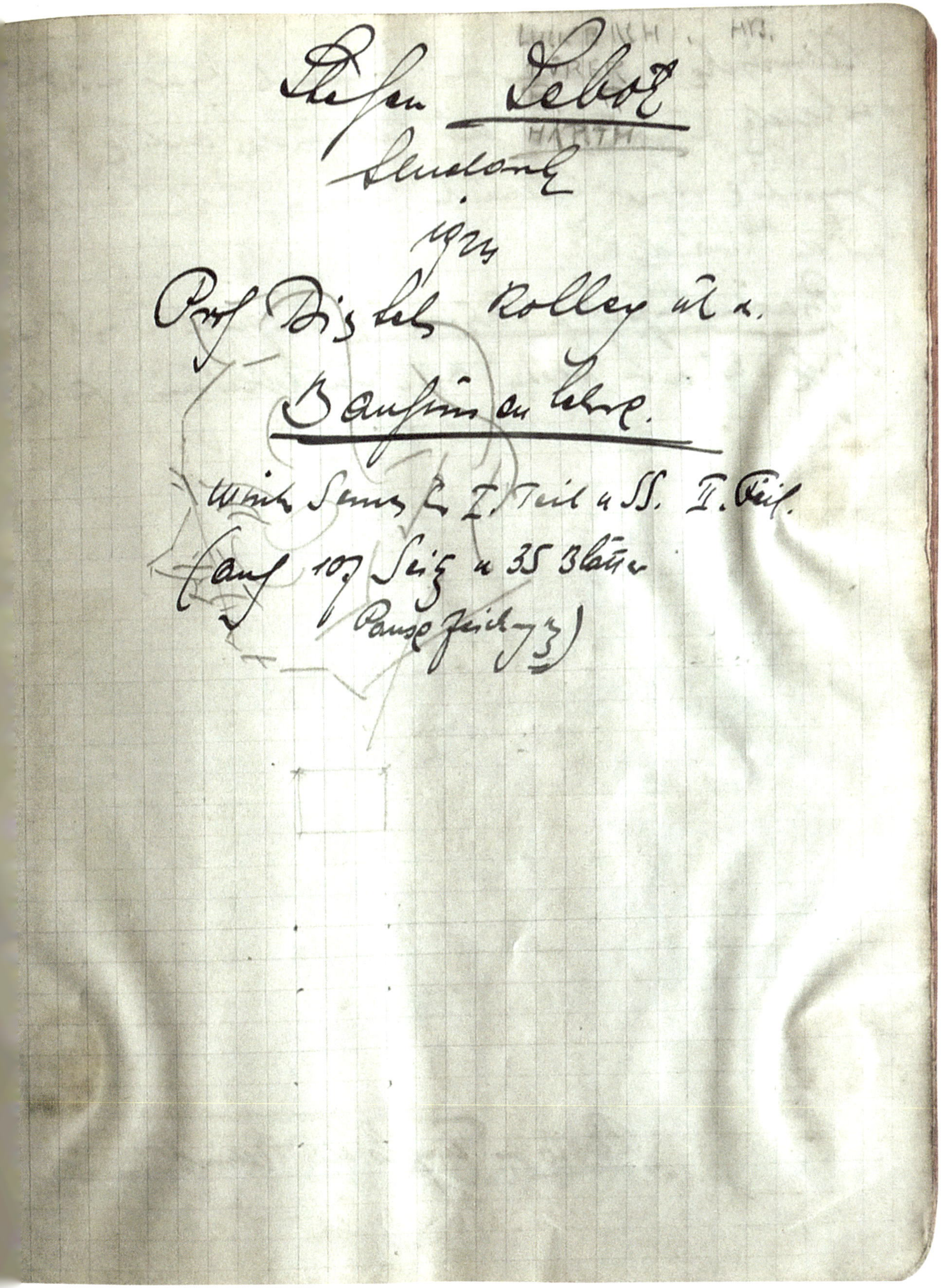

Above and overleaf: Stefan Sebök, pages from his *Bauformenlehre* sketchbook, *c* 1924

Abb. 101
Abb. 103

...teren Geschütze
...Abb. Merseburg
...rm Abb. 107.

(Abb 101 Schloss Beschaffenheit 102
103 Ratskeller Halle.) Originelle
Abb. 106
Gemeinde Schule

Abb. 104

Abb. 105

Portal

Schlosshof.

Portal

Rathaus-Portal
Abb 107 Würz-
burg Julianus
Institut.

...ens

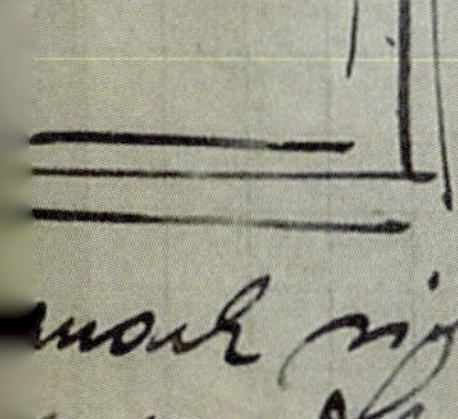

5
Abb. 108
8

Ursprüngliche Profilierung
Abb 108. ursprünglich Abb. 109.
nach Holz
konstruktio-
nen angefertig-
te Rahmen

...noch richtig ausgebil-
...ete Steinprofile.

...ndsen Öffnungen selbst beständig, selbst manchmal
...ichtig! Türstürze. Die Sehne fühlt ausgebildeten Türumrahmungen als bei aegyptischen Bauten (Abb 82, 83) Die Rosetten auf den Türsturz sind nicht auf die Lücken Gewicht zu fühlen. Sie entstammen aus dem Orient. Die **Schwebenden** Türumrahmungen bildmässig ...lich, möchte ...

...liothek ... in Venedig. ...sind nur

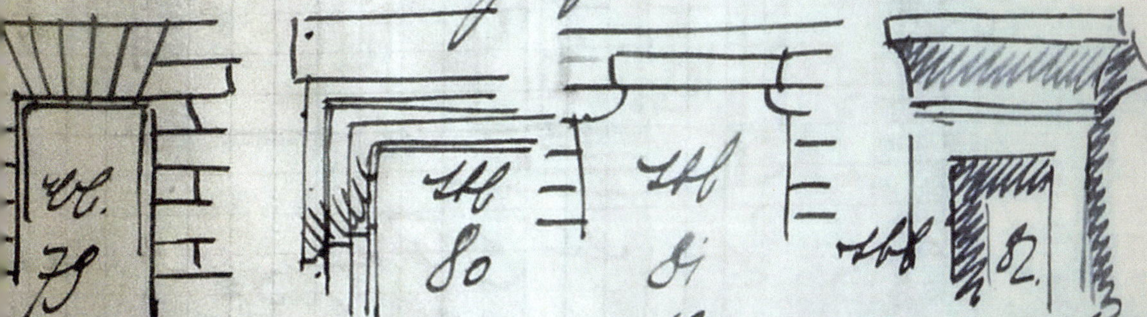

...b 2 aegyptische ganze Schlagprofil - rolle.

Abb 84 Erklärung.

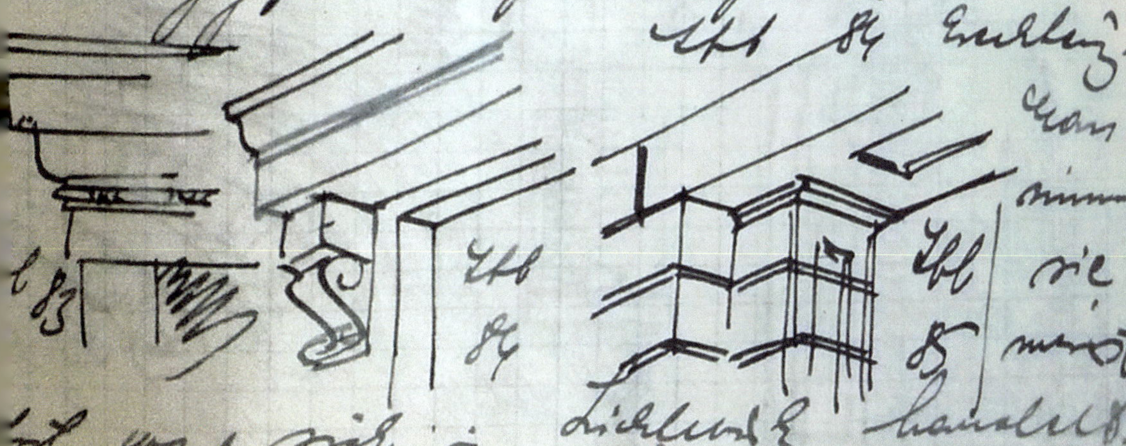

Man nimmt sie meist

...f wo es sich - Lichtwirkung handelt.

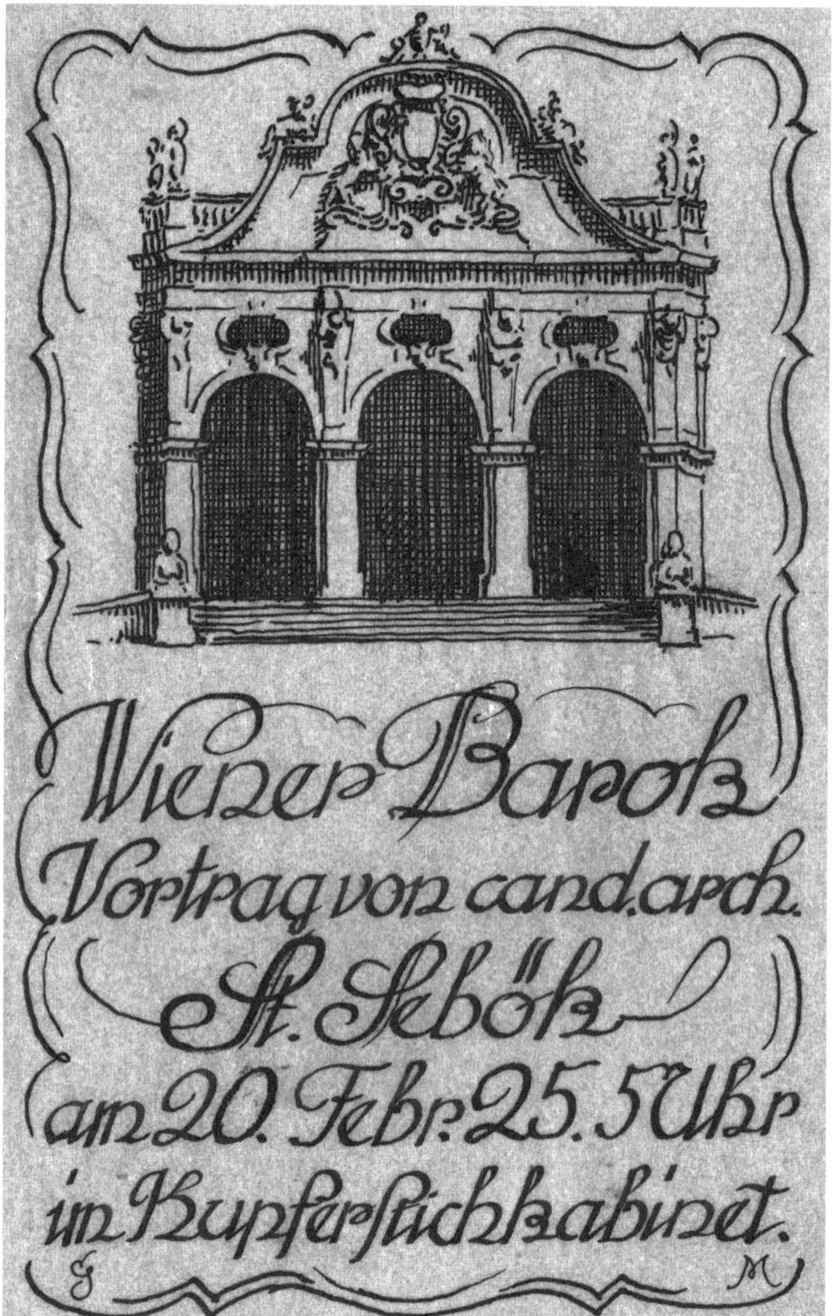

Manuscript of lecture on the Viennese baroque by Stefan Sebök, 1925

I later learned that talented students like Sebök were often assigned research projects like this by their professors and were encouraged to present the results in the form of a lecture. The other important finds at the Akademie were three student sketchbooks containing a mixture of drawings of buildings and portraits. A particularly fascinating one was a notebook inscribed *Bauformlehre* ('Formal Studies'), which seemed to be a collection of lecture notes interleaved with small, exquisite tracing paper drawings of various buildings in and around Dresden. Another one labelled *Ungarn* ('Hungary') had many sketches of his hometown.

Also in Berlin, at the Bauhaus archive, I met the new director Annemarie Jaeggi and came across the patent that Gropius had taken out for the Totaltheater – there seems to have been considerable rivalry between Gropius and Piscator as to who had originated the idea. In other files, the Bauhaus kept an original copy of the catalogue for the 'Section allemande' at the twentieth annual Salon of the Société des Artistes décorateurs exhibition held at the Grand Palais in Paris in 1930 – a show that has come to be known simply as the Werkbund exhibition. In the book Sebök is listed as one of the participants and a number of very fine axonometric drawings of Gropius's apartment are illustrated.[16] The catalogue also contains some descriptions and illustrations of the *Light-Prop for an Electric Stage* (*Lichtrequisit einer elektrischen Bühne*), a project Sebök worked on with Moholy-Nagy. However, there was very little descriptive information in the Bauhaus archive about this, apart from a construction drawing and a copy of the *Light-Prop* itself.

I also discovered the last of the competition projects Sebök undertook with Gropius – a design proposal for the Kharkov Theatre. These preliminary sketches survived in the package that Hoffmann had passed on to the Bauhaus. They featured copious annotations, which were incredibly difficult to decipher, not only because of Sebök's somewhat illegible handwriting, but because his command of the German language was not all that it should have been, even after living in the country for more than ten years. The grammar and spelling are pretty woeful – although his mistakes now seem typical of dyslexia, a condition which happens to be a speciality of my family. (Interestingly, as I later discovered at the Shchusev Museum archive in Moscow, it was Sebök's misspelling of various project titles that actually helped the archivists identify unsigned drawings as his. His dyslexia, then, may well have preserved his historical legacy.) The theatre itself, which was awarded seventh place in the competition, was designed to accommodate an audience of up to 4,000 people for both theatre and circus performances. Unfortunately, very few of the original drawings survive, as they were probably sent off to Kharkov. However, many good photographic records of these architectural renderings and posters for the competition attributed to Sebök remain in the Bauhaus archive.

16
Catalogue for the Werkbund Exhibition in Paris, Bauhaus-Archiv, Berlin, BA Inv No 1740, sign T Paris 1930–32.

Above, right and overleaf: Walter Gropius, project for a state theatre in Kharkov, Russia, 1930–31
Cover of invitation to participate and sketches, sections, plans and perspectival views
(featuring the reintroduced Shevchenko monument) by Stefan Sebök

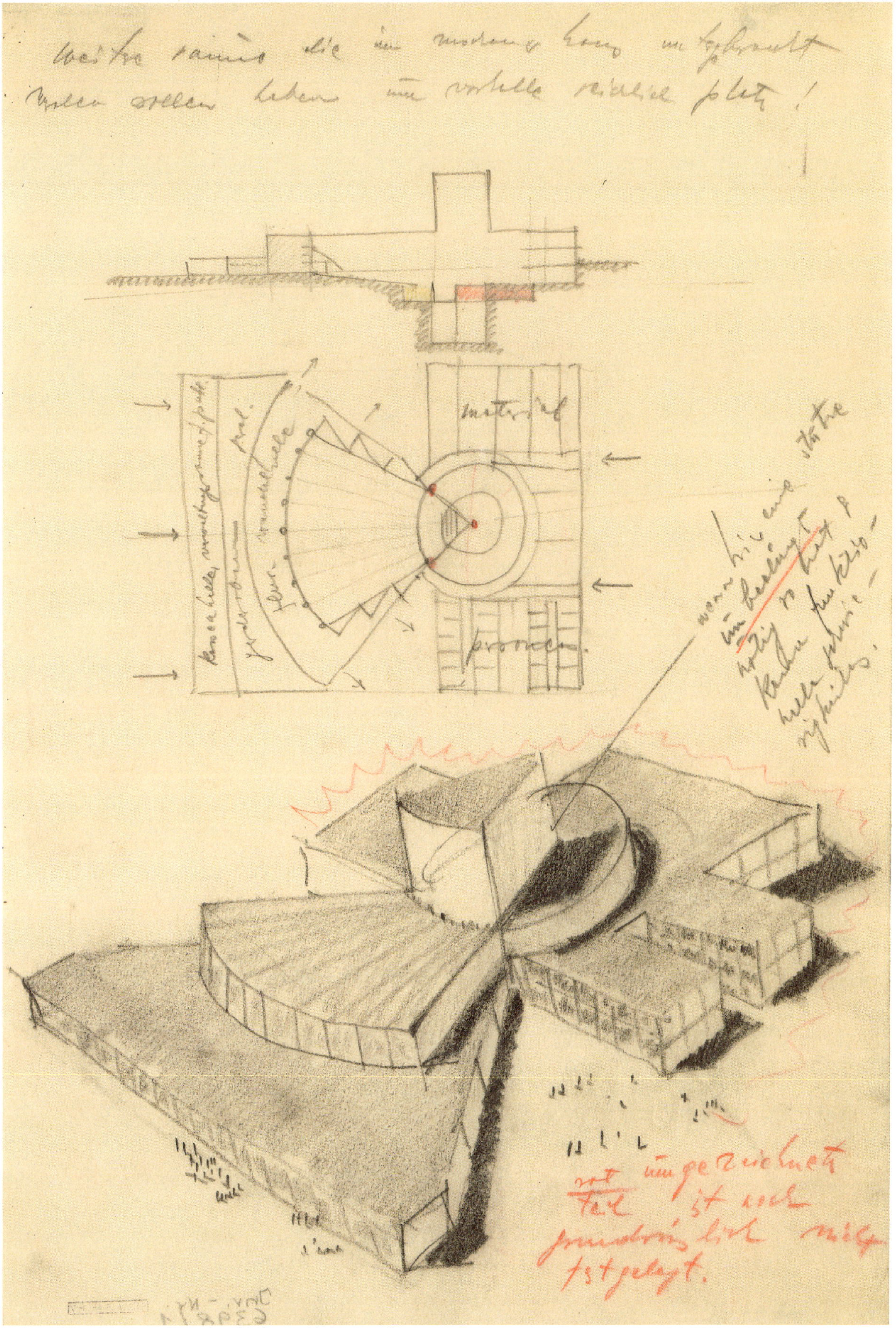
material

schnürboden, prospekte.

drehscheibe, die unterhalb der schnürboden liegenden teil versenkte.

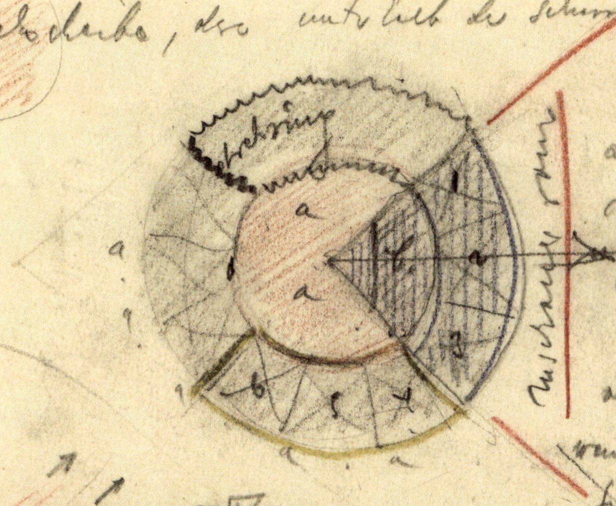

auf der „drehring" schieben sich bühnenwagen

auch über orchesterraum, wenn orchester versenkt, so kann schnell durch lautsprecher verbreitet werden.

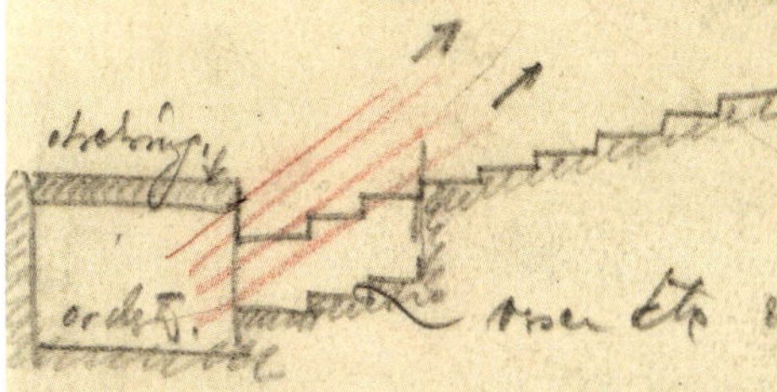

über die rote sitzreihe.

aufbau der drehscheibe findet in der bühnen niveau auf die flächen a a statt,

die aufbau der bühnenwagen auf der bühnen drehring geschieht auch auf die fläche a-a-a — jedoch eine umrangierung kann durch versenkung ein teil des ring-teil finden.

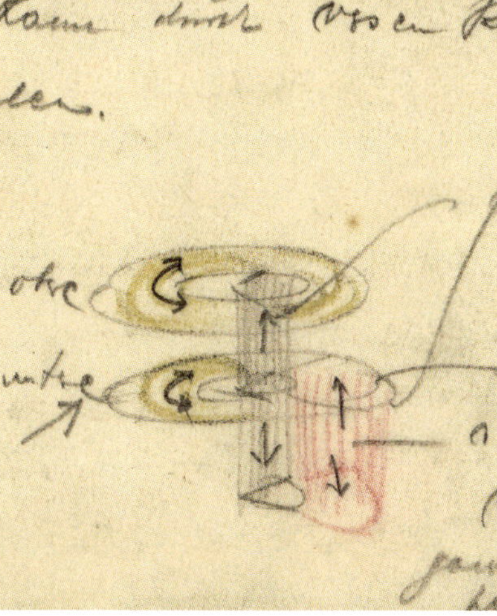

durch drehung der ring kann orchester verschoben werden, wonach dann ganze vorplatz ringteil [illegible] werden.

dazu:

kleine
schematische
perspektiven

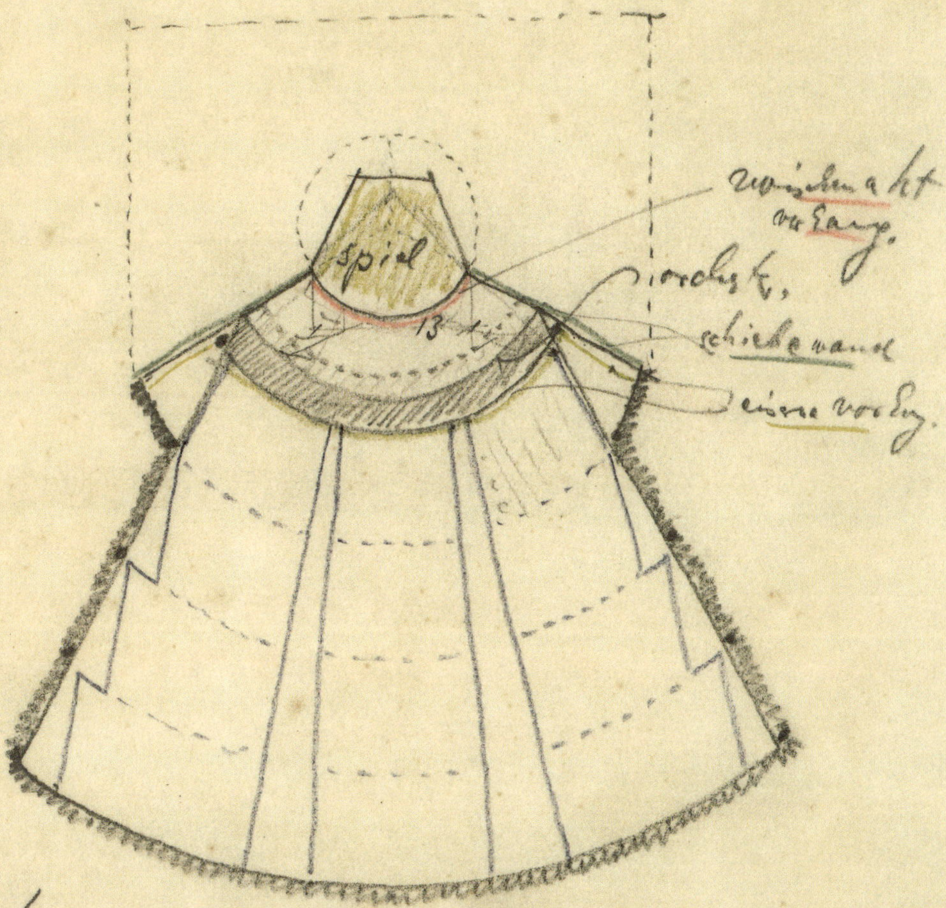

hier kommt dazu:
1.) intimes spiel auch
vorgerückt
2.) " spiel in 3 teilen

intimes spiel
auf drehscheibe
aufgebaut.

массовый центр

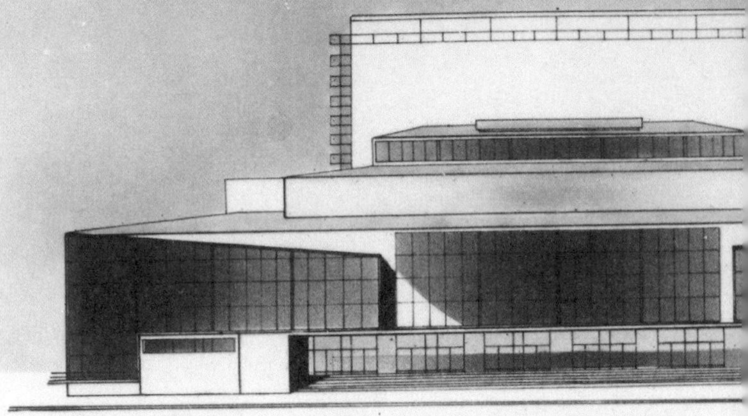

10. вид с ул. карла либкнехта 1:200

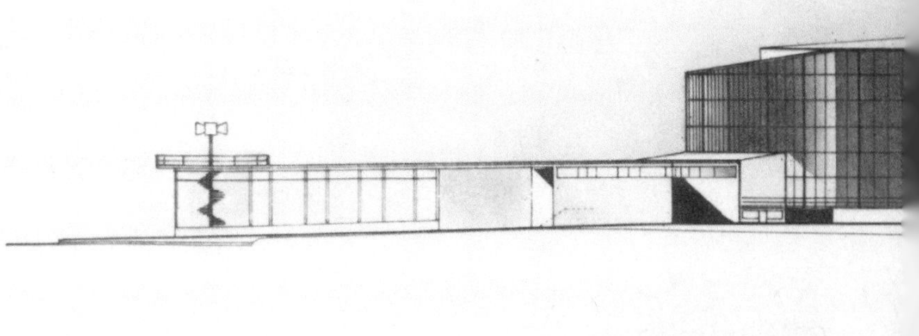

вид с сердюковского пер-ка 1:20

массовый центр

16. перспектива вестибюля и фойе

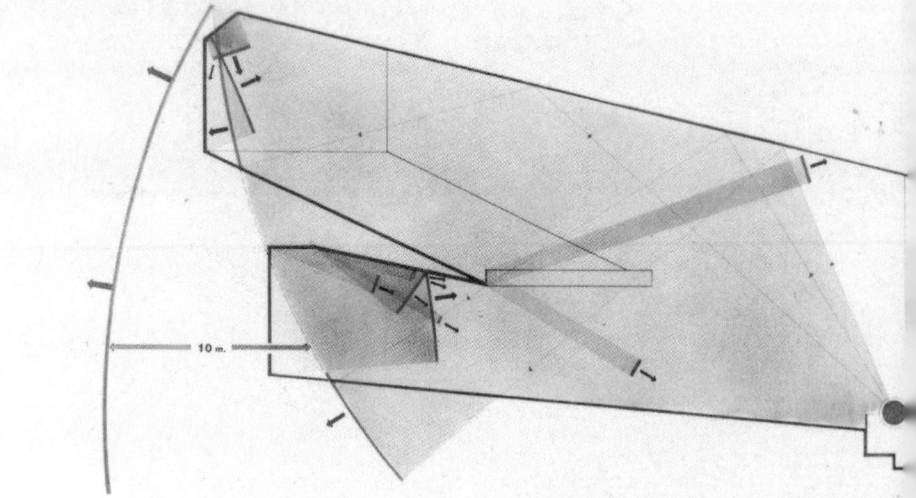

таблица звуко-поглощения:

1. пол в партере, линолеум	1 273,0 x 0,03	= 16,37
2. " яруса, линолеум	[illegible]	[illegible]
3. бок.стены, стенных лепка	[illegible]	[illegible]
4. задние стены, стенных лепка	[illegible]	[illegible]
5. потолок, укрыш. из плет. проволоки	[illegible]	[illegible]
6. ниж. плоск. яруса, плет. проволока	[illegible]	[illegible]
7. барьеры партера, бетон	[illegible]	[illegible]
8. барьеры балкона, бетон	[illegible]	[illegible]
9. двери, деревянные	[illegible]	[illegible]
10. отверстие сцены	[illegible]	[illegible]
11. стулья, деревянные	[illegible]	[illegible]
12. люди	[illegible] x 0,50	= 1928,00
13. отверстия отопления и вентиляции	70,0 x 0,50	= 11,00
сумма всех поглотителей		3587,78

вычисление времени отдачи звука (эхо):
при вычислении объёма зала осталось неучтенным объёмное помещение по ту сторону наибольшего сцен. отверстия, зато звуко-поглотательное число наибольшего отверстия вводится в общую сумму всех звуко-поглотителей.

время отдачи звука высчитывается по формуле: $T = \frac{0,164 \cdot V}{A}$

объём зала V: ... 25 185,16 m³
сумма всех звуко-поглотителей: ... 3 587,78

$$T = \frac{0,164 \cdot 25\,185,16}{3\,587,78} = 1,1\ldots$$

вычитанное возможное время отдачи звука: 1,15 сек.

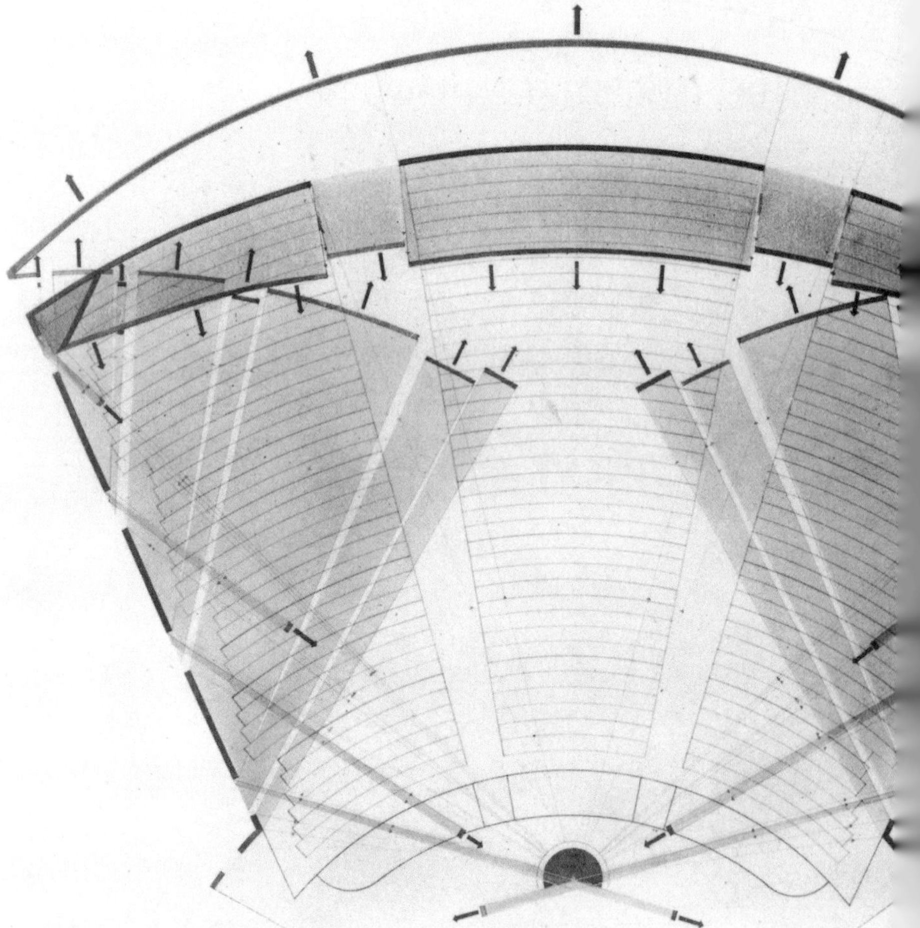

12. слышимости (акустики) 1:1oo

массовый центр

.сцена.

сцена построена как индустриальный монтажный зал или сортировочный вокзал с различными возможностями переставлять и передвигать в каждом направлении.

платформы с площадью в 25 квадратных метра каждая могут, как непрерывный лифт-/патерностер/-благодаря соединению с трюмом, подниматься, опускаться и передвигаться. центральный поворотный круг окружен поворотным кольцом. весь поворотный круг и отдельные части могут опускаться и подниматься.

магазины таким образом примыкают к нижней стороне сцены, что все части могут, без больших изменений, легко в'езжать на сцену при помощи под'емных кранов и [illegible].

управление всеми механическими устройствами производится из одного центрального командного пункта с центральной клавиатурой.

все уборные артистов могут быть наблюдаемы инспектором с одного главного командного мостика.

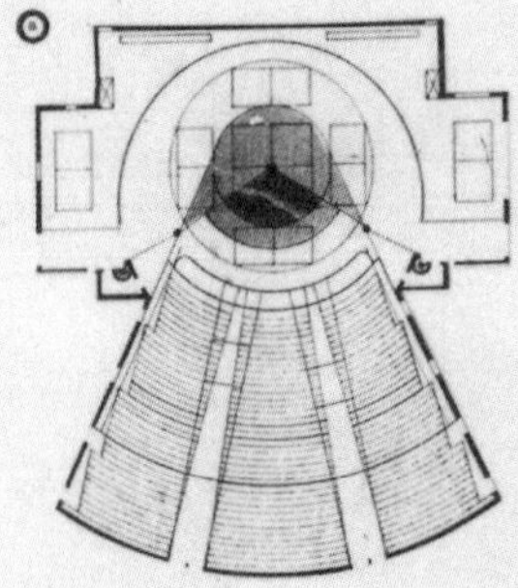

игральные площади и игральные пути

сцена должна быть приспособлена для всякого рода представлений, как интимных, так и массовых.

(а) есть вид маленькой игральной площади для интимных представлений.

(б) увеличивает переднее поле-/авансцену/-и дает возможность перенесения единичных артистических представлений в проходы зрительного зала и на боковые рампы до балконов сцены. одновременно могут сценические платформы, привешенные к балконам потолка, в'езжать со сцены в свободное пространство зрительного зала.

(в) указывает расширение сцены б/ возможность ее увеличения в глубину.

(г) ставит наибольшую сценическую площадь с максимальным ее расширением и дает одновременно возможность перемещения постановок через всю сцену из одного бокового портала здания в другой.

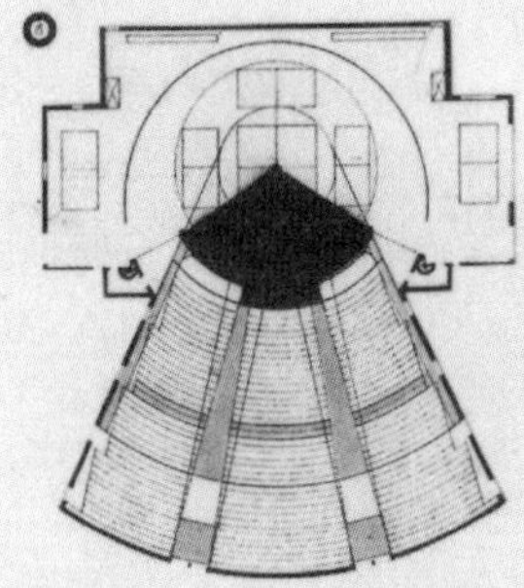

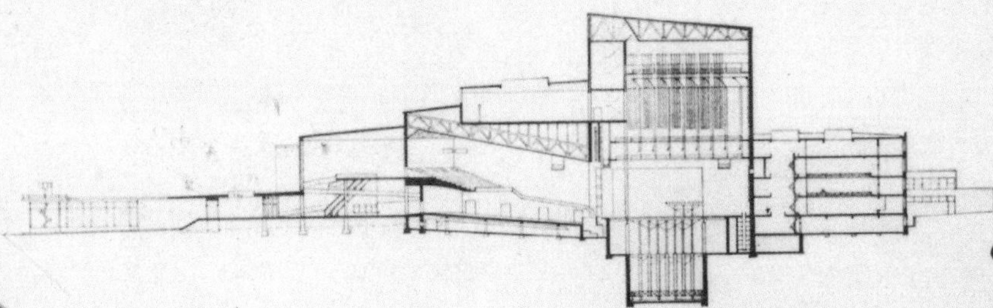

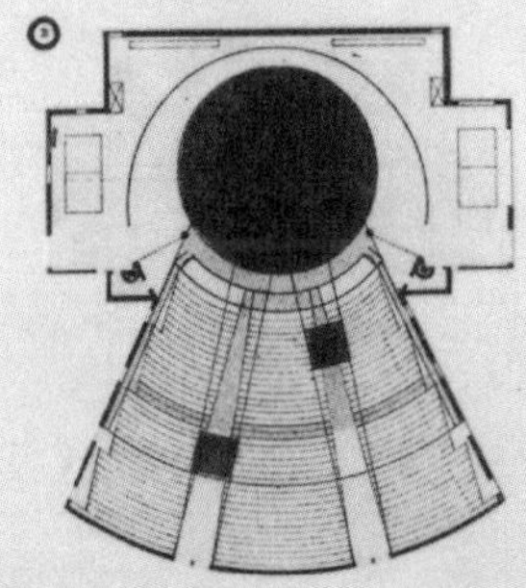

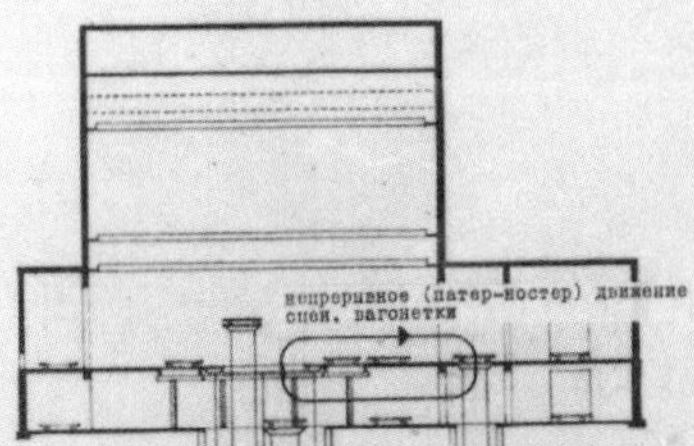

поперечный разрез через сценическое помещение

фильм и проекция.

с целью ввести зрительные массы в сценическое действие и одновременно охватить сценой весь зрительный зал, установлен целый ряд источников световых эффектов, которые позволяют не только собственно-сценическое пространство за пожарным занавесом, но и потолки и боковые стены зрительного зала заполнять проекциями и фильмами.

существенное средство охватывающее сцену и зрительный зал и об'единяющее зрителя и актера

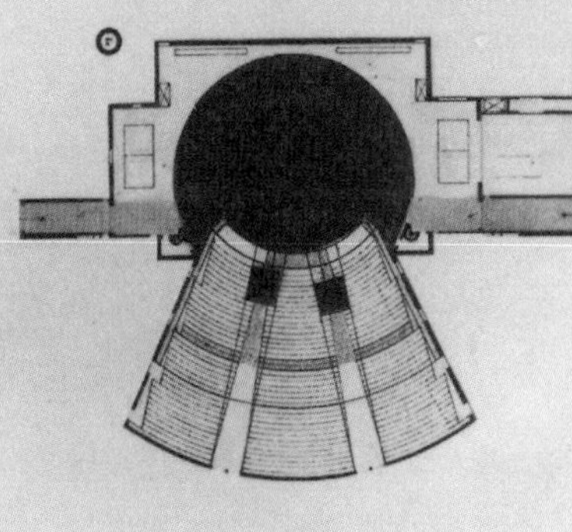

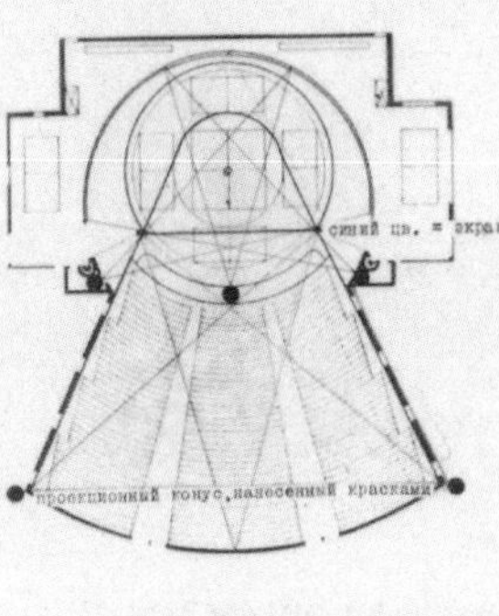

площадок для игр 1:500

массовый центр

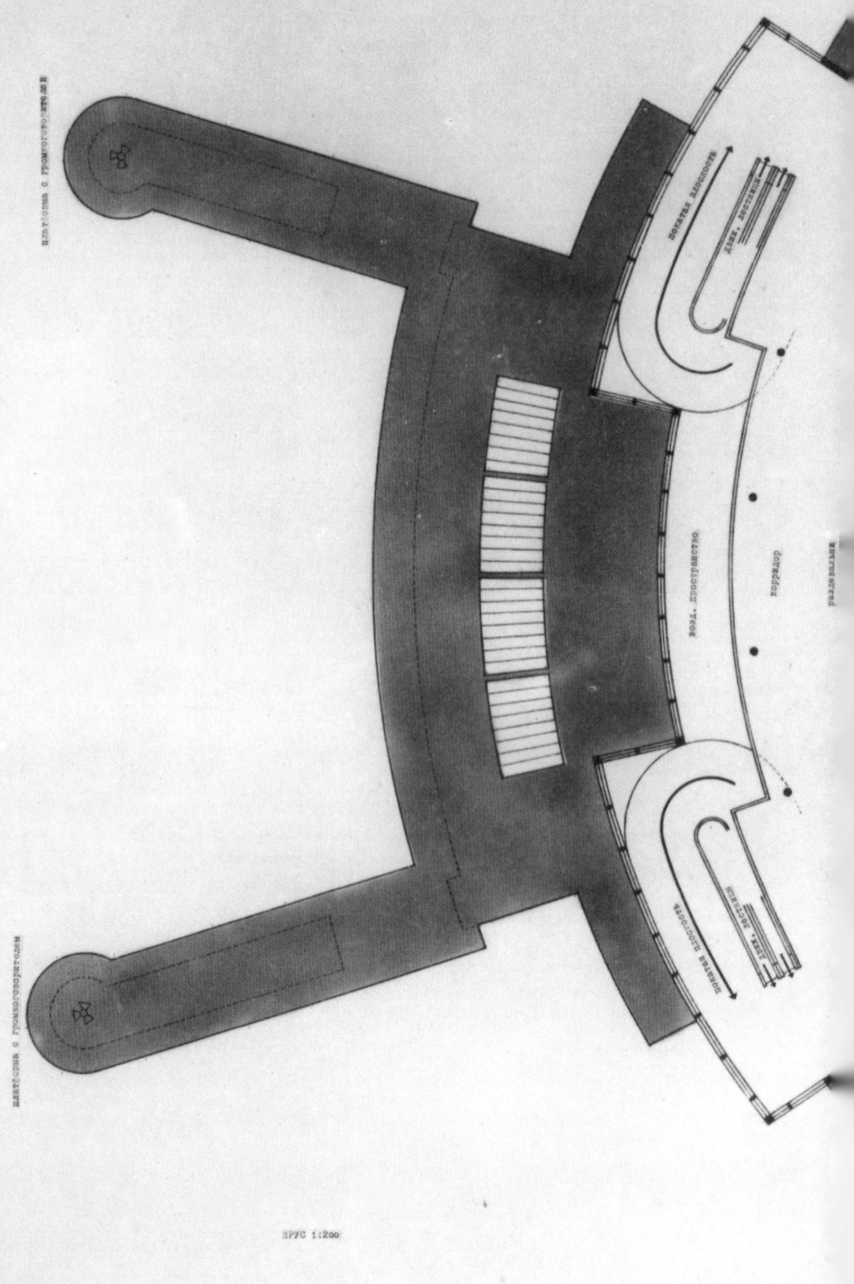

5. горизонт. проекция яруса 1:2оо

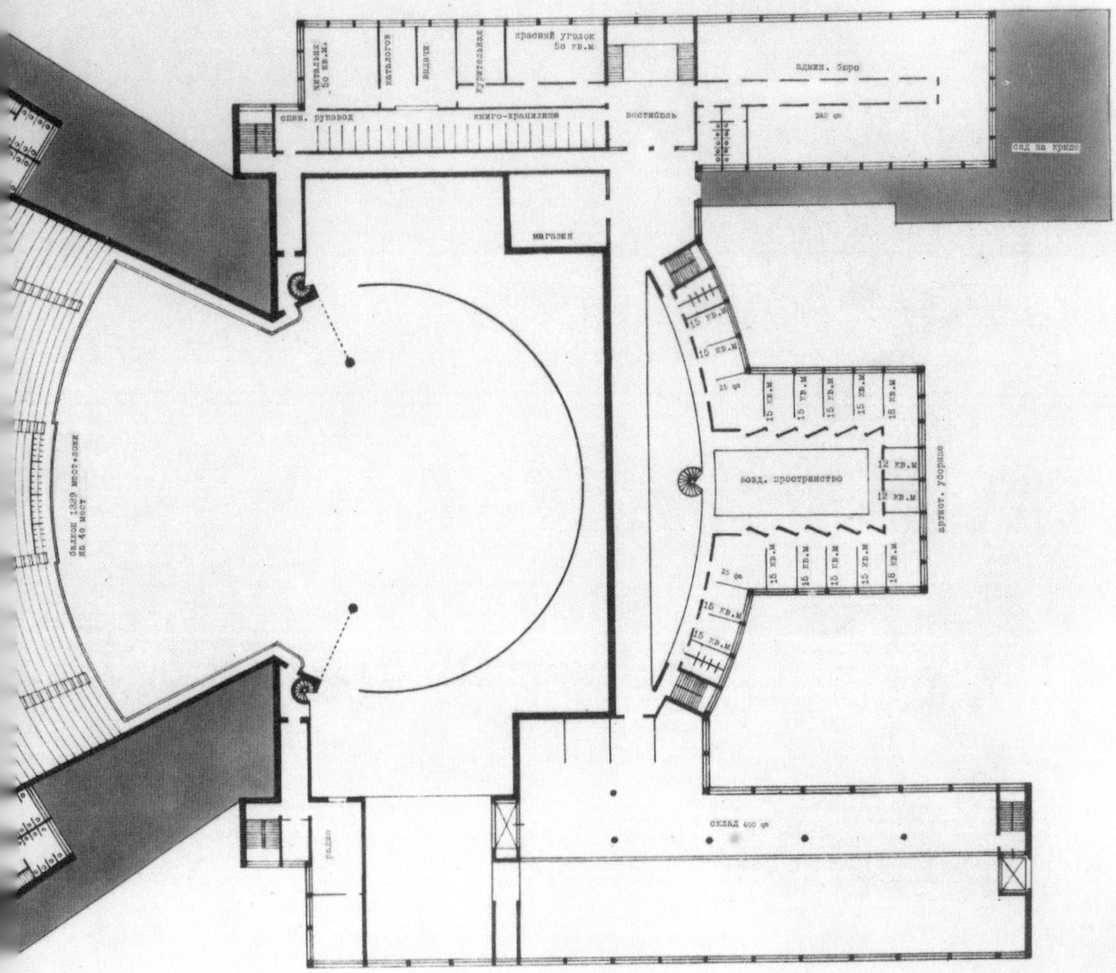
читальня 50 кв.м.
каталогов
выдачи
курительная
красный уголок 50 кв.м
админ. бюро
спец. руковод
книго-хранилище
вестибюль
240 qm
сад на крыше
магазин
15 кв.м
25 qm
18 кв.м
12 кв.м
возд. пространство
артист. уборные
склад 400 qm
радио
балкон 1329 мест+ложи из 40 мест

Inspired by these theatrical projects, I later went to visit the Theatre Museum in Cologne. This was on the recommendation of Hubertus Gassner, but also to follow up what I had learned on my trip to Boston and the Bauhaus archive about Sebök's involvement with Moholy-Nagy during his time spent working in Gropius's office in Berlin. László Moholy-Nagy, a fellow Hungarian, was an artist, photographer and studio master at the Bauhaus (1923–28). Strongly influenced by Russian constructivism, which he first came into contact with in Berlin in the early 1920s, he soon developed an expertise in the fields of photography, typography, sculpture, painting and industrial design, focusing always on the idea that photography could go beyond the limitations of the human eye in creating a whole new way of seeing the world – an ambition that manifested itself in his experiments with photograms and abstract light effects, and two artworks that explored the effect of movement on the senses, the *Lichtrequisit einer elektrischen Bühne* (Light-Prop for an Electric Stage) and the *Kinetisch-Konstruktives System* (Kinetic-Constructive System). Sebök was involved in the design and construction of both these pieces. A drawing for the design of the Kinetic-Constructive System is in the Cologne Theatre Museum, signed Moholy-Nagy, with a label 'Durchkonstruiert von Stefan Sebök'.

This project, as described by Chris Salter in his book on the technology of performance, *Entangled*, envisioned a huge vertical cylinder in which both the audience and performers would be kept in constant motion by a series of conveyor belts and escalators mounted on the structure's exterior and interior. Performers could also ascend via a central elevator and descend by sliding down a fire station-like pole, while the entire structure itself turned in a circular motion. A virtual construction of the Kinetic-Constructive System was recently developed by the New York architect Peter Yeadon, who argued that the various colours and shading illustrated in the collage did not simply serve an aesthetic purpose, but offered colour-coded indications relating to the tower's structural load and assembly.[17] This, in turn, begs the question as to whether the collaged drawing always associated with this project and attributed to Moholy-Nagy may also have been the result of Sebök's more technical, architectural and structural understanding of its construction.

Later came the collaboration on the famous *Light-Prop*, the mechanical, kinetic sculpture first exhibited at the 1930 Paris Werkbund exhibition. The *Prop* was constructed with the aim of producing an array of coloured light, while the machine itself rotated on its central axis. The shadows it produced were projected against the wall of the installation space in a kind of theatrical production of itself – something that intrigued Moholy-Nagy no end. The original model for the machine is at the Busch-Reisinger museum and the only surviving drawing of its construction, accredited to Sebök, sits in the Bauhaus in Berlin.

17
Peter Yeadon, 'A Note on the Kinetic-Reconstructive System' in Oliver Al Botar (ed), *Technical Detours: The Early Moholy-Nagy Reconsidered* (New York: The City University of New York, 2006), p 204.

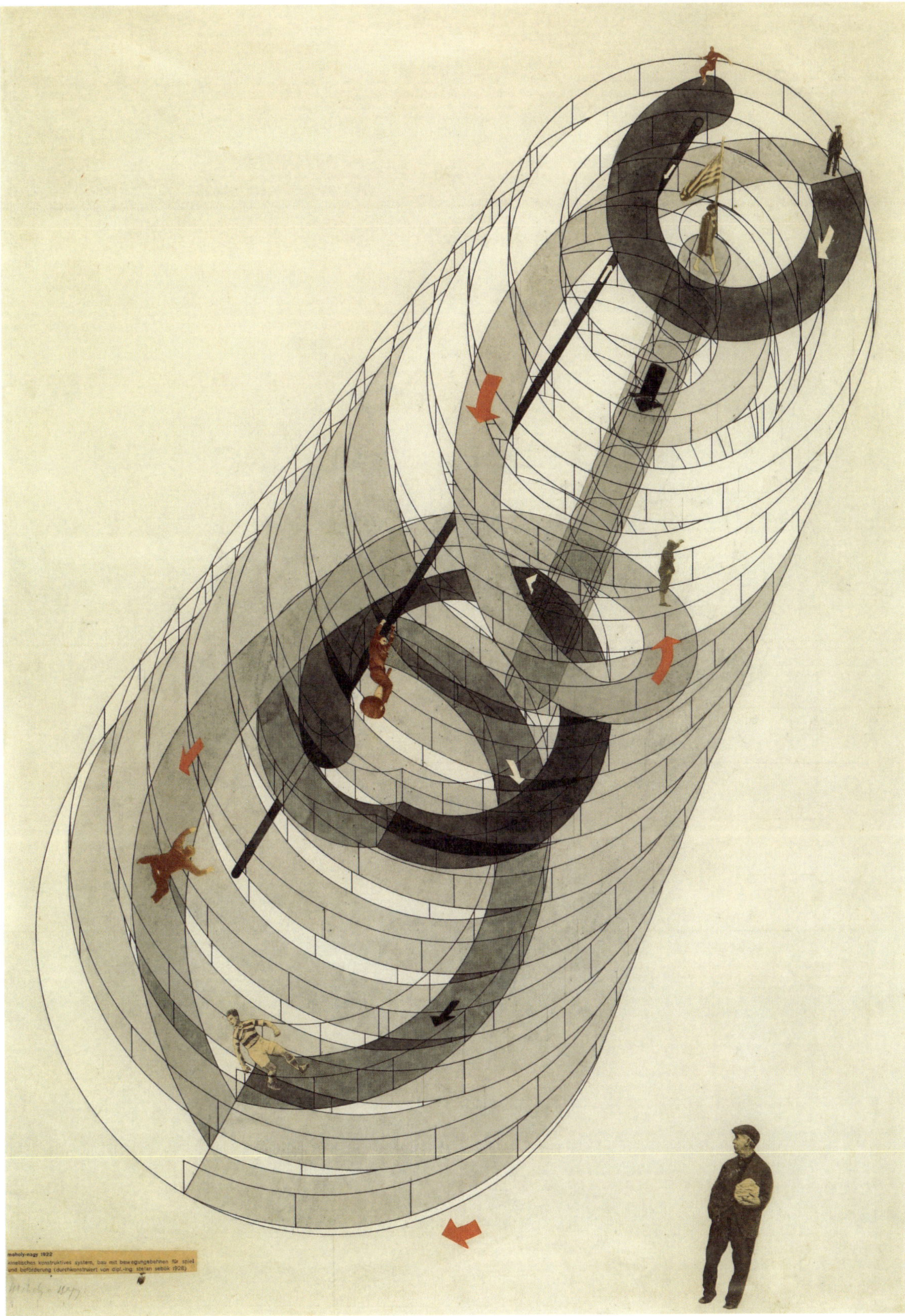

László Moholy-Nagy, with Stefan Sebök, Kinetic Constructive system, 1928

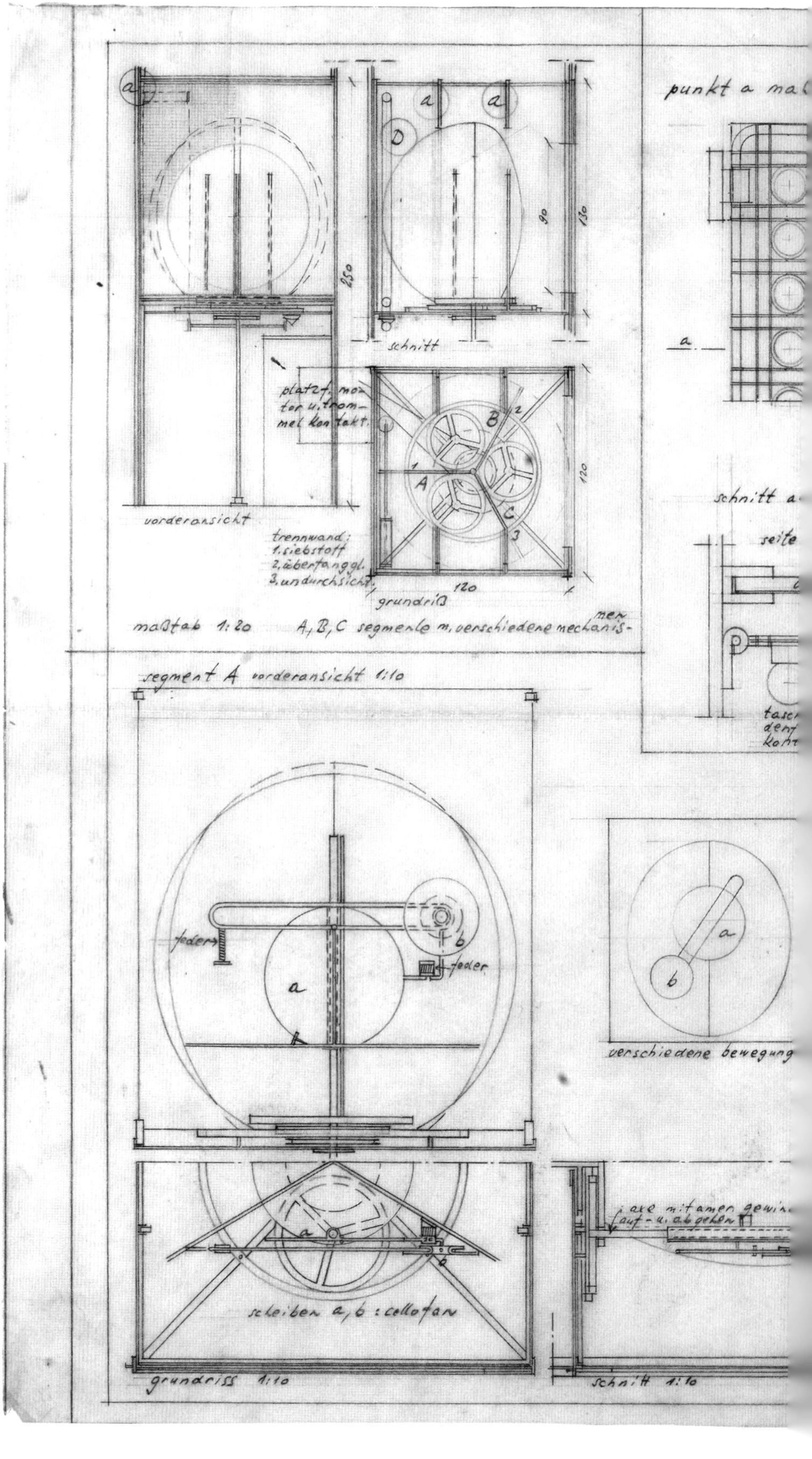
punkt a
a
a
a
D
250
90
130
schnitt
platz f. motor u. trommel kontakt.
B
2
1
A
C
3
120
vorderansicht
trennwand:
1. siebstoff
2. überfanggl.
3. undurchsicht.
120
grundriß
maßtab 1:20
A, B, C segmente m. verschiedenen mechanismen
a
segment A vorderansicht 1:10
feder
b
feder
a
a
b
verschiedene
a
b
scheiben a, b : cellofan
grundriss 1:10
axe mit einem
auf- u. abgehen
schnitt 1:10

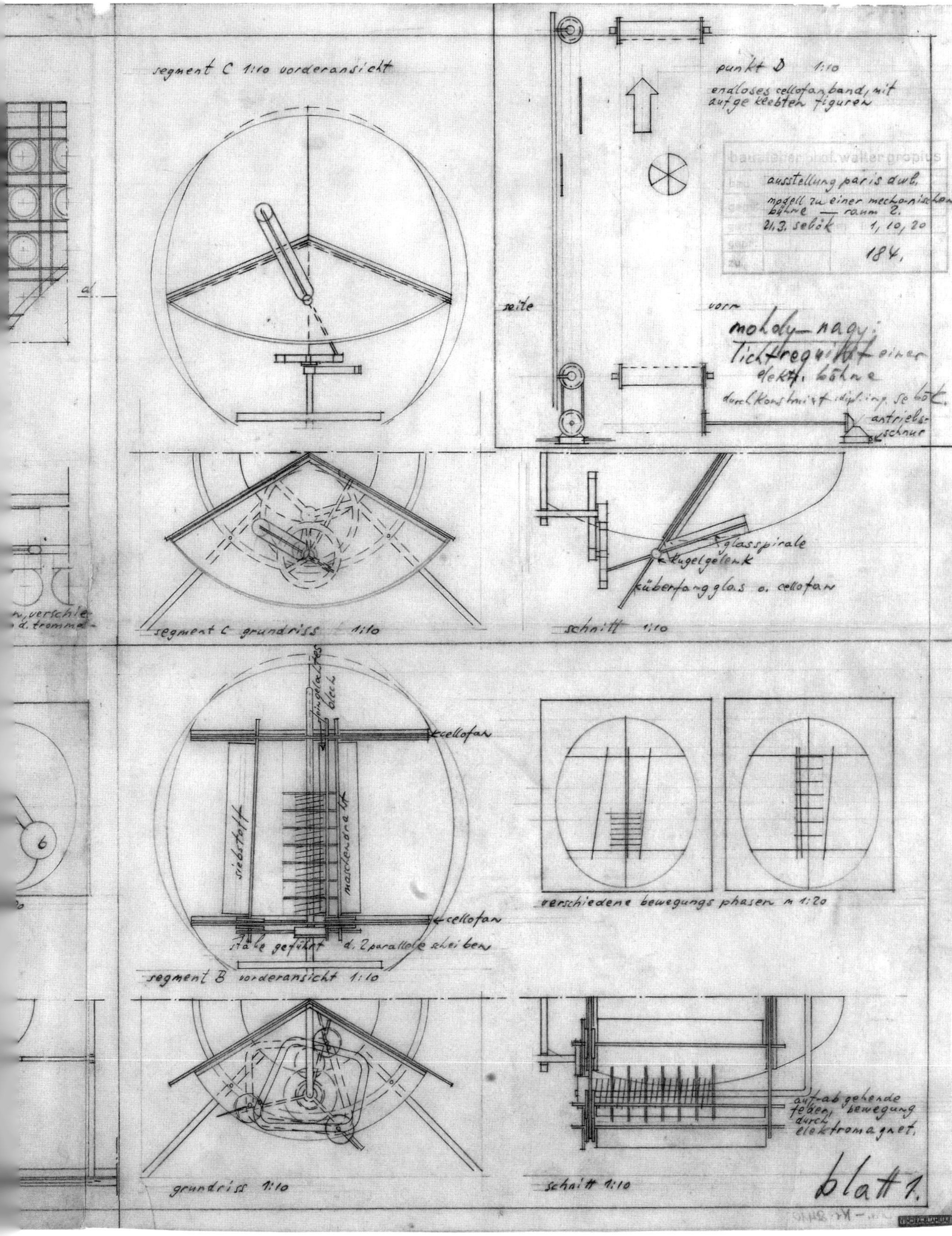

Above and overleaf: László Moholy-Nagy, Lightmodulator, technical drawing and collages with Stefan Sebök

moholy-nagy:
lichtrequisit einer elektrischen bühne
1922-193o
(durchkonstruiert von dipl.ing.stefan sebök)
darstellung eines bewegungsspiels auf dem
ersten sektor (werkzeichnung)

moholy-nagy:
lichtrequisit einer elektrischen bühne
1922-1930
(durchkonstruiert von dipl.ing.stefan sebök)
darstellung des gesamtmodells

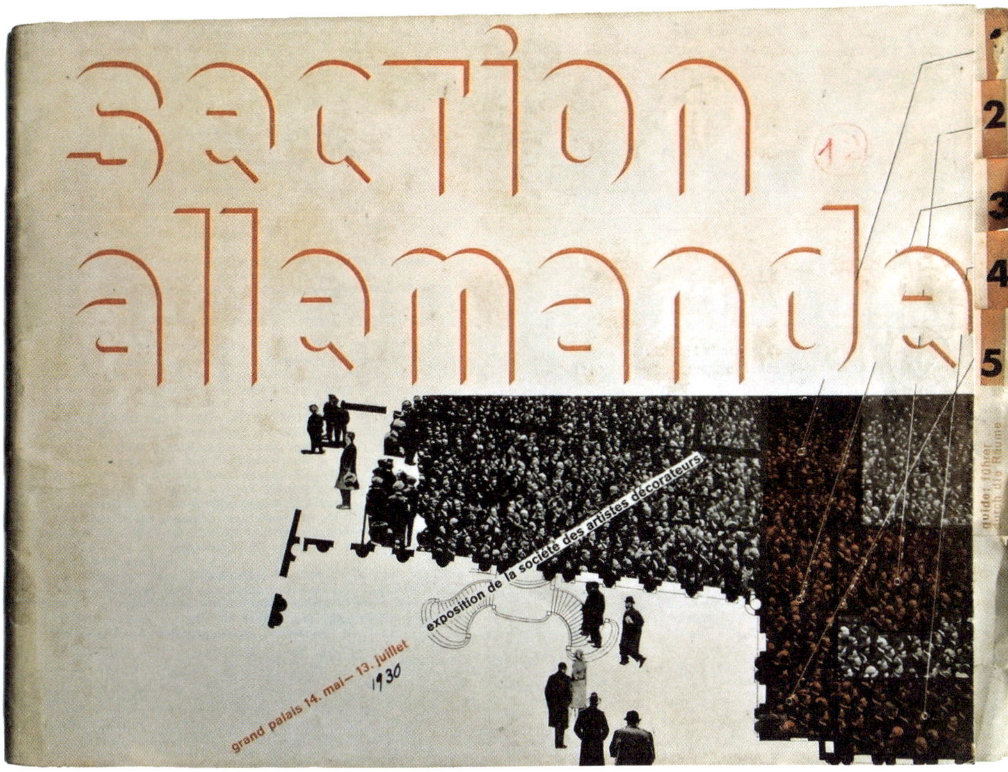

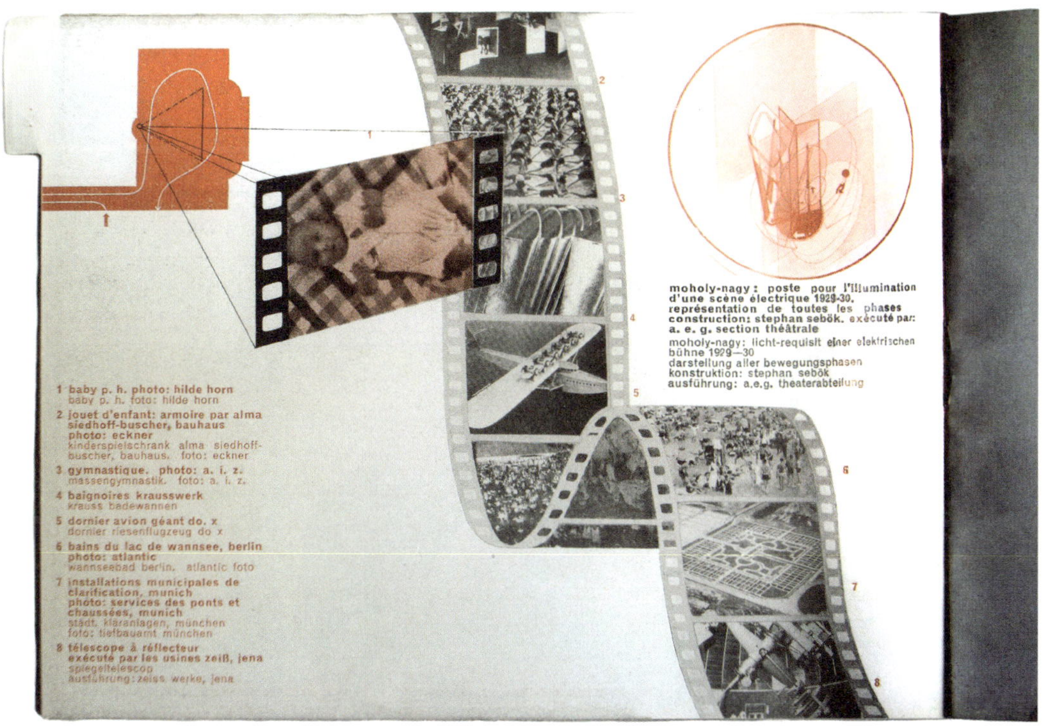

Paris Werkbund exhibition catalogue, featuring the Lightmodulator, 1930

Above and overleaf: Walter Gropius, communal room for a high-rise apartment, 1930
Perspectival views by Stefan Sebök

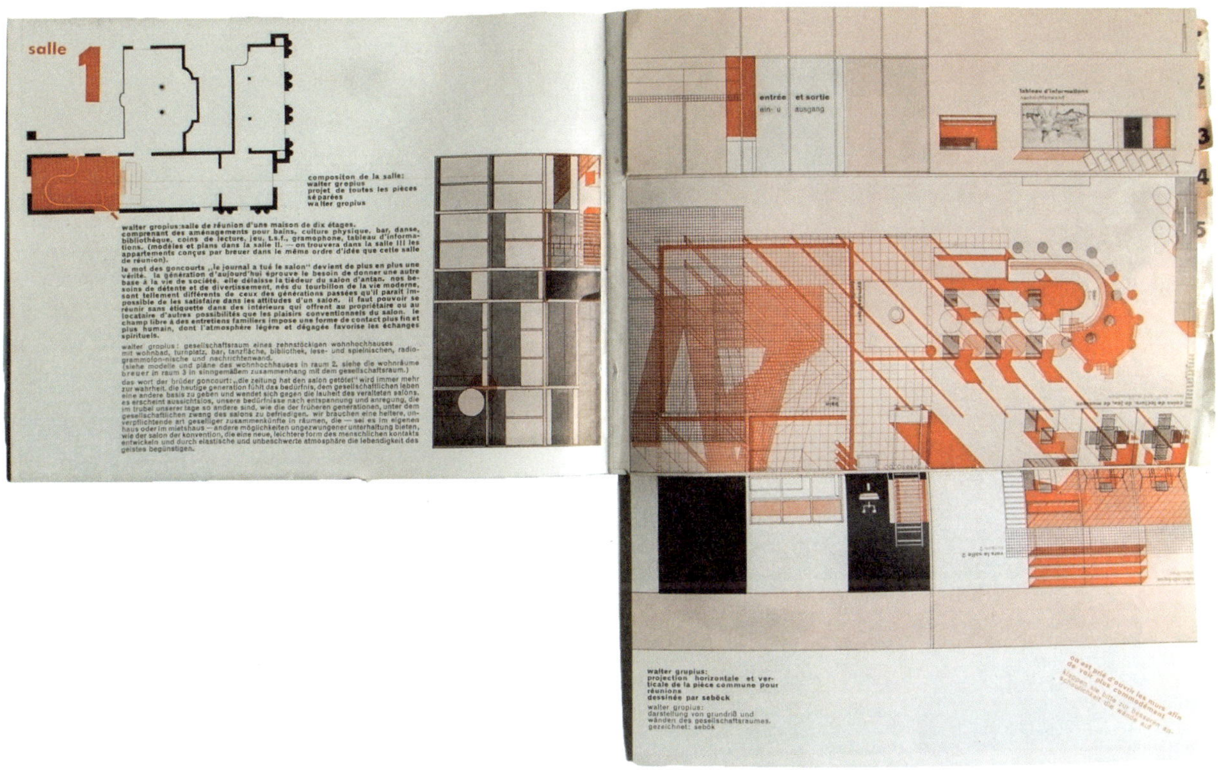

Gropius's high-rise apartment project in the catalogue for the Paris Werkbund exhibition, 1930

Above and overleaf: photograph of the production team for *The Merchant of Berlin*, 1929

The construction of the *Light-Prop* was reviewed in great detail by the art historian Nan Rosenthal whose graduate thesis on the *Light-Prop* was published in the *Harvard Graduate Journal*. In this paper, she points out that there is no reference to the *Light-Prop* in the writings of Moholy-Nagy prior to its construction with Sebök. And that contrary to the commonly held view, the *Prop* was built by the mechanic Otto Ball in whose workshop Moholy-Nagy had first seen the machine perform and whose name is on the plaque of the *Light-Prop* on display at the Bush-Reisinger Museum. It was Otto Ball who would have required Sebök's construction drawings (AEG, usually credited with its construction, were in fact only responsible for the lightbox built into the machine).[18] Rosenthal also revealed the little-known fact that the two *Props* currently in existence – in the Bauhaus archive and the Eindhoven Museum – were constructed by Woody Flowers from MIT with some safety modifications for the Venice Biennale only after Moholy's death. Flowers never got properly acknowledged for it.

In addition to these mechanical installations Sebök was involved with Moholy-Nagy in a number of Piscator's plays. The first of these was a set design in early 1929 for a production of Offenbach's *Tales of Hoffmann*. Sebök was employed as leading technician and stage designer, a role well documented by Max Gebhard in the *Wechselwirkungen* catalogue. According to Gebhard, 'all hell let loose' when Moholy-Nagy met up in the studio with his friend Sebök. With lively debates between them, all the original sets, props and lighting were dismantled, changed around, reassembled and then taken apart yet again. Everyone would work late into the night until finally, to the accompaniment of wild applause and whistling, they achieved the desired effects.

In August that same year Moholy-Nagy got a second commission from Piscator for the set design of Walter Mehring's *The Merchant of Berlin*, which was to be the opening production in Piscator's new theatre on Nollendorfplatz. Again, Sebök was responsible for the construction, which according to reviews, surpassed anything previously realised, with a stage that could spin or be raised or lowered hydraulically, and with horizontal carts on which the actors slid through the space at different heights, as well as additional film projections. It produced a technical spectacle that met with mixed reviews from the public but wild enthusiasm from the critics, who praised its ability to evoke the movement and vitality of the city street.

On my return to London I thought I should try again to track down Sebök's university records. This was partly in response to a question from Matthias Schirren at the Berlin Akademie – when, exactly, was Sebök born? – a key question, given that he was considering curating an exhibition timed to coincide with the centenary of Sebök's birth. I had phoned the TU in Dresden several times in the past with various enquiries, but no palpable success. This time I tried a different tactic. Instead of asking directly about Sebök, I simply said that I would like to know something about the curriculum of the architectural school in 1925.

18
Nan Rosenthal, 'László Moholy-Nagy's Lichtrequisit, 1930', Harvard University Graduate School of Arts and Sciences, 1969.

Stefan Sebök (right) in Dresden, 1921

Immediately I was put through to the TU Dresden archive department, whose existence had never before been acknowledged. I was informed that they did indeed have records for some of their students, as 10,000 archives had survived the burning of Dresden. It turned out that Sebök's was among them.

The Dresden records turned out to be voluminous.[19] They included Sebök's original application to the university, his matriculation certificate, student card and documentation of his admission and graduation, together with the subjects he studied, the grades he was awarded and his internships or *Praktikums* (none of which were with Gropius, as suggested by Peter Nisbet). In addition, they also revealed some interesting biographical details about why he was unable to study in Budapest and how he spent time working in various architectural offices and as a stonemason to gain practical experience. In his application, Sebök explains that he was frustrated by his circumstances and that his burning desire had always been to become an architect. He states political reasons for not being able to study in Hungary. There is a remark pencilled next to his statement – '*numerus clausus*' – referring to the fact that in Hungary only a very small number of Jews were allowed into higher education, in contrast to the Weimar Republic which had no such restrictions at the time.

One of the documents in the archive which intrigued me most was an affidavit, translation of a Hungarian document, signed by a notary, stating that my grandfather was very sympathetic towards the German Reich, as evidenced by the fact that he had sent his three children to study in Germany before the war. This sort of affidavit was apparently an indispensible part of the application process. He was admitted in 1921 to the Hochbau division for the winter term, and graduated with the Tanztheater diploma project submitted in December 1926.

Alongside these records, the TU's archivist Matthias Lienert also offered great insights into the structure of the architecture course. He explained that in Dresden, in contrast to the other universities, three different faculties offered an architectural training. Besides the traditional, arts-based Kunstakademie, there was the Fakultät Bauingenieurwesen, whose students typically enjoyed careers working on the construction of railways and other large engineering and infrastructural projects, and the Hochbau-Abteilung, the youngest faculty, founded in 1875 on the initiative of Rudolph Heyn and Gustav Zeuner, whose students could choose whether they wanted an art- or an engineering-orientated training.[20] In Sebök's time certain subjects were compulsory, whilst others were elective. Sebök chose the engineering-orientated course but took art subjects and drawings for his free choices – giving him a well-rounded training that stood him in good stead in his later career. According to Lienert, in these early decades of the twentieth century the students and staff of all three Dresden faculties were heavily influenced by the teachings of the architectural historian Cornelius Gurlitt, who had been appointed to the school in 1903.

19
Stefan Sebök, Dresden Technische Hochschule Student Archives, Inv No 9548.

20
Matthias Lienert, *Geschichte der Technischen Universität Dresden in Dokumenten und Bildern* (Dresden: Technische Universität Dresden, Band 2), p 41.

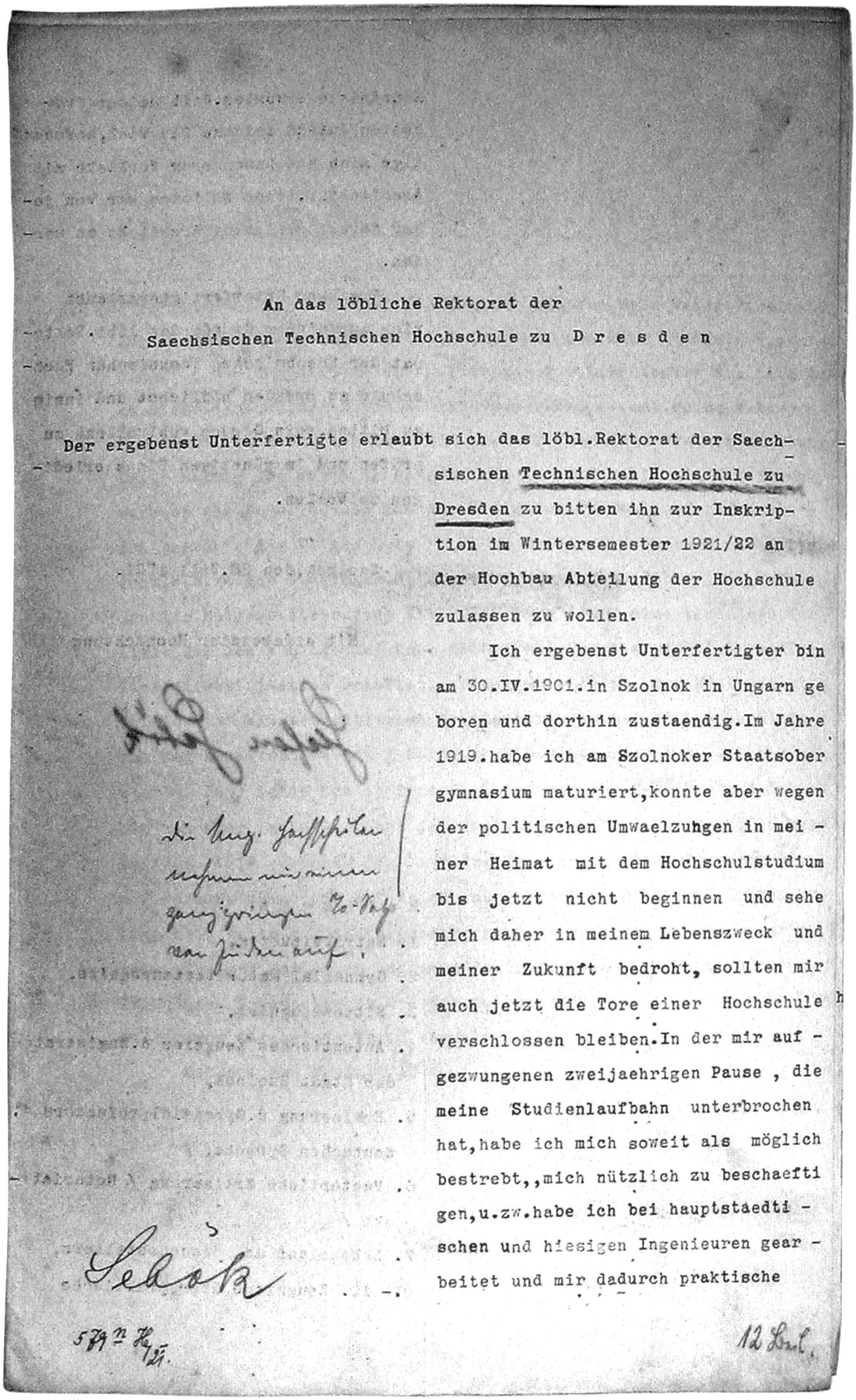

An das löbliche Rektorat der

Saechsischen Technischen Hochschule zu D r e s d e n

Der ergebenst Unterfertigte erlaubt sich das löbl.Rektorat der Saechsischen Technischen Hochschule zu Dresden zu bitten ihn zur Inskription im Wintersemester 1921/22 an der Hochbau Abteilung der Hochschule zulassen zu wollen.

Ich ergebenst Unterfertigter bin am 30.IV.1901.in Szolnok in Ungarn geboren und dorthin zustaendig.Im Jahre 1919.habe ich am Szolnoker Staatsobergymnasium maturiert,konnte aber wegen der politischen Umwaelzuhgen in meiner Heimat mit dem Hochschulstudium bis jetzt nicht beginnen und sehe mich daher in meinem Lebenszweck und meiner Zukunft bedroht, sollten mir auch jetzt die Tore einer Hochschule verschlossen bleiben.In der mir aufgezwungenen zweijaehrigen Pause , die meine Studienlaufbahn unterbrochen hat,habe ich mich soweit als möglich bestrebt,,mich nützlich zu beschaefti gen,u.zw.habe ich bei hauptstaedtischen und hiesigen Ingenieuren gearbeitet und mir dadurch praktische

Sebök

Stefan Sebök's application for admission to the Sächsische Technische Hochschule, Dresden, 1921

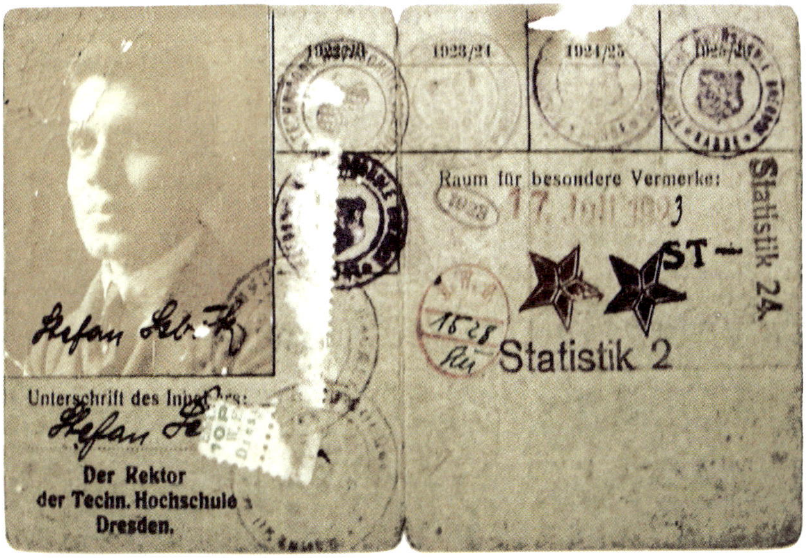

Stefan Sebök

Unterschrift des Inhabers:

Stefan Sebök

Der Rektor
der Techn. Hochschule
Dresden.

1922/23 | 1923/24 | 1924/25 | 1925/26

Raum für besondere Vermerke:

17. Juli 1923

ST–

Statistik 24.

Statistik 2

Matrikel
bis 15. 11. 1931 verlängert

Matrikel Nr. 16666

Herr ... Sebök

geboren am 30.4.01 zu Szolnok, Ungarn

ist heute als Studierender der Sächsischen Technischen Hochschule zu Dresden eingeschrieben worden.

Dresden, den 15ten November 1921.

Der Rektor der Sächsischen Technischen Hochschule

Form. III, 1.

Stefan Sebök's student card at the Sächsische Technische Hochschule, Dresden (top), matriculation certificate (bottom), practicum certificate from Szolnok, 1923 (overleaf left), Dresden transcripts, 1926 (overleaf right)

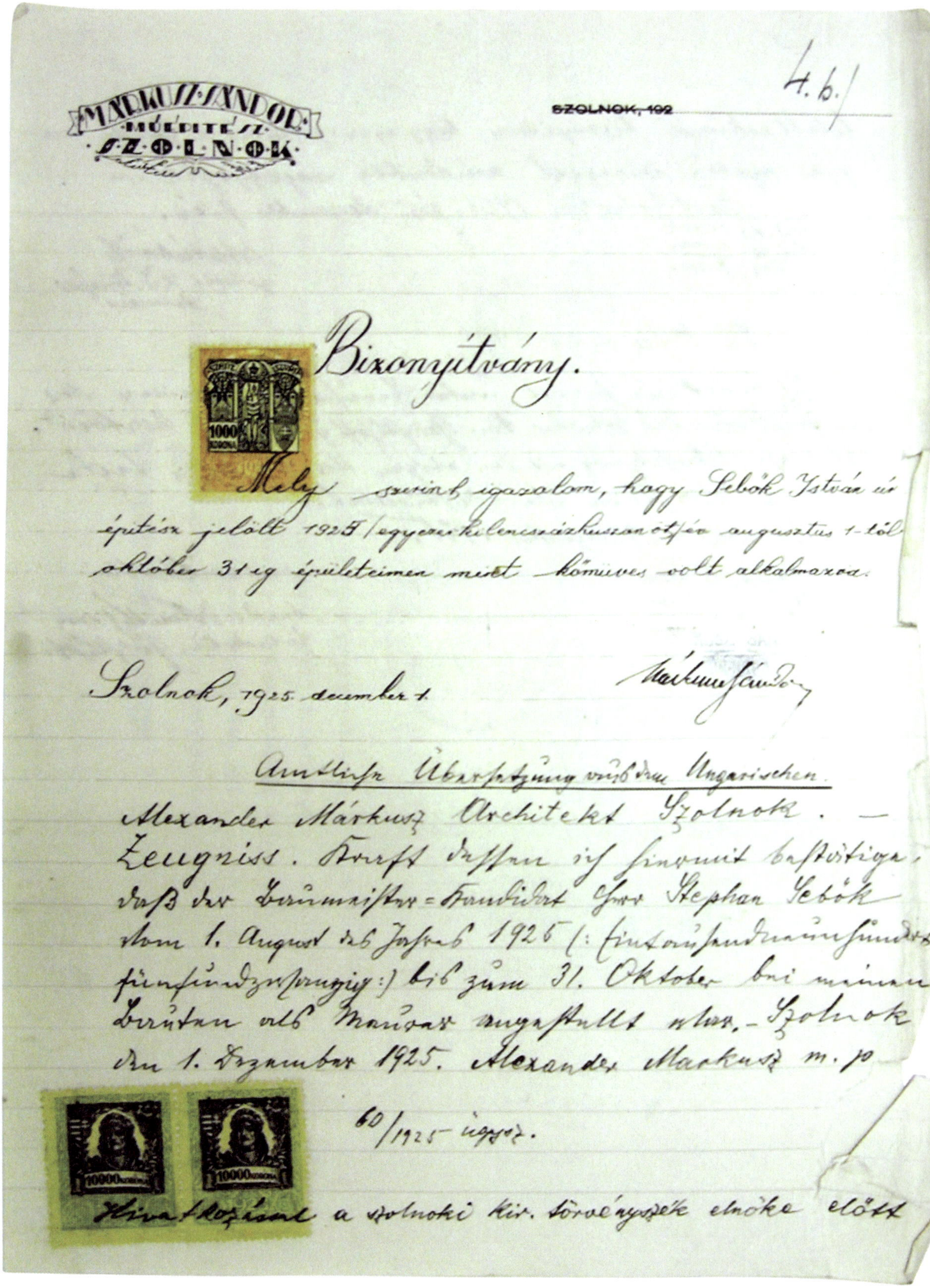
MÁRKUSZ SÁNDOR
MŰÉPITÉSZ
SZOLNOK

SZOLNOK, 192

4. b./

Bizonyitvány.

Mely szerint igazolom, hogy Sebők István úr épitész jelölt 1925 (egyezerkilencszázhuszonötös) augusztus 1-től október 31-ig épületeimen mint kőmüves volt alkalmazva.

Szolnok, 1925. december 1.

Márkusz Sándor

Amtliche Übersetzung aus dem Ungarischen.

Alexander Márkusz Architekt Szolnok. — Zeugniss. Kraft dessen ich hiermit bestätige, daß der Baumeister-Kandidat Herr Stephan Sebők vom 1. August des Jahres 1925 (: eintausendneunhundertfünfundzwanzig :) bis zum 31. Oktober bei meinen Bauten als Maurer angestellt war. — Szolnok den 1. Dezember 1925. Alexander Markusz m. p.

60/1925 ügysz.

Hivatkozással a szolnoki kir. törvényszék elnöke előtt

47.2.10

×

Hochbau – Abteilung.

Diplom-Schlussprüfung aus Lehrgang A.

Studienbelege.

des Studierenden . . Stefan Sebök . . . .

Zeichnungen	Dozenten	Note	Unterschrift des Dozenten.
a.) Grundfächer:			
1.) Höhere Baukonstruktion.	Prof. R. Müller	1b	Rmüller
2.) Statik der Baukonstruktionen u. Eisenkonstruktionen des Hochbaues.	" M. Foerster	1b	gz. M. Foerster
3.) Entwerfen von Hochbauten.	" Dülfer	1b	[illegible]
	" Schneegans	2a	[illegible]
	" Muessmann	1b	Muessmann
4.) Raumkunst Entwerfen.	" Högg	2a	E Högg.
	" Hempel	1a	O Hempel
5.) Architektonische Perspektive.	" Diestel	1a	Diestel
6.) Baugeschichtliche Arbeit.	" Reuther	1a	Reuther
7.) Architektur-Aufnahmen	" Reuther	2a	Reuther
b). Wahlfächer:			
1.) Architekturmalerei II.	Prof. Beckert	–	
2.) Architekturplastik	" Gross	–	
3.) Städtebau	" Muessmann	–	
4.) Figürliches und Aktzeichnen	" Hempel	1b	O Hempel
5.) Gartenarchitektur-Entwerfen	" Hempel	–	
6.) Architektonisches Skizzieren nach der Natur II.	" Hempel	1b	O Hempel.
	Durchschnittsnote:	1b	i.V. [illegible]

F. XXXIII, 16b

Stefan Sebök, caricatures of his Dresden professors, *c* 1924

Gret Palucca, 1923, photo Charlotte Rudolph

As a result of Gurlitt's influence, many of the Dresden professors had a strong leaning toward neo-classical architecture – an interest not only reflected in the buildings they designed, such as the Berlin Reichstag, but also in their teaching (this presumably also explains the drawings in Sebök's notebooks and perhaps even his lecture at the Kupferstichkabinett in 1925). Given his interest in the baroque, I was always puzzled by Sebök's choice of subject for his graduating diploma – a contemporary dance theatre – compared to the more traditional projects produced by his contemporaries. Again, Lienert came up with a very plausible explanation, pointing out that the famous dancer, Gret Palucca, had been performing in Dresden at exactly that time. The idea that she was the Tanztheater's most likely inspiration became even more convincing when I discovered from the Palucca archives in Berlin that in 1925 she was holding gymnastic classes at the Dresden TU. This connection was cemented more recently when I came across a Hungarian journal from 1926 with a short essay by Sebök on Palucca, accompanied by a striking, almost emblematic photograph of her in flight.

As my search gained pace, buoyed by this material, I contacted the public archives office in Szolnok again, in the hope of finding a record of Sebök's birth certificate. The personal files were not available, but it turned out that they held records from the town's secondary schools. Among these, the archivist M S Gulyas uncovered Sebök's school examination records. Judging from these his best marks were for drawing, and from his fifth year on, he was allowed to have extra drawing lessons instead of ancient Greek. These lessons were given by his form master, Gyula Ruszti, a well-recognised Hungarian artist, who was a member of the Szolnok circle – a renowned group of painters in Hungary at the beginning of the twentieth century who exhibited widely in the national salon in Budapest. And also buried within these examination details and marks for drawing exercises was a record listing his date of birth – 30 April 1901 – which was great for me, to finally have an official record of his birth, but bad news for Schirren, whose centenary exhibition was already too late.

With the addition of the details of his birth, high school and university education to the material I had already uncovered through the various archives in Berlin, Boston and Dessau, the picture of Sebök's life seemed much more complete. The only aspect that I was still in the dark about was the time he had spent in the Soviet Union and his eventual fate. This was initially hampered by the fact that I didn't even know the Russian spelling of his name. This minor but crucial detail was finally resolved when the late Catherine Cooke, a renowned specialist in Soviet and Russian architectural history, became involved with my search. Catherine was an architectural historian and academic, and an international authority on constructivism and socialist urban planning. Through her frequent visits to Moscow and other parts of the Soviet Union she uncovered many of the country's modern architectural masterpieces, by architects such as Melnikov, Shukhov and Vesnin, and fought for their preservation. The fact that many of these buildings have survived is very much due to her writing and influence.

АРХИТЕКТУРА СССР

Arkhitektura SSSR

БРАТЬЯ ВЕСНИНЫ

"The Vesnin Brothers"

January 1940

1 • ЯНВАРЬ • 1940

Ленинизм бессмертен • 175 лет Всероссийской Академии художеств • Гаражи и автомагистрали • Мастера советской архитектуры — братья Веснины • Архитектура кирпичных зданий • Пропорции в древнерусской архитектуре • Справочник архитектора — сборные детали в крупноблочном строительстве

Article on the Paveletskaya scheme by Stefan Sebök with Vesnin and Liashchenko, *Arkhitektura SSSR*, issue 1, 1940

от наследства мировой архитектуры, но используют это наследство лишь там, где оно в какой-либо мере соприкасается с нашим временем.

Отсюда непосредственно вытекает и следующая значительная черта архитектуры Весниных. Их сфера — это большие здания. Умение дать архитектурную организацию сооружениям значительного масштаба, не прибегая к средствам гигантомании и нарочитой монументальности, выделяет произведения Весниных. Дробность, мелочность разделки им органически чужда. Здание Днепровской ГЭС, промышленные объекты Днепростроя, автозавод имени Сталина в Москве стали образцовыми произведениями нашей промышленной архитектуры. Глядя на них, поражаешься тому искусству, с которым Веснины придали выразительность этим, казалось бы, чисто «инженерным» объектам. Но именно в этом умении Весниных эстетически облагораживать утилитарные формы, поднять промышленную архитектуру до уровня общественной наиболее ярко сказалось то, что они являются подлинно советскими архитекторами.

Значение и ценность творчества братьев Весниных, научивших дружно работать большой коллектив своих сотрудников, заключается в том, что оно проникнуто молодой, здоровой и жизнерадостной силой, той целеустремленностью и ясностью мысли, которую можно пожелать каждому советскому архитектору

В. и А. Веснины. Проект станции метро «Павелецкая». Вестибюль. 1939 г.

V. et A. Vesnine. Projet de la station du metro „Pavéletskaia à Moscou. Vestibule. 1939

Перронный зал. В. и А. Веснины. Соавторы: С. Лященко и С. Зебек

Salle du perron. V. et A. Vesnine avec collaboration de S. Liaschenko et S. Zébec

I first met Catherine through my son, Daniel, who had asked her for some expert help with an architectural design project he was proposing on the Moscow metro while a student at Sheffield University (at the time he had no idea that 70 years earlier his uncle had been designing exactly the same thing). Seeing the expertise and encouragement she had offered him, I wrote to her about my own interest in finding more information on the Soviet architectural scene in the early 1930s. She replied immediately, and became even more enthusiastic (cycling over to see me) when I told her about Sebök and his connection with Ginzburg.

Catherine's help was invaluable. She was not only able to throw light on various aspects of the letter Sebök wrote to Gropius in 1936, but with her vast knowledge of resources on Russian architecture in the 1920s and 1930s, was able to search for projects Sebök might have been involved with through the architects he mentions in his letter – El Lissitzky, Ginzburg and the Vesnin brothers. In no time at all she came up with some extremely exciting information. In particular, she uncovered a project in a catalogue on the Vesnin brothers relating to the Moscow metro. Four architects and one engineer were credited as having worked on it, with the name of one of them listed as S F Zebek. She pointed out that Zebek could be a transliteration from Sebök in German to Zebek in Russian. She was convinced that Zebek was not a Russian name. A few days later, in a meticulous search through back issues of the architectural daily *Arkhitektura SSSR*, Catherine spotted that in late 1939 the Vesnins, Liashchenko and a S F Zebek were working on a scheme for the Paveletskaya metro station.[21] She later confirmed this spelling when she found both the German and Russian spelling of Sebök/Zebek in a supplement to the German edition of a Russian architectural exhibition catalogue.

This discovery was the vital key in allowing me to apply to the archives of the Russian Federal Security Bureau (FSB) and gain access to the former KGB files.[22] The FSB are now required by Russian law to make available to surviving relatives the contents of the arrest files and records of those people caught up in Stalin's purges. Erwin Nagy, Moholy-Nagy's nephew, who had similar experiences with his father, had already written several letters to a number of Russian authorities on my behalf, but his Russian spelling of Stefan's surname was incorrect, as he had translated Sebök from the Hungarian, while the Russians did it from the German. Immediately a new letter had to be dispatched to all of the authorities with the correct Russian name.

I received a response in London six months later via the Russian embassy. Accompanying a prison photograph of Stefan the letter informed me that:

> From the materials of the archival file it emerges that Zebek, Stefan Ferdinandovich, born 1901, native of the town of Szolnok in Hungary,

21
'Paveletskaya Metro Station', *Arkhitektura SSSR* (January 1940), p 49.

22
Stefan Sebök, KGB (NKVD) Interrogation about the Kharkov Project, 2 August 1941, S F Zebek Arrest Files, FSB Archives, No P-45964, p 30.

Stefan Sebök, USSR arrest portrait, 23 June 1941

citizen of the USSR, was prior to his arrest an architect in the design studio of the People's Commissariat for the Soviet oil industry, Narkomneft, and lived at the following address: city of Moscow, 4–6 Novo-Basmannaya Street, apartment 204. He was arrested on 23 June 1941 by the organs of the NKGB of the USSR on accusation of spying. At a special meeting of the NKVD of the USSR he was sentenced to be shot. Before the sentence was carried out he died in the hospital of the NKVD administration's prison in Saratov on 18 March 1942. The cause of death was enterocolitis. In 1997 Stefan Ferdinandovich Zebek was rehabilitated.

With the help of Erwin Nagy and Sergei Lar'kov from the Russian Memorial Foundation (a human rights organisation and archive that looks to assist victims of Russia's political repression), I immediately wrote back, in the rigidly set formula requested by FSB bureaucracy.

1. What was the date of the trial and the date when the sentence was passed?

2. How was S F Zebek's charge formulated?

3. What institution rehabilitated S F Zebek and how was the rehabilitation formulated?

4. Inform us on the basis of the prisoner's questionnaire and the records of the first interrogation of the following:

a. biographical details
b. any information about his family and their fate (if these details are absent, could you make an enquiry about this to the Main Information Centre of Ministry of Internal Affairs).

5. Are there any documents or personal effects of S F Zebek that were confiscated at the time of the arrest?

6. Have there been any enquiries from any relatives or organisations?

7. Could you also supply copies of:

a. the prisoner's questionnaire
b. the bill of indictment
c. the Special conferences 'guilty' verdict
d. the cause of death
e. the decision about his rehabilitation

ХРАНИТЬ ВЕЧНО

СССР

Государственной Безопасности

НАРОДНЫЙ КОМИССАРИАТ ВНУТРЕННИХ ДЕЛ

Спецчасть НКГБ Управление

ЭКУ Отдел

0114694

Центральный архив ФСБ РФ

ДЕЛО № 2693

По обвинению Зебек Стефана Фердинандовича

Начато „23" июня 1941 г. В 1 томах

Окончено „5" декабря 1941 г. Том № 1

После судебного рассмотрения и вступления приговора в силу, настоящее дело подлежит немедленному возвращению в 1-й Специальный отдел НКВД СССР (гор. Москва). К делу должна быть приобщена копия приговора.

Основание: приказ НКВД, Прокуратуры и НКЮ Союза ССР № 2 от 5 августа 1938 года.

Передача находящихся в производстве следственных дел, а также взятых из архива дел в другие отделы или органы НКВД, хотя бы и временно, производится исключительно через 1-й Специальный отдел НКВД.

Передача следственного дела оформляется постановлением, утверждаемым начальником соответствующего управления НКВД, или его заместителем.

Р-45964

~~0114694~~

Арх. № Н 16083

Сдано в архив „ " 19 г.

Н-16083 Р-45964

Stefan Sebök, NKGB arrest file

The file I received in return comprised some 30-odd pages, though judging from its numbering the original document may well have been much longer.[23] The whole of the file, meticulously translated by Catherine Cooke, contained an immense amount of incredibly valuable information relating to Sebök's life and work in Hungary, Germany and Russia. From his initial interrogation, for example, I learned that he first moved to the Soviet Union in July 1931, not as part of any touring architectural group but to complete a contract with the Bureau of Foreign Specialists of the Trade Representation of the USSR in Germany, and then after the appropriate formalities, went to the USSR to work as an architect. Also in the file is a detailed first-person account of how Sebök met his wife Mariya Levina:

> I became acquainted with Mariya in Berlin. Her father worked in the USSR trade representation in the city and she was studying at the Institute [he does not say which institute]. In 1930 a competition was announced for a memorial to the Ukrainian poet Shevchenko in Kharkov. Keen to take part, I wanted to find out more details about the location for the monument in order to have the opportunity to draw up a design which could take account of its site and context. I went to the tourist office in Berlin to familiarise myself with Kharkov through any books or journals they might have. I was told that they didn't have any such books but that there was, in Berlin, a Soviet student (female) who lived in Kharkov. They gave me her name and phone number and in this way I became acquainted with Mariya.

He was also asked how his relation with Maria developed and what her parents did, to which he replied, 'her father, Moïsei Semenovich Levin, an agronomist by training, worked in the trade representation of the USSR in Berlin, but I did not know his precise job. Her mother, Evgeniya Efimovna Golubitskaya, was a dentist by training, but at that time she wasn't working.' To questions about his marriage, he replies that they had 'no special understanding about living together', and that he came to the USSR in August 1931 and Levina in the summer of 1932, and after numerous meetings in Moscow in 1932 they married in the autumn of the same year.

The rest of the interrogation centred around Sebök's presumed spying activities. He is asked who he met in the course of his intelligence work. He answers that he has never engaged in any intelligence work. This question is asked again and again and again. Each time he repeats, 'I have not conducted intelligence work, hostile work.' The file also contained this statement:

> I, the undersigned, Investigator from the Fifth Section of the First Department of the Interrogation Section of the NKVD USSR – M GOIKMAN, declare by this present statement that on this date

23 Ibid.

СССР

3

НАРОДНЫЙ КОМИССАРИАТ ГОСУДАРСТВЕННОЙ БЕЗОПАСНОСТИ

ОРДЕР № 526

Июня 23 дня 1941 г.

Выдан .... Центральный архив ФСБ РФ ....
.... государственной безопасности

тов. Сергееву

на производство: ареста и обыска

Зебек

Стефана Фердинандовича

по адресу Ново-Басманная ул

дом 4/6 кв. 204

Народный Комиссар
Государственной Безопасности СССР

Место для печати

Начальник Третьего Отдела
НКГБ СССР

справка: 65 Арест санкционирован Прокурором СССР.

Stefan Sebök, NKGB arrest order

НКВД СССР

2643

4

Анкета арестованного

ВОПРОСЫ:	ОТВЕТЫ:
1. Фамилия	Зебек
2. Имя и отчество	Стефан Фердинадович
3. Год и место рождения	Родился в 1901 год; Венгрия область (край) ___ район; село ___ гор. Сульнок
4. Постоянное местожительство (адрес)	Москва: Ново-басманная ул дом 4/6 кв 204.
5. Профессия и специальность	Архитектор
6. Последнее место службы и должность или род занятий	а) учреждение Архитектурная предприятие мастерская № 1 б) должность Архитектор. в) звание ___ г) в систему какого Наркомата, или другого руководящего органа входит учреждение (предприятие) Наркомнефтепром д) если не работает—когда уволен „—" ___ 194 г.
7. Партийная принадлежность	а) в прошлом б/п б) в настоящее время —/— билет № ___
8. Национальность	Венгерец.
9. Гражданство (при отсутствии паспорта, указать какой документ удостоверяет гражданство)	а) гражд. (подд.) С.С.С.Р б) паспорт № ___ кем выдан 68 о/м. г. Москва.

Центральный архив ФСБ РФ

Stefan Sebök, USSR arrest questionnaire, 1941

СССР

НАРОДНЫЙ КОМИССАРИАТ ВНУТРЕННИХ ДЕЛ

ПРОТОКОЛ ДОПРОСА

К ДЕЛУ № —

Допрос начат в „00" час. „45" минут. Окончен в „01" час. „40" минут.

1941 г. июня мес. 25 дня. Я следователь I отдела (должн., наимен. органа, фамилия)

Следчасти НКГБ ... допросил в качестве арестованного

1. Фамилия Зебек
2. Имя и отчество Стефан Фердинандович
3. Дата рождения 1901 года
4. Место рождения гор. Сольнок, Венгрия
5. Местожительство Ново-Басманная ул. д. 4/6 кв. 204.
6. Нац. и гражд. (подданство) венгерец, гр-н СССР
7. Партийность (в прошлом и в настоящем) беспартийный. Состоял кандидатом в члены Германской компартии в 1930–1931 г. Документов не имею.
8. Образование (общее, специальное) высшее, окончил Дрезденское (Германия) высшее техническое училище в 1926 году
9. Паспорт отобран при аресте. (когда и каким органом выдан, номер, категор. и место прописки)
10. Род занятий Архитектурно-проектная мастерская Наркомнефти — архитектор (место службы и должность)
11. Социальное происхождение отец, торговец в гор. Сольнок до 1936 г. (в настоящее время умер) (род занятий родителей и их имущественное положение)
12. Социальное положение (род занятий и имущественное положение):

а) до революции учился, на иждивении родителей

б) после революции до 1926 года учился, а с 1926 по день ареста работал по найму.

Центральный архив ФСБ РФ

Stefan Sebök, record of NKGB interrogation, 1941

221

А К Т

гор. Москва, 1941 года, июля "2" дня.

Я, Нижеподписавшийся, Следователь 5 Отделения I Отдела Следчасти НКГБ СССР – ГОЙХМАН, составил настоящий акт в том, что сего числа, мной произведено уничтожение, путем сожжения, в соответствии с постановлением по следделу № 2693 от 1 июля 1941 года на Зебек С. Ф. следующих документов и разных бумаг:

1. Дипломные работы – одна папка.
2. Разные планы и проекты – 27 папок
3. Топографических военных карт – три штуки
4. Почтовая переписка – две папки
5. Папка (одна) с перепиской и рукописными заявлениями
6. Записные книжки – четыре штуки.
7. Фотокарточки – 7 шт. [redacted]

В чем составлен настоящий акт.

СЛЕДОВАТЕЛЬ 5 ОТД. I ОТДЕЛА СЛЕДЧАСТИ НКГБ СССР
ЛЕЙТЕНАНТ ГОСБЕЗОПАСНОСТИ –

М. Гойхман

Присутствовали:

NKGB statement of destruction of Stefan Sebök's documents and papers found on his arrest at his home at Novo-Basmannaya, 1941

has been executed by me the destruction, by means of burning, in accordance with the instruction of Investigation Department number 2693 of July 1941 concerning Zebek S the following document and various papers:

1. diploma work (one folder)
2. various plans and projects (17)
3. topographic, military maps (three items)
4. postal correspondence (two folders)
5. one folder of correspondence and handwritten statements
6. notebooks (four items)
7. photographs (seven items). A camera (Leica) and typewriter were confiscated and later returned.

After reviewing all of this new material I had no doubt that the Russian archives must contain even more information. Soon it became obvious that the only option available to me was to go to Moscow myself and see what I could find out personally. I started to plan a visit. My two prime targets there were the Shchusev Museum of Architecture and the FSB archives. Two years later I arrived in the city – a visit greatly facilitated by two friends: Tiina Talvik from Estonia and Nikolas Zavadenko from Russia.

I'd built up an image of the place from my talks with Clara Kernig, whom I'd met in Boston. Clara was a Hungarian dancer married to a Hungarian engineer working in Moscow at the same time as Sebök. She described life in Russia in the 1930s with great zest, speaking about the physical difficulties of everyday life, about the food shortages and their delight when they were assigned a one-room apartment (which they moved into immediately, realising it might be the only chance they got, even though it was not yet completed and still without windows, in the middle of the bitter Moscow winter). In spite of all these difficulties, Clara described Moscow as infused with a real intellectual buzz, with superb opera, concert and theatre performances which everybody could afford. People also held endless discussions – political and cultural – with their friends in their tiny homes, caught up in the infectious enthusiasm of feeling that they were building a new society. Then things started to go sour with the rising Stalinist terror. In 1937 Clara told her husband she was going home to Hungary. He was still keen to stay on, but could not do so for long. She described the unbelievable circumstances surrounding his departure. A Hungarian architect called Pap (no relation to Gyula Pap) was living in Moscow at the time. During Stalin's purges he was arrested. The authorities tried to get him to confess that he and some of his acquaintances were planning to assassinate Stalin. In an attempt to get off the hook, Pap apparently incriminated Clara's husband, but he was alerted by one of the managers at his work and advised to leave for Hungary by the first available train. This he did, and in 1938 arrived back in Budapest.

"УТВЕРЖДАЮ"

Нач. Отдела ЭКУ НКВД СССР
Лейтенант Госбезопасности

"6" декабря 1941 года.

Утверждаю: Нач. 1го Отд. 2го Отд. Военпрокуратуры 25/XII

ОБВИНИТЕЛЬНОЕ ЗАКЛЮЧЕНИЕ

По следственному делу № 2693, по обвинению ЗЕБЕК Стефана Фердинандовича в преступлениях, предусмотренных ст. 58 п. I-а УК РСФСР.

В 1941 году в НКВД СССР поступили данные о том, что проживающий в гор. Москве ЗЕБЕК Стефан Фердинандович - архитектор проектной мастерской Наркомнефти СССР, занимается шпионской работой в пользу германской разведки.

На основании этих данных, ЗЕБЕК 23 июня 1941 года был арестован.

В процессе следствия по делу установлено, что ЗЕБЕК в 1931 году, под видом изучения в СССР архитектурных работ, при содействии быв. работника Торгпредства СССР в гор. Берлине КИРСАНОВА Петра Николаевича (осужден), приехал в Советский Союз и при его содействии устроился на работу в систему НКПС.

(л.д. 26-36, 103-110).

Проживая в СССР, ЗЕБЕК занимался разведывательной работой в пользу германской разведки и привлекал новых лиц для шпионской работы.

По этому поводу, арестованный бывш. председатель дорожного общества изобретателей, [illegible] на допросе 5 августа 1938 года показал:

"...Мне известны следующие агенты германской фашистской разведки: ... ЗЕБЕК Стефан, по национальности венгерец, бывш. архитектор Ленинской железной дороги"...
(л.д. 137-141).

Показаниями осужденного бывш. главного инженера проектного бюро по реконструкции Московского железнодорожного узла - [illegible] Алексея Матвеевича, ЗЕБЕК также изобличается, как агент германской разведки.

"... Директивы, которые дал мне ЗЕБЕК в [illegible] [illegible] встречи, сводились к следующему:
1. Я должен сообщать ему шпионские данные о техническом вооружении и [illegible] [illegible] [illegible] [illegible]

Indictment of Stefan Sebök as a member of German intelligence, spying in the USSR, 1941

Surprisingly, Pap was released from prison in 1939 and also returned with his family to Hungary, where he practised as an architect. On his return to Budapest he confessed this story to Clara and her husband. She could still recall, more than 60 years on, the full horror and disgust she felt on hearing his confession. Although Pap is a relatively common name, it is unlikely that there were many architects with this name in the USSR. It is quite probable, therefore, that this is the same person that Gyula Pap, in his interview with Julia Szabó, describes as the director of the Soviet Pavilion in Germany. If this is the case, he must have had some connection with Sebök.

With Clara Kernig's recollections fresh in my mind, Moscow came as a real surprise. The city I found in 2005 was vibrant and full of life. People were very open, friendly and helpful, and not at all what I had expected. My first port of call was the Shchusev Museum of Architecture. As a result of an earlier call by Zavadenko, the red carpet was laid out for me. The director, David Sarkisyan, had arranged for a senior archivist to help me with my search – Arkadi Krasheninnikov, a sprightly 84-year-old who had acquired his knowledge of German as a prisoner of war. With Arkadi and Dottina Alexandrova, custodian of the archives, I was shown a beautiful drawing Sebök produced of the Paveletskaya metro station while he was working for the Vesnin brothers; Arkadi also speculated that Sebök may well have had a hand in the design of his own Novo-Basmannaya apartment complex. At the same time, they warned me that I was unlikely to find many additional sketches, renderings and plans by Sebök, as hundreds of thousands of drawings of architectural and infrastructural importance were strategically destroyed by the Russians when the German army was nearing Moscow in the Second World War. As someone arrested and sentenced for espionage, Sebök's name would also have been removed from anything that did survive.

The following day, after various bureaucratic hurdles had been overcome, I was finally able to visit the archives of the FSB, though I had some difficulty finding the place. I had imagined the archives as an imposing Soviet-style neo-classical structure, but they are actually located in a residential neighbourhood, in an unassuming building that looks exactly like all the other houses around it. Waiting for me there was a friendly and very helpful archivist who first explained to me what my rights were and also informed me that any personal material I might find was legally mine to keep. She asked to see my passport, gave me a quick questionnaire to fill in and then handed me the discoloured FSB file. My emotion in holding it in my hands was indescribable. I asked her if I could make a Xerox or scan but was told that only 10 percent could be copied. My face dropped but on seeing my disappointment she immediately reassured me that as soon as I received the first 10 percent, I could apply for another and another and so on, until I had the whole thing. And so I immediately set to work.

"УТВЕРЖДАЮ"
Начальник отдела 5 Управления ГВП –
помощник главного военного прокурора
полковник юстиции Л.П.Копалин

"24" марта 1997 г.

З А К Л Ю Ч Е Н И Е

по делу в отношении
Зебека С.Ф.

г. Москва

"24" марта 1997 г.

Особым совещанием при НКВД СССР от 8 апреля 1942 г.
~~Военным трибуналом~~

осужден/а/ ~~по ст.ст.~~ за шпионаж (статья УК РСФСР не указана)
УК РСФСР к расстрелу, с конфискацией имущества

Фамилия, имя, отчество Зебек Стефан Фердинандович

Центральный архив ФСБ РФ

Год и место рождения 1901 г., г.Сцолонок (Венгрия)

Гражданин/ка/ какого государства СССР
Национальность еврей
Место жительства до ареста г.Москва

Дата, каким органом арестован/а, краткая суть обвинения /осуждения/, последующие изменения судебных решений и мер наказания: арестован Зебек 23 июня 1941 г. по обвинению в шпионской деятельности на территории СССР в пользу германской разведки.

Posthumous summary of the Stefan Sebök trial, 1997

Доводы, по которым лицо подлежит реабилитации:

На предварительном следствии Зебек виновным себя не признал и заявил, что он агентом германской разведки не был и шпионской деятельностью на территории СССР не занимался. Каких-либо доказательств, подтверждающих то, что Зебек являлся агентом германской разведки и на территории СССР занимался сбором сведений, содержащих государственную тайну, не истребовали и к делу не приобщено. Восполнить в настоящее время эти пробелы не представляется возможным. В действиях Зебека состава преступления, предусмотренного ст.58-6 УК РСФСР (шпионаж), не имеется. Осужден Зебек по политическим мотивам.

На Зебека Стефана Фердинандовича

распространяется действие ст.3 Закона РФ "О реабилитации жертв политических репрессий от 18 октября 1991 г. с последующими изменениями и дополнениями.

Дело пересмотрено по обращению в порядке надзора

/в порядке исполнения закона/

Военный прокурор
отдела реабилитации
полковник юстиции М.Лиходий

Исп.вх. №

ГЕНЕРАЛЬНАЯ ПРОКУРАТУРА
РОССИЙСКОЙ ФЕДЕРАЦИИ

ГЛАВНАЯ
ВОЕННАЯ ПРОКУРАТУРА

24. марта 1997 г.
№ 5ук-3969-92

103160, Москва, К-160

При ответе ссылайтесь на наш номер и дату

СПРАВКА

/о реабилитации/

Гражданин /ка/ Зебек Стефан Фердинандович

Год и место рождения 1901 г., г.Сцолонок (Венгрия)

Гражданин /ка/ какого государства СССР

Национальность еврей Место жительства до ареста г.Москва

Место работы и должность /род занятий/ до ареста Архитектор проектной мастерской Наркомнефти СССР

Дата ареста 23.06.1941 г.

Когда и каким органом осужден/а/ (репрессирован/а/) Особым совещанием при НКВД СССР от 8.04.1942 г.

Центральн… [illegible] …ва ФСБ РФ

Квалификация содеянного и мера наказания /основная и дополнительная/ за шпионаж (статья УК РСФСР не указана) к расстрелу, с конфискацией имущества

Дата освобождения Зебек умер 16.03.1942 г. в тюрьме г.Саратова

На основании ст.3 Закона РФ "О реабилитации жертв политических репрессий" от 18 октября 1991 г. гражданин/ка/ Зебек Стефан Фердинандович реабилитирован/а/.

Главная военная прокуратура

Начальник
отдела реабил…
Главной военной прокуратуры [signature] Л.П.Копалин

ЦА ФСБ России, Р-45964, л. 170.

Stefan Sebök, certificate of rehabilitation, 1997

The file consisted of pages numbered sequentially from 1–136 and 156–179, with a closed file inserted between them. On the last pages I noticed that the first digit of the numbers was overwritten. Could this mean that the original file was much bigger – 379 pages instead of 179? As soon as I started reading, I realised that the file was full of extensive and vital information on all of the places Sebök had worked and the people he had met from his days at the Bauhaus onwards. Piecing this information together with what I already knew, I was able to generate a comprehensive picture of his working life since leaving Germany.

In the USSR, as Sebök tells us, he worked first for the architectural department of the Soviet railways, where he was initially involved with the design of various apartment buildings and then later on a number of railway and metro stations. Over the course of his interrogation he gives a detailed account of the buildings themselves. One of the commissions he was involved with was the Khazan railway station in Moscow, a building that still exists, and one I was therefore very interested in seeing while still in Moscow. On pulling up outside, I immediately recognised it as the same facade depicted in a drawing on the wall behind Sebök in a photograph sent to my mother from Moscow in 1932 (see overleaf). Yet again, the information in the files had solved what until then had been something of an architectural puzzle.

Besides the Khazan station, the majority of buildings listed in the files are those he produced alongside the Vesnin brothers, who he joined in 1936, and include the design of buildings for the Socialist Industry exhibition, a fire depot at the Yaroslav rubber factory, the Paveletskaya metro station, a waiting room for the Leninskaya metro station, a design for the reconstruction of the Pavelsk railway station in Moscow, a plan for the refurbishment of several buildings inside the Kremlin, a sketch design for a second building for the People's Communist Party Committee in Moscow and a design for the yard in front of Factory No 402 in Moscow, as well as drawings and models of the ball-bearing factory in Moscow and the Copper Combinate factory in the Urals, produced for the Paris international exhibition. At the time of his arrest he was still working with the Vesnin brothers.

Sebök's work with the Vesnins is also confirmed in a letter written by B A Vesnin to Koganovich, the People's Commissioner of Communications, on 4 September 1939, produced at a time when Sebök was threatened with eviction from his apartment. The letter was spotted in the Russian State Archive of Art and Literature by the American scholar Richard Anderson, who passed the information on to me as he knew of my search into Sebök's activities in Russia. Richard also advised me how to obtain material from the archives. Thanks to his advice, on a later visit to Moscow and the State Archive I was able to obtain a copy of this letter and some other documents relating to Sebök. In this letter, Vesnin lists all the metro projects on which Sebök has collaborated and concludes that the 'timely and high-quality fulfilment of these projects depends to a significant degree on the uninterrupted involvement of architect Zebek'.

Stefan Sebök in Moscow, photograph sent by him to his family, 1932

Vesnin brothers, Leninskaya station (top) and Sovnarkom building (bottom)

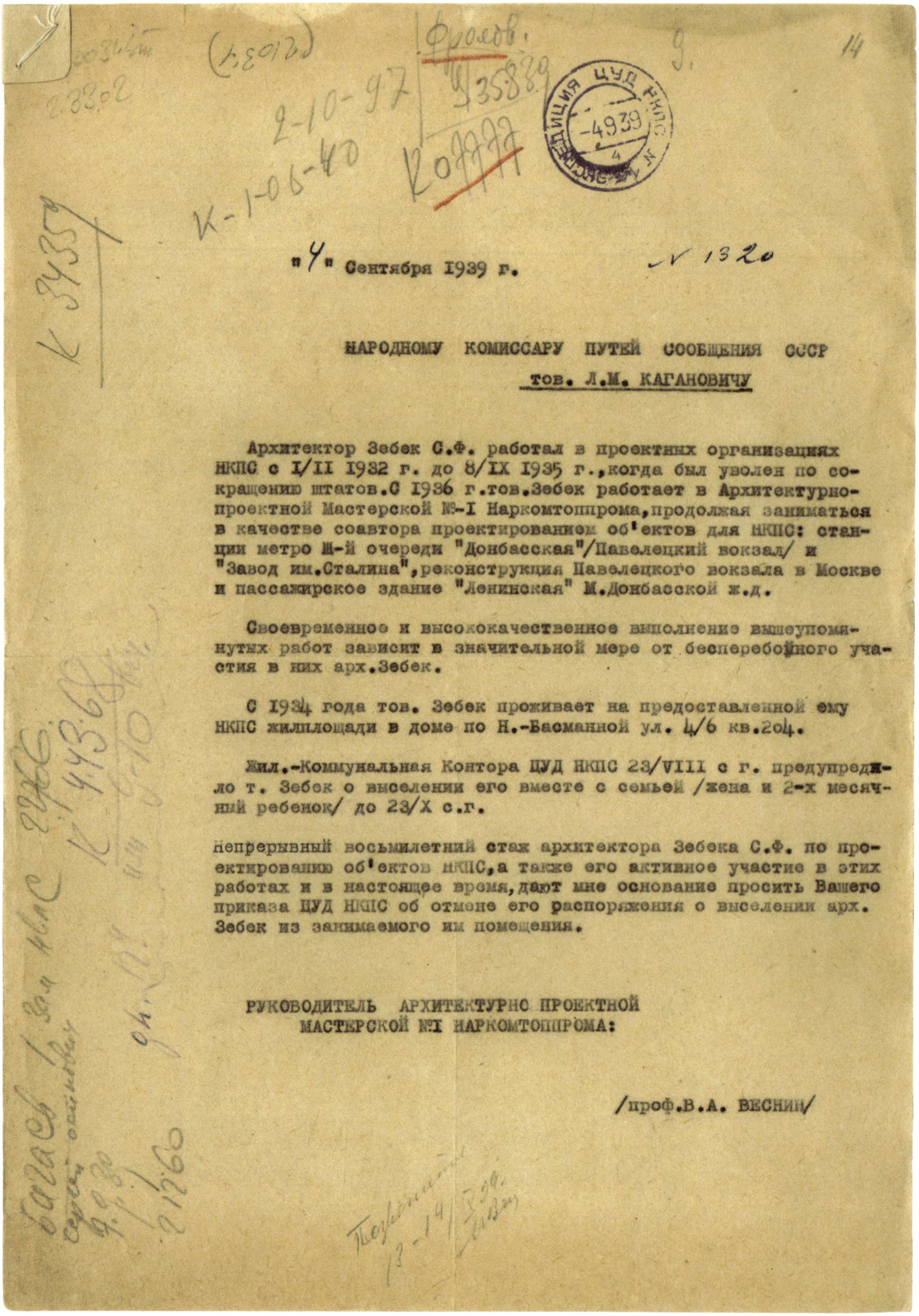

"4" Сентября 1939 г. № 1320

НАРОДНОМУ КОМИССАРУ ПУТЕЙ СООБЩЕНИЯ СССР
тов. Л.М. КАГАНОВИЧУ

Архитектор Зебек С.Ф. работал в проектных организациях НКПС с I/II 1932 г. до 8/IX 1935 г., когда был уволен по сокращению штатов. С 1936 г. тов. Зебек работает в Архитектурно-проектной Мастерской №-I Наркомтоппрома, продолжая заниматься в качестве соавтора проектированием об'ектов для НКПС: станции метро Ш-й очереди "Донбасская"/Павелецкий вокзал/ и "Завод им. Сталина", реконструкция Павелецкого вокзала в Москве и пассажирское здание "Ленинская" М. Донбасской ж.д.

Своевременное и высококачественное выполнение вышеупомянутых работ зависит в значительной мере от бесперебойного участия в них арх. Зебек.

С 1934 года тов. Зебек проживает на предоставленной ему НКПС жилплощади в доме по Н.-Басманной ул. 4/6 кв. 204.

Жил.-Коммунальная Контора ЦУД НКПС 23/VIII с г. предупредило т. Зебек о выселении его вместе с семьей /жена и 2-х месячный ребенок/ до 23/X с.г.

Непрерывный восьмилетний стаж архитектора Зебека С.Ф. по проектированию об'ектов НКПС, а также его активное участие в этих работах и в настоящее время, дают мне основание просить Вашего приказа ЦУД НКПС об отмене его распоряжения о выселении арх. Зебек из занимаемого им помещения.

РУКОВОДИТЕЛЬ АРХИТЕКТУРНО ПРОЕКТНОЙ
МАСТЕРСКОЙ №I НАРКОМТОППРОМА:

/проф. В.А. ВЕСНИН/

Letter from B A Vesnin to Koganovich re Stefan Sebök's eviction, 1939

Above and overleaf: Vesnin brothers, with S Liashchenko and S F Zebek (Stefan Sebök), Paveletskaya station, 1939

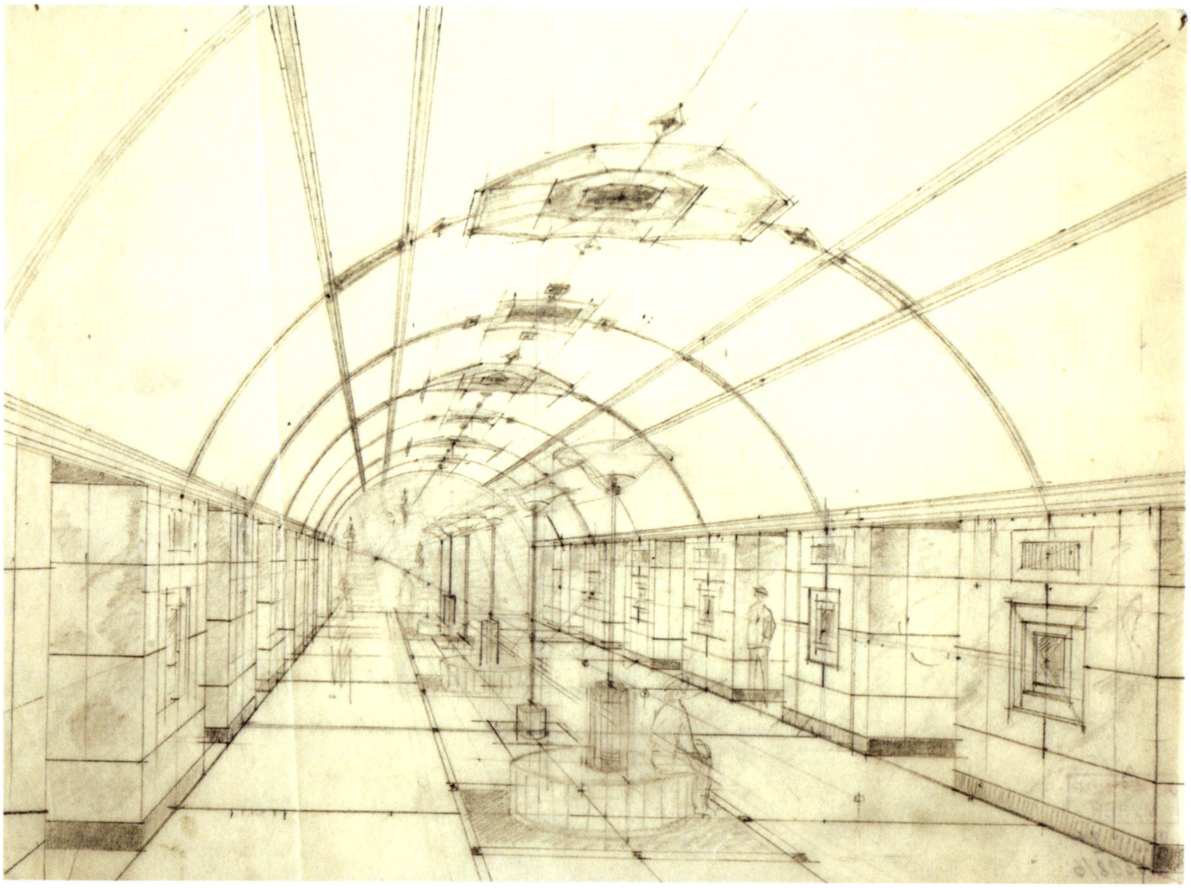

С.Т. ПОВЕЛЕЦКАЯ

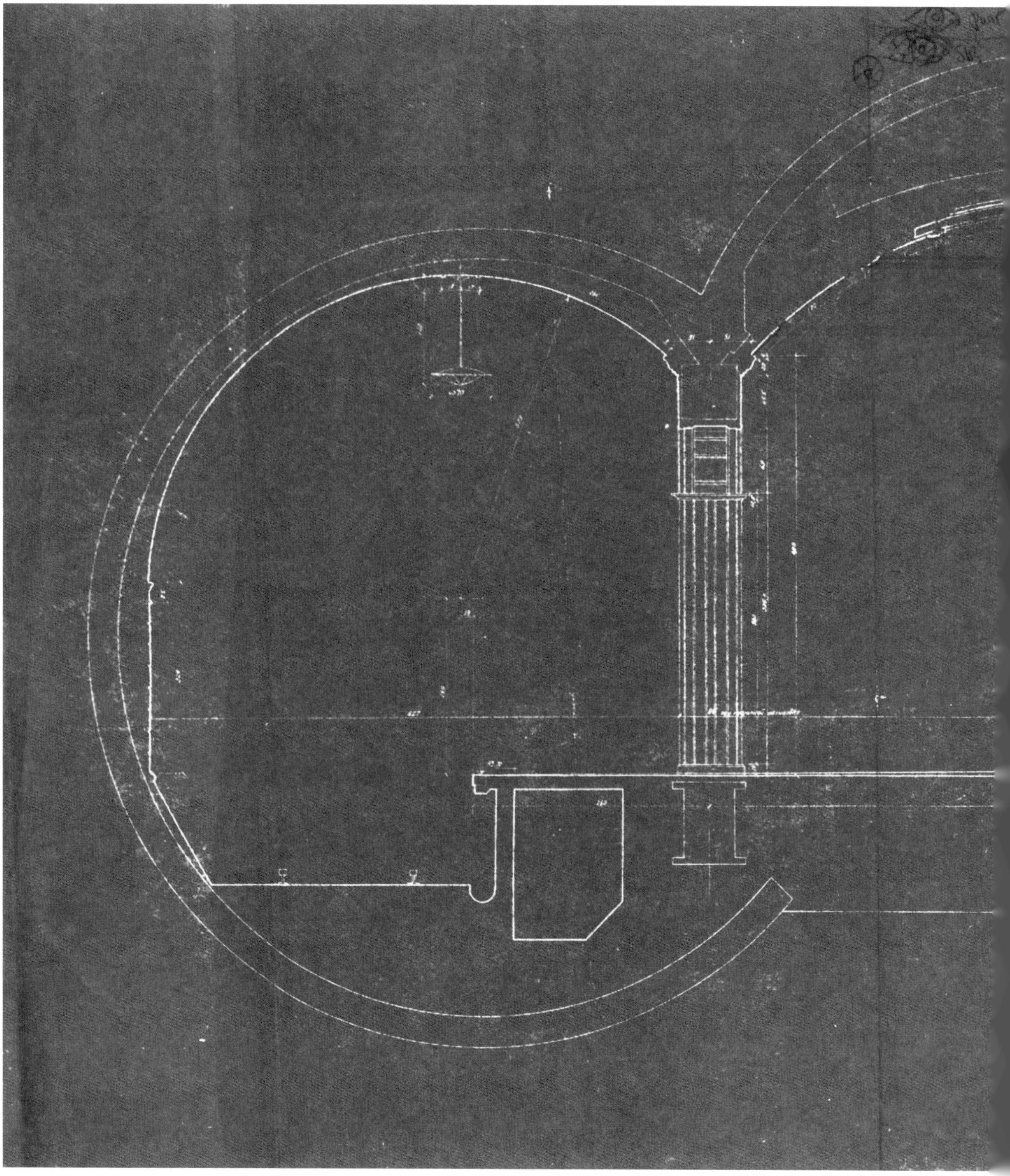

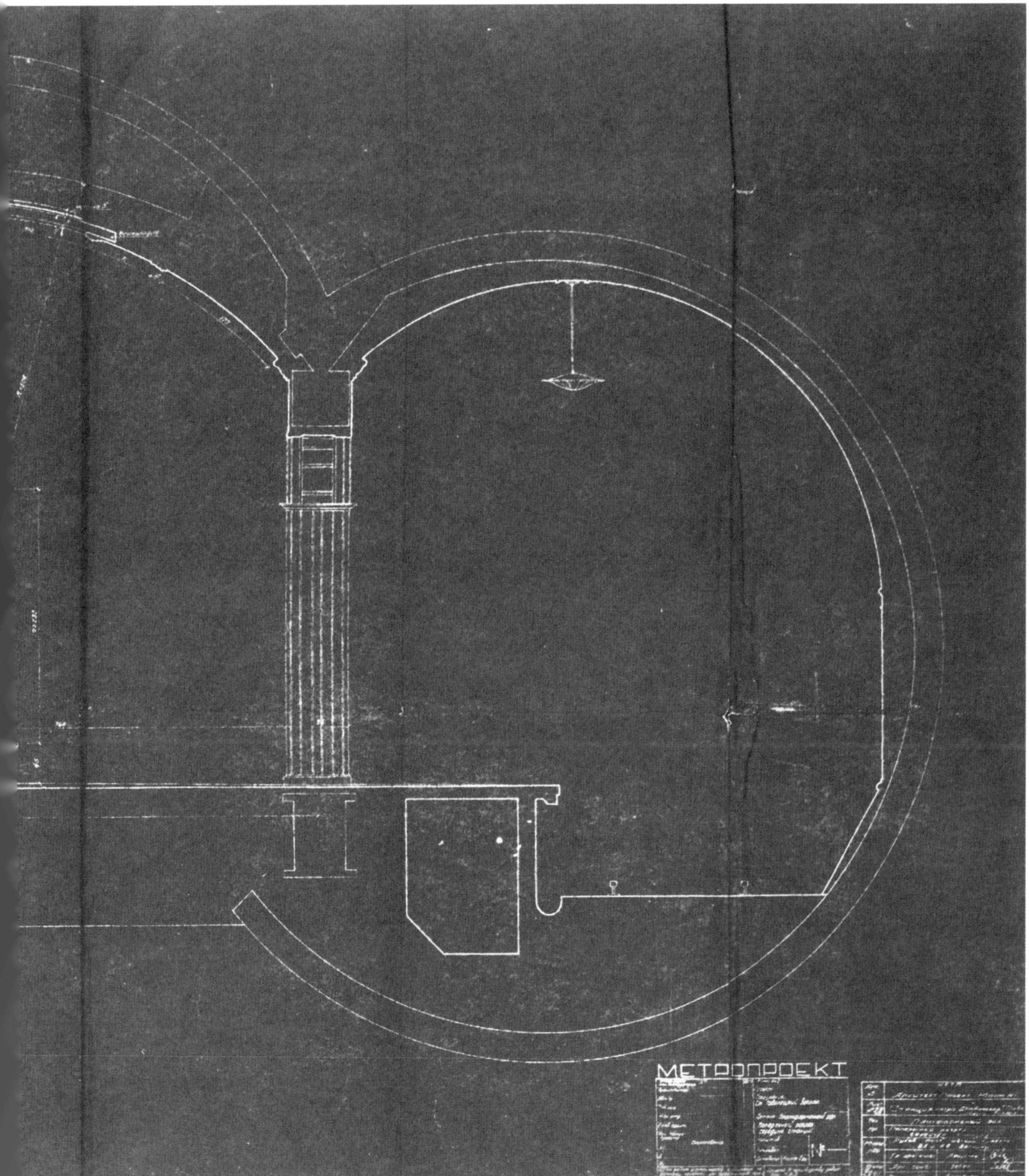
МЕТРОПРОЕКТ

ПАВЕЛЕЦКАЯ

YAD VASHEM
Institutul pentru comemorarea
martirilor şi eroilor Holocaustului
P.O.B. 3477 Jerusalem, Israel

דף-עד
עדות-בלאט
Foaie de Mărturie

יד ושם
אינסטיטוט צום אנדענק
פון אומקום און גבורה

LEGEA PENTRU COMEMORAREA
MARTIRILOR SI EROILOR 5713-1953
stabileşte în articolul 2 că:
Yad Vashem are misiunea de a strînge în ţară documente cu privire la toţi fiii poporului evreu care şi-au pierdut viaţa, care au luptat şi s-au revoltat împotriva duşmanului nazist şi a colaboratorilor săi, şi de a păstra memoria şi NUMELE lor şi ale comunităţilor, organizaţiilor şi instituţiilor distruse pentru că aparţineau poporului evreu.

דאס געזעץ אנדענק פון אומקום און גבורה - יד-ושם, תשי״ג 1953
שטעלט פעסט אין פאראגראף נומ׳ 2 :
די אויפגאבע פון יד-ושם איז איינזאמלען אין היימלאנד דעם אנדענק פון אלע יידן, וואס זענען געפאלן, האבן זיך מוסר נפש געווען, געקעמפט און זיך אנטקעגנגעשטעלט דעם נאצישן שונא און זיינע ארויסהעלפער, און זיי אלעמען, די קהילות, די ארגאניזאציעס און אינסטיטוציעס, וועלכע זענען חרוב געווארן צוליב זייער אנגעהעריקייט צום יידישן פאלק — שטעלן א דענקמאל.
(געזעץ-בוך נומ׳ 231, י״ז אלול תשי״ג, 82.8.3591)

דאטען וועגן אומגעקומענעם: יעדן נאמען אויף א באזונדער בלאט, מיט קלארער שריפט
DATELE VICTIMEI: UN FORMULAR PENTRU FIECARE PERSOANĂ, CU LITERE DE TIPAR

בילד פון דעם
אומגעקומענעם
שרייבט אן דעם נאמען
אויף דער ריקזייט
פון דעם בילד

FOTOGRAFIA VICTIMEI
RUGĂM SCRIEŢI
NUMELE PE VERSO

Numele de familie: Левина — 1. פאמיליע-נאמען:

Prenumele: Мария Моисеевна — 2. פארנאמען:

Nume înainte de căsătorie: — 3. פאמיליע-נאמען פאר דער חתונה (פאר א פרוי):

6. פאראייראט? Stare civilă — 5. מין Sex — 32 года — 4. געבורטס-דאטע (ווי אלט) Data naşterii/Vîrsta apr.

Locul naşterii şi ţara: Харьков - Украина — 7. ארט פון געבורט (שטאט, לאנד):

Mama victimei - Prenumele: - פארנאמען: — 8. מוטער פון דעם אומגעקומענעם
- Numele de fată: - מיידלשע-פאמיליע:

Tatăl victimei - Prenumele: - פארנאמען: — 9. פאטער פון דעם אומגעקומענעם

Soţul/Soţia victimei - Prenumele - פארנאמען: — 10. מאן/פרוי פון דעם אומגעקומענעם
- Numele de fată: - מיידלשע-פאמיליע:

Domiciliul permanent Oraşul şi ţara: Россия г. Москва — 11. סטאבילער וואוינארט (שטאט, לאנד):

Domiciliul in timpul războiului Oraşul şi ţara: — 12. וואוינערטער בעת דער מלחמה (שטאט, לאנד):

Data/Anul morţii: 14. צייט פון טויט: — Profesiunea victimei: 13. בערוף אדער פאך:

Împrejurările morţii: 16. אומשטענדן פון טויט: — Locul morţii: октябрь 1941 г. г. Харьков - расстреляна немцами. 15. ארט פון טויט:

Completat de către: — געשריבן פון:
Eu, subsemnatul Богатырева Эстер. איך, דער אונטערגעשריבענער
Cu locuinţa (adresa) Бенсямина Цвьль ha халяв 5/с וואס וואוינט (אדרעס)
Rudă/Prieten cu victima (specificaţi) ______ קרובשאפט
דערקלער דערמיט, אז די עדות מיט אלע פרטים איז א ריכטיקע לויט מיין בעסטען וויסן
DECLAR CĂ DUPĂ CUNOŞTINŢA MEA ACEASTĂ MĂRTURIE ESTE CONFORMĂ ADEVĂRULUI
Locul şi data Бенсямина [illegible] ארט און דאטע — Semnătura Богатырева אונטערשריפט
În timpul războiului am fost în: lagăr/ghetou/rezistenţă: Эвакуац[illegible] — ווערנד דער מלחמה בין איך געווען אין: לאגער/געטאָ/פארטיזאנער

"...ונתתי להם בביתי ובחומותי יד ושם..אשר לא יכרת". ישעיהו נו ה
"... le voi da în Casa Mea si înlauntrul zidurilor Mele un loc si un nume ... care nu se va stinge." Isaia, 56,5

Yad Vashem report on Mariya Levina Sebök, *c* 1972

In the same archives is also located a second letter, offering further testimony to Sebök's work on the design of metro stations, written by his work colleague on the Paveletskaya station, S V Liashchenko. As much as attesting to Sebök's role as an architect, the letter, somewhat inadvertently, also offers interesting insights into its design. Liashchenko writes that:

> In the design of the architectural form of the metro station 'Stalin Works' the authors of the project faced an extremely difficult problem: to provide an architectural solution appropriate to the great name that the station will bear; to emphasise the greatness of the Stalin five-year plan and the industrial character of the Moscow district that it will serve: the Stalin Works, the Kirov Dynamo Plant, the Kaganovich Ball-bearing Plant and others. From this perspective the authors took on themselves the challenge to design the station in a simple, austere, triumphant style, free of petty decorations and half measures. It appeared that in order to achieve the goal the station design should consist of a great spacious hall without corridors, passages or columns. Such a free design also corresponds to its functional purpose. Considering its location close to Moscow's largest factories, which employ and release in a given shift tens of thousands of workers, the authors consider it most expedient to design this station as one free and open hall in order to avoid crowding on platforms and in passages between columns. Thus, the architectural solution was based on a new construction principle of solid framing that never before has been applied to metro construction. This approach is relatively easy to employ considering the surface depth of the station. Underlying the design was the desire to provide a feeling of ease, airiness and opulent space, free of anguish and the heaviness associated with other underground spaces.

Despite these entreaties, Sebök was convicted as a Gestapo spy on 11 October 1941, mainly on the basis of material found in his apartment. This material would have been drawings he produced with the Vesnin brothers, as well as projects he designed for the Russian railways. Architecture, therefore, was the thing that incriminated him. In particular, the KGB saw the plans of the railway stations as strategically sensitive material, but were blind to the fact that Sebök had these in his possession only because he designed these stations. More than the absurdity of this myopia, though, and much more than architecture, the irony and paradox of a Russian archive ultimately preserving the very thing they had originally sought to terminate, is overwhelmed by the tragedy of Stefan Sebök's end. In the same week in October 1941 when he was convicted and sentenced to be executed as a Gestapo spy, his wife, daughter and mother-in-law were shot by the Gestapo in the massacre of Kharkov Jews (information I discovered through the Yad Vashem archives).

On my last day in Moscow – and if not the ultimate end of my search then at least as a kind of *dénouement* – I wanted to see for myself the Novo-Basmannaya apartment where Sebök and his wife Mariya lived. With Arkadi Krasheninnikov coming along to help me find my way, we travelled north-east from the city centre to the Basmannaya district. The Novo-Basmannaya itself is a classic 1930s building, six to eight storeys high and somewhat along the lines of one of Le Corbusier's urban blocks. Built in a U-shape, around three sides of a square with trees and a small playground in the middle, it houses some 360 apartments, all originally built for technical staff who worked for the Russian railways. After a few furtive glances and walks around the block, we came across apartment 204, a ground-floor flat that ran from the street-side to the garden side and which appeared really quite spacious. Arkadi pointed out that this would have been considered a highly desirable apartment at the time and would only have been allocated to somebody held in quite high esteem. I rang the buzzer and knocked a few times but the only response I got from inside were the barks from a ferocious-sounding dog. Slowly, and somewhat reluctantly, I started to walk away. Meanwhile Arkadi had met one of the neighbours in the square, who told him that the present owner moved into the apartment at the end of July 1941 – a period that would have been very soon after Sebök's wife and child were forced to leave Moscow. In view of the circumstances of the Sebök family departure, they must have left practically all their possessions behind. As furniture and effects were in short supply in the Soviet Union at that time, many of their things could very well still be inside. For now, though, it seemed right to leave number 204 alone. There will always be more leads to follow and things to uncover, and as I stood outside the apartment, watching children play in the snow, the sense of my own relief at finally being so close to Stefan was mirrored by the ease with which I could imagine a day in his life there: happy, at least in that moment, his drawings pinned to the wall of the apartment and his wife and child close by.

Stefan Sebök and his wife Mariya, *c* 1930, photo Gyula Pap

The Bauhaus and Hungary's Émigré Artists' Last Illusions of Modernity

Éva Forgács

The story of István (Stefan) Sebök's life and career is emblematic in more ways than one. It is the story of many Hungarian Jews who believed in the power of education, and of many European intellectuals who believed in communism. Sebök's family took seriously the promise of Jewish assimilation into Hungary's commercial and economic life. They had good reason to be optimistic about the future. The emerging urban middle classes of the Kingdom of Hungary – governed independently since the Austro-Hungarian Compromise of 1867 – were known, like their counterparts in Vienna and Berlin, as the *Bildungsbürgertum,* or 'bourgeoisie of education'. The generation born in the late 1880s and 1890s benefited from excellent schools. Education provided the key to social integration and advancement. Institutes in Budapest such as the Sociological Society, the Free School of Social Sciences and the Galileo Circle hosted free lecture series, organised by the young people themselves, which attracted the best scientists and scholars. Yet for all this, Sebök would feel compelled to leave his country, joining a mass tide of emigration that the historian Tibor Frank has described as the 'Hungarian Trauma'.[1] And so what, then, had prompted this trauma? In short, the answer is war, revolution and counter-coup.

In the last days of October 1918, in the wake of the disintegration of the Austro-Hungarian Empire, returning soldiers expressed their unwillingness to go on fighting by putting flowers in their helmets. The 'Aster Revolution' had begun. The swift pacifist uprising led to the left-leaning Count Mihály Károlyi – the 'Red Count' – being appointed Prime Minister on 31 October, and then President on 16 November, after the last Habsburg emperor, Charles IV, renounced the throne. But barely four months later, the new Hungarian People's Republic was dealt a fatal blow: the loss of two thirds of its territories under the terms of the peace treaty with the Allies. Unable to negotiate better terms – or to contain the deteriorating internal situation – the Károlyi government ceded power on 21 March to a coalition of communists and social democrats led by the communist Béla Kun. The Hungarian Soviet Republic was proclaimed the same day.

In the early post-revolutionary period, communism held few negative connotations for the young idealists. On the contrary, it was an attractive social and political concept for a large part of the intelligentsia. Many were self-conscious socialists who contributed enthusiastically to educational programmes to help the underprivileged. A few committed themselves more fully to the communist cause, among them the philosopher György Lukács, who served as Vice-Commissar for Public Education during the Commune.

The Hungarian Soviet Republic lasted just 133 days. In August 1919 a Romanian military invasion toppled Kun's government and installed a new regime. Its governor, Admiral Horthy, dispatched troops across the country to root out enemy communists and subversive Jews (the two were seen as synonymous) – Christianity and nationalism ruled. In 1920 Hungary passed a law limiting the number of Jews admitted to higher education to six per cent of the total. This *numerus clausus* was effectively the first anti-Jewish law in Europe in the twentieth century.[2]

The new regime's zeal for retribution meant that those who were suspected of having cooperated with the Commune in any way, or who were simply Jewish, and thus deprived of access to higher education, fled the country. This wave of emigration drained Hungarian culture in an unprecedented way. The émigrés included internationally recognised scientists such as mathematician John von Neumann, physicists Leo Szilárd, Eugene Wigner and Edward Teller, biochemist and sociologist Michael Polányi and his brother, the economist Karl Polányi; photographers Robert Capa, André Kertész, Brassai, György Kepes and Éva Besnyö; writers Arthur Koestler and Béla Balázs; composers Béla Bartók and Zoltán Kodály; philosopher and essayist György Lukács, philosopher and art critic Lajos Fülep, artist, critic and essayist Leo Popper, poet and artist Anna Lesznai, painters Róbert Berény, Lajos Tihanyi, Dezsö Orbán, Béla Czóbel, László Moholy-Nagy, László Péri; the entire avant-garde group of Hungarian activists led by writer, artist and publisher Lajos Kassák; architects Stefan Sebök, Alfred (Fred) Forbát, Farkas Molnár and several later Bauhaus students of architecture such as Tibor Weiner or Béla Scheffler; art critics Ernö (Ernst) Kállai and Alfréd Kemény, musicians Georg Solti, Joseph Szigeti, Antal Doráti and George Széll, not to mention film director and producer Alexander Korda and most of the originators of the Hollywood film studios. The list could go on and on.[3]

The Bauhaus – a school where no restrictions were imposed on the imagination or religious or national background – held a special allure for many of the émigrés. During this period Hungarian participation in the Bauhaus was more conspicuous and intense than that of any other national group. In addition to the Hungarian students and faculty who were active in the school, there were several others who worked directly for Gropius, or who, like the painters Sándor Bortnyik and Andor Weininger, were informally related to the school.

Sebök joined Gropius in 1927 and through him became part of the colourful Hungarian community gathered around the Bauhaus. Farkas Molnár had worked in Gropius's office in 1921, while he was still a student – he was almost certainly among the first to participate in the architectural design course set up in the 1920/21 winter semester. Gropius taught the theoretical part of the course, and his closest colleague and draughtsman Adolf Meyer the practical part. Fred Forbát was probably one of Molnár's teachers there – Adolf Meyer had asked him to assist as the course developed into an intensive seminar by the summer of 1922.[4] Forbát had worked in Gropius's office since 1920, and participated in collaborative Bauhaus projects such as the Adolf Sommerfeld House (where he designed the chauffeur's house). By the time Sebök arrived, however, he had already departed for Berlin.

Paths to the Bauhaus or to Gropius's office originated in many different locations and in a variety of chance encounters. For example, Molnár and the painters Hugó Johann and Henrik Stefán – all from Forbát's native Pécs – heard about the Bauhaus from a German painter, Werner Gilles, who they happened to meet in Fiesole, Italy. Among the earliest Hungarian Bauhaus students were Margit Téry-Adler and Gyula Pap. Téry-Adler had studied with Johannes Itten in Vienna, and was among the 14 students who followed their master to Weimar in 1919. Pap had also gone to Vienna that same year, with the intention of enrolling in Itten's private art school. When a friend told him that Itten was now in Weimar, in a new art school called the Bauhaus, Pap immediately sent his portfolio to Weimar and soon got notification that he had been accepted for a one-semester probation period. After he had completed this he stayed on and studied in the metal workshop throughout 1922 and 1923.

In the mid-1970s I had a series of conversations with Pap in Budapest, and he gave me an illuminating account of how Itten had won over the students on day one of the *Vorkurs*. They all had high expectations because of Itten's reputation, Pap said, and so they were slightly put out when he came into the classroom at 8.00am and gave them an assignment instead of launching right away into 'teaching'. Dryly, and in a hurry, he asked them to think about their favourite colours, and then to paint two compositions by 2.00pm, reducing their palette only to these colours. One composition had to be free, the other geometric. Having said this, he left, leaving them puzzled. When he returned a little after 2.00pm he did not look at the works – did not even seem interested in them. Instead he asked the students to stand up and form a circle, holding their works up high. Take a good look at your fellow students' paintings, he said, because you will never again see each other so naked or so sincere – not that semester or, for that matter, at any time in the future. Then he stormed out of the room. Gradually, the lesson they had just learned started to sink in – the full significance and the enigmatic nature of colour, its intimate ties to the personality and the unconscious. The students realised that if you 'showed your colours' you revealed more of yourself than you perhaps intended – and in a direct way unmatched by most other kinds of communication. Itten had learned this kind of approach from his own teachers, who had followed Pestalozzi, Rousseau, Goethe and Rudolf Steiner – none of whom featured in higher education in Hungary at the time. As his writings indicate, Moholy-Nagy was also interested in teaching methods based on intuition.

One of the young stars of the Bauhaus was another Hungarian student from Pécs, Marcel Breuer, a friend of Forbát's. Breuer enrolled in the Bauhaus in 1920, when he had just turned 19, and studied there until 1925, when he was appointed a 'Young Master'. He had started out as a painter but soon switched, on Forbát's advice, to the cabinet-making workshop. He first designed expressionist furniture, such as the recently recovered African Chair, made of painted wood with a colourful textile weave, then copied Gerrit Rietveld's early chair designs, before settling on a rudimentary modern functionalist style of his own, which dominated the interior design of the 1923 Haus am Horn. Fascinated by the lightweight tubular structure of a bicycle he had purchased in Dessau in 1926, he started to use nickel-plated aluminium tubes for chairs that could be industrially mass produced – a major breakthrough in modernist furniture production – and designed the chair that would become his signature piece: the 'Wassily'.

Another young artist from Pécs, Andor Weininger, attended Itten's *Vorkurs* in 1921, then studied in the mural painting workshop. Gropius appreciated Weininger's many talents – besides

Soldiers and civilians celebrating the victory of the revolution, Deák Square, Budapest, 1918

Count Mihály Károlyi giving away plots of land, Kálkápolna, Hungary, 1919

painting, he was involved in both the Bauhaus band and the Bauhaus theatre – and made the special gesture of inviting him to come back to the school to do whatever he pleased, releasing him from his workshop obligations. Like other Hungarian Bauhaus artists, Weininger attended private classes taught by Theo van Doesburg, who after being denied an official platform for spreading the ideas of De Stijl – in the form of a teaching post at the Bauhaus – had set up his own alternative course that was fiercely critical of the Bauhaus tendency towards expressionism and romanticism, arguing instead for objectivity, impersonality and technology. Like several other students of painting in the Bauhaus, Weininger also made forays into architecture. He designed De Stijl-inspired rectangular houses and a geometrical design for a mechanical stage review.

The Russian connection that was so decisive in Sebök's life was, to a great extent, mediated by Hungarians in Germany. In the famous photo taken in September 1922 of the participants at the Constructivist-Dadaist Congress organised by van Doesburg in Weimar, we see not only Moholy-Nagy, who was not yet at the Bauhaus, but also his friend, the Berlin-based Hungarian art critic Alfréd Kemény, who had already travelled to Moscow the previous year, at the invitation of the Komintern, and was the first to report back directly on the Constructivists of the INKhUK (Institute of Artistic Culture). A few others, for example the poet Franz Jung or the painter George Grosz, got there by smuggling themselves across the Finnish border. Kemény emigrated to the Soviet Union in 1933. More fortunate than Sebök, he was able to return to Hungary in 1945.

In 1922 a group called KURI – in German the initials stand for 'Constructive, Utilitarian, Rational, International' – was set up by some of van Doesburg's Hungarian followers at the Bauhaus: Molnár, Weininger, Johann and Stefán. KURI drew its inspiration from van Doesburg's teaching, with its emphasis on the objective and the universal, and from Russian constructivism. Its manifesto, published in the Hungarian journal *ÚT* ('road', 'way') in December 1922, consigned all the 'isms' of modern art, including those represented by the Bauhaus faculty, to the past. The way forward lay in 'technology, sociology and medicine'. Weininger's *De Stijl*-inspired *Mechanical Stage – Abstract Revue*, along with Molnár's *Red Cube House* and other designs, illustrate points 23–25 of the manifesto:

- At long last the mechanical image and the mobile sculpture will become reality, and all this will culminate in an architecture that will constantly change its place and forms.
- At long last direct, unmediated mobility will replace the hitherto static arts.
- The regular will replace the accidental.
- Instead of the decorative and the strongly expressive we will have the Constructive, the Utilitarian, the Rational, the International. Long live the new Cube – the first cubic house in the world!

Weininger offered his own gloss on the origins of 'KURI' in an interview with Katherine Jánszky-Michaelsen.[5] The name did not begin life as an acronym formulated by some high-minded Bauhaus students, he said, but was a word he had learned during the war, in a nonsense song that blended several of the southeastern European languages spoken by the Austro-Hungarian soldiers. It had no intrinsic meaning, but was gibberish.

More Hungarian students arrived at the Bauhaus after Sebök. Otti Berger studied textile design from 1927 to 1930, and was head of the weaving workshop in 1931–32. Ruth Hollós was a student in 1926–27. The painter, poet and musician Henrik Neugeboren, also known as Henri Nouveau, was there from 1927 to 1929; and a number of women enrolled to study photography: Etel Fodor 1928–30, Mása Baranyai 1929, Zsuzsa Bánki 1930, Zsuzsa Markos-Ney 1931, Judit Kárász 1931–32 and Irena Blühová 1931–33. Another future architect, Tibor Weiner, enrolled in the Bauhaus after Gropius's resignation, in 1929, graduated from Hannes Meyer's class in 1930, and followed him to the Soviet Union in 1931.

The first Hungarian member of the Bauhaus faculty was Moholy-Nagy, hired by Gropius to replace Johannes Itten early in 1923. Gropius wanted a representative of constructivism who did not entirely restrict himself to a purely geometric style; a progressive yet undogmatic new Bauhaus master. Sebök worked on some of Moholy-Nagy's technical details. Like Weininger, Moholy had a free-roaming imagination, but needed specific technologies to realise his ideas. Early on, he experimented with the idea of so-called 'telephone pictures', where he would communicate the exact parameters of the picture – its measurements and industrial colour code names – to a factory over the telephone. The idea was that the picture could be manufactured in an entirely industrial way without the artist touching it at all. Moholy-Nagy saw the possibility of translating the system of visual signs into the system of numbers, and then reversing the whole process to produce the picture. This seems remarkably prescient – a forerunner of the kind of data transfer from one system to another that we now see all the time on our computers. By a similar token, Weininger's *Mechanical Stage – Abstract Revue* was only adequately realised in Kassel in 1986, when its design sequences were written into a computer program that synchronised the rhythmical horizontal, vertical and rotating movements of the geometric panels with the music and the changing lights that accompanied their movements. The unbridled free atmosphere of the Bauhaus, allowing playfulness and encouraging experiments without heed for failure, led to such leaps of the imagination into the unknown. And Sebök's technical expertise would prove indispensible in actually bringing some of these works into being.

The art critic Ernő Kállai – who came from a German/Serbian/Hungarian family – was an astute observer of the changing political and cultural scene in Germany. Quitting his teacher's job in Budapest in 1920, he moved to Berlin, where he started writing art reviews for a number of successful journals, as well as Lajos Kassák's avant-garde monthly *Ma,* published from exile in Vienna. Kállai discerned the new aspiration to 'objectivity' and a 'new classicism' long before anyone else. He reviewed the 'First Russian Exhibition' in autumn 1922, wrote about El Lissitzky, Kazimir Malevich and Naum Gabo, and the new developments in German and international art. Kállai was also the very first critic to notice the decline of constructivism as early as 1923 – when it was still the most celebrated new style among the young progressives – and to criticise what he saw as the self-serving aestheticism of geometric abstraction, both Dutch and Russian. He reviewed books, photography, design and film, and in 1927 participated in the 'Painting versus Photography' debate launched by Moholy-Nagy on the pages of the Dutch avant-garde journal *i 10.* Kállai planned to collaborate with Kassák on a book about the activities of the *Ma* group to be published as volume 18 of the Bauhausbücher series, but this never got beyond the planning stage.

The Bauhaus's second director, Hannes Meyer, brought in Kállai to edit the *bauhaus zeitung* and the catalogues of the school's travelling exhibitions, and he stayed there from 1928 until Meyer's dismissal in 1930. Kállai was progressive, like Sebök, but experience had taught him not to pin too many hopes on the potential of art and design to improve society. At the time of the rise of Nazism, siding with the Bauhaus was a matter of course for him, even if he criticised the school in its internal forums for its new dogmatism of the straight line and its puritan functionalism, comparing this to the promises it had first made. 'The new Berlin', he wrote in 1930:

> despises the swollen marble and stucco showiness of the 'Wilhelmine' public buildings and churches ... but it revels in the hocus-pocus of megalomaniac motion-picture palaces, department stores, automobile 'salons' and gourmet paradises with their shrieking advertisements. This new architecture, the slender nakedness of its structure shining far and wide and bathed in an orgy of lights at night, is by no means, so we are told, ostentatious; it is rather 'constructive and functional' ... Bauhaus style. But let us take heart. For small homeowners, workers, civil servants and employees the Bauhaus style also has its social application. They are serially packaged into minimum standard housing.[6]

Progressive architects and artists in Germany and Holland felt disillusioned, caught between the relative affluence of society in the late 1920s (prior to the 1929 stock market crash) – which they welcomed – and the betrayal of their ideals of the immediate postwar years. As the avant-garde began to fade – both as art and as a mindset – they looked to the Soviet Union as the possible future. This was the place where the world was being redesigned and society was being reshaped – rather than being merely 'packaged into minimum standard housing', with no higher ideals in sight.

Recent scholarship has revealed that the ties between the Bauhaus and the Soviet Union were more extensive than previously thought. Annemarie Jaeggi relates that in the autumn of 1927 – ie, still during Gropius's tenure – a number of official Soviet delegations visited the Bauhaus. The visitors included the writer Ilya Ehrenburg and the cultural commissar Anatoly Lunacharsky, as well as a group of Russian students who came to study construction technologies. The following year a delegation of Bauhaus students headed by Gunta Stölzl paid a return visit to Moscow. The former Bauhaus student

Bela Kun talking to workers at the Csepel factory after its nationalisation, Budapest, April 1919

Soldiers and young men around a decorated car, Budapest, October 1918

Hinnerk Scheper worked in Moscow for two years, from 1929 to 1931. Also in 1931, a Soviet government delegation visited Gropius in Berlin and 'nourished expectations that he would be called to Moscow, presumably as the head of Giprogor, the State Institute of Urban Design'. In the end, however, a three-day lecture trip to Leningrad in 1933 was the sole concrete outcome of Gropius's Russian plans (together with a competition entry for the Ukrainian State Theatre in Kharkov in 1930–31, in which Sebök was also involved).[7]

As the Nazis rose to power, socially engaged German and Dutch architects flocked to the Soviet Union. Among them was Ernst May, who in 1930 took practically all of his Frankfurt staff to Russia – including Fred Forbát and Mart Stam. 1930 was also the year when Hannes Meyer was ousted from the Bauhaus because of his communist sympathies. In an interview given to the Soviet daily *Pravda* shortly before his departure he said:

> After many years of working within the capitalist system I am convinced that working under such conditions is quite senseless. In view of our Marxist and revolutionary conception of the world we, revolutionary architects, are at the mercy of the insoluble contradictions of a world built on animal individualism and the exploitation of man by man. I have said, and I say again, to all architects, all engineers, all builders: Our way is and must be that of the revolutionary proletariat, that of the communist party, the way of those who are building and achieving socialism. I am leaving for the USSR to work among people who are forging a true revolutionary culture, who are achieving socialism, and who are living in that form of society for which we have been fighting here under the conditions of capitalism. I beg our Russian comrades to regard us, my group and myself, not as heartless specialists, claiming all kinds of special privileges, but as fellow workers with comradely views ready to make a gift to socialism and the revolution of all our knowledge, all our strength, and all the experience that we have acquired in the art of building.[8]

Meyer may have been a more committed and self-conscious communist than many of his colleagues, but his words reflect the dominant view among progressive architects. How these architects were betrayed we know from their individual fates, including that of István Sebök.

The recent research that has uncovered Sebök's substantial contribution to some of the Bauhaus's signature products and designs, as well as his important work in Moscow, reflects the current trend towards a more nuanced examination of the legacy of modernism. This new work highlights figures who were indispensible in inspiring and realising many first-rate projects, but were long overshadowed by the signatories of those projects. Sebök's career path, from Hungary to Germany and the Soviet Union, combined with his commitment to the rational, international outlook in architecture and kinetic art, epitomises the journeys of those capable young specialists who offered their professional expertise and imagination to the community, wherever life took them.

1
Tibor Frank, '"All Modern People Are Persecuted": The Hungarian Trauma, 1918–1920', in Victor Karady and Maria M Kovács (eds), *The Hungarian Numerus Clausus: Law and Academic Anti-Semitism in Interwar Central Europe* (Budapest, 2011).

2
The small town of Pécs, home to many of the Hungarian Bauhaus members, had a special status until the end of the Commune as part of the short-lived Serbian-Hungarian Republic that enjoyed independence from Hungary. Pécs was a multi-ethnic town with a German, Serbian, Croatian and Hungarian population of Roman Catholic, Protestant, Jewish or Serbian Orthodox faith. An Artists' Circle offered artistic education to aspiring young artists and the local journal *Krónika* (Chronicle) was a well-informed forum for contemporary cultural developments.

3
For a detailed discussion see Tibor Frank, *Double Exile: Migrations of Jewish-Hungarian Professionals through Germany to the United States, 1919–1945* (Oxford/New York: Peter Lang, 2009).

4
Annemarie Jaeggi, *Adolf Meyer: Der zweite Mann* (Berlin: Bauhaus Archiv Museum für Gestaltung, 1994), p 469.

5
The interview is cited and included in a CD by András Koerner, *The Stages of Andor Weininger* (New York: Alma on Dobbin, 2008).

6
Ernst Kállai, 'Zehn Jahre Bauhaus', *Die Weltbühne*, January 1930. English translation by Wolfgang Jabs and Basil Gilbert, in Timothy O Benson and Eva Forgacs (eds), *Between Worlds, A Source Book of Central European Avant-Gardes 1910–1930* (Cambridge, MA: MIT Press and LACMA, 2002), p 637.

7
Available at http://www.international.icomos.org/risk/2007/pdf/Soviet_Heritage_34_V-4_Jaeggi.pdf.

8
From *Pravda*, Berlin dispatch dated 10 October 1930, http://rosswolfe.wordpress.com/2011/04/28/the-german-avant-garde-architectural-journals-wasmuths-monatshefte-fur-baukunst-und-stadtebau-1926-1931.

Congress of Constructivists and Dadaists (Theo van Doesburg and friends in Weimar), 1922

The International Fronts of
Soviet Architecture, 1919–1939

Richard Anderson

On 3 April 1935 the newspaper of the Union of Soviet Architects published a casual group portrait – a snapshot taken at a recent event in Moscow. Eleven figures crowd together, vying for space within the frame. At far right, the Czech architect Jaromír Krejcar leans into Nikolai Kolli, a veteran Soviet architect who was at the time overseeing the completion of Le Corbusier's Tsentrosoyuz building in Moscow. Hannes Meyer, the Swiss-born former Bauhaus director, stands behind Kolli. Hans Schmidt (also Swiss) fiddles with his tie at the centre of the image. Antonín Urban, a communist architect from Czechoslovakia who studied under Meyer at the Bauhaus, stands between Schmidt and Nusim Nessis, another Czech-born architect. At the far left, partially cropped, is István Sebök. A record of a meeting between foreign and Soviet architects, this photograph documents the international front of Soviet architecture as it was constituted in the mid-1930s. The persons assembled here had come to the Soviet Union for a variety of reasons: some in search of what Le Corbusier called the 'mystique' of the USSR, some fleeing the financial collapse of 1929 and the unemployment it created, some fleeing the rise of right-wing dictatorships in Central Europe. And some, like Meyer, drawn to the Soviet Union out of political conviction.

Sebök described the contours of this international front to Walter Gropius in a letter written in January 1936. He was at pains to convince his former mentor that architecture had made great progress in the USSR.[1] In the mid-1920s, Erich Mendelsohn had described the USSR as a major pole of the emerging industrial civilisation – 'Russia and America – the future of Utopia!' – but by the middle of the 1930s, the progress of Soviet architecture was not self-evident to western observers.[2] International hopes were dashed by the outcome of the 1932 competition for the Palace of the Soviets. Despite the long list of modern architects invited to submit proposals – among them Gropius and Le Corbusier – it was Boris Iofan's, Vladimir Shchuko's and Vladimir Gel'freikh's monumental tower that was ultimately selected. Gropius had himself surveyed the architectural scene in Leningrad in 1933 and was reportedly 'horrified and shaken by what he had seen and experienced'.[3] Sebök assured Gropius that after a short phase marked by the celebration of Renaissance prototypes and classical orders, Soviet architects had recognised the frivolity of such concerns in the face of the vast construction projects projected in Stalin's Second Five-Year Plan. 'I believe, dear Gropius, that you yourself would acknowledge that of late architecture has come very, very far here', Sebök wrote. But he also reported that not everyone among the diverse group of foreigners working in the USSR was satisfied with Soviet architectural production: Le Corbusier, Ernst May, Bruno Taut and Hannes Meyer numbered among those who 'after a certain time became disgruntled'. Disgruntled indeed – Meyer would return to Switzerland only months after Sebök's writing. Yet others, including Grete Schütte-Lihotzky, Werner Hebebrand, Hans Schmidt, Kurt Meyer and André Lurçat, 'live here and, if they at first found it somewhat difficult, now manage, and they and the public are satisfied with their work'. There was tension on the international front.

Sebök's text provides a critical map of the aspirations that collide just below the surface of the otherwise casual snapshot of 1935. The particular mixture of disappointment and satisfaction he identified among the foreign architects working in the USSR can be attributed to the dynamism of the Soviet architectural imaginary. Throughout the interwar decades, the relationships between architects working inside the Soviet Union and architects outside underwent a series of transformations. The revolutionary romanticism of the early years both incited Soviet architects to new forms of practice and, in the minds of western architects, conjured visions of a synthesis between the social and aesthetic. The images of workers' clubs, communal houses and urban plans that poured out of the Soviet Union throughout the 1920s fuelled the reformist agendas of western architects in an era when, in the words of Anatole Kopp, 'modernism was not a style but a cause'.[4] But collaboration and integration of the international front of modern architecture gave way to estrangement and suspicion during the 1930s, when the worlds of politics and culture were transformed by political radicalisation throughout Europe. Tracing the intricate lines of the architectural front, the following episodes provide a background to the tension Sebök diagnosed among his colleagues. Together, they describe how the architectural culture of the Soviet Union could engender both passionate commitment and utter alienation, utopian brotherhood and puzzled incomprehension, economic opportunity and bureaucratic coercion.

Встреча иностранных архитекторов с советскими
проф. Н. Я. Колли, проф. Ганнес Майер, арх. Ба
арх. Не

A meeting of Soviet and foreign architects at the House of the Architect, Moscow, 1935

архитектора. Справа налево: Яромир Крейцар, х. Нингупс, арх. Ганс Шмидт, арх. Антоний Урбан, рх. Зебек.

'Art is dead: long live Tatlin's new machine art!'

This provocative slogan was made public at the First International Dada Fair, which took place in Berlin in 1920. It was proudly displayed on a placard that George Grosz and John Heartfield held aloft in a memorable photograph. The 'machine art' to which they referred was Vladimir Tatlin's Monument to the Third International (1919–20), a 400m-tall steel spiral that was to straddle the Neva River in Petrograd and house rotating government offices. Although it is unlikely that the two had actually seen Tatlin's revolutionary tower at the time of the Dada fair, they clearly sought to capture some of the energy emanating from the East for their own purposes. Richard Huelsenbeck, the poet, drummer and later chronicler of Dada activities, upplemented this enthusiasm for the new Russia when he declared Dada to be a 'German Bolshevist affaire'.[5] Conflating the Bolshevik's toppling of the Tsarist regime with Dada's destructive impulse, these artists capitalised on the polemical force of all things Soviet. As a subject of broad popular interest in Weimar culture, the idea of Russia became an unstable and mobile discursive figure that lent a revolutionary flair to the contexts in which it appeared.

While the Berlin Dadaists drew upon such German-language publications on Soviet art as Konstantin Umanskij's *Neue Kunst in Russland* (1920) and his earlier essays in *Der Ararat*, other German artists and architects were engaged in direct communication with their Russian colleagues. As early as 1919, David Shterenberg, the chairman of Russia's newly created Section of Fine Arts, had issued a call for artistic exchange between German and Russian artists. 'Russian artists turn first to their immediate neighbours, their German colleagues, and invite them to the discussion and exchange of news regarding that which is attainable by artistic means.'[6] Among the many recipients of this call were members of the Berlin-based Workers' Council for Art, an organisation whose very name was derived from the Russian word *sovet*, or workers' council. Gropius, Taut and other members of the group responded with utopian enthusiasm: 'We feel at one with you in the firm desire to do everything in our power so that the rift that power politics has opened between peoples may be once again closed.'[7] Against nationalism, which had unleashed devastation on European societies during World War I, the Workers' Council for Art asserted the primacy of socialist internationalism.

More than any of his colleagues, Taut promoted a romantic vision of Soviet socialism in his texts and sought to tie this to a programme for a new architecture. 'Ex oriente lux', Taut wrote in 1919, 'the light comes from the East even today and its credence finds new nourishment as it sees itself propagated further west.'[8] He coupled his interest in the luminous spread of socialism with a call for the socialisation, or unification of the arts under the wing of architecture. Already in 1914 Taut was seeking ways to lend architecture some of the brilliance and rhythms he found in the abstract paintings of Wassily Kandinsky and Franz Marc, or in the sculpture of Alexander Archipenko. In order to create a new total work of art, architecture would have to rise above purely economic and functional considerations. Just as abstraction freed painters of the need to reflect the world, 'architecture too can set itself free from utilitarian demand'.[9] This anti-utilitarianism pervaded the work shown at the Exhibition of Unknown Architects that the Workers' Council for Art sponsored in 1919. The crystalline and amorphous forms of the expressionist projects of Hermann Finsterlin, Wenzel Hablik, Johannes Molzahn and others flew in the face of bourgeois notions of design.

The anti-utilitarianism Taut espoused resonated in Russia, where artists and architects were exploring the unification of the arts as well. SINSKUL'PTARKh, a group of sculptors and architects, was founded by Boris Korolev in 1919 in order to analyse the means of artistic synthesis. Nikolai Ladovskii and Vladimir Krinskii, who would each make significant contributions to Soviet architectural culture, were active members of the group. SINSKUL'PTARKh's emphasis on the non-utilitarian aspects of design would lead Ladovskii to undertake a rigorous analysis of architecture's formal laws and their relations to human perception. He would later assemble his theory of architectural rationalism from the material generated by the nexus of German expressionism and the scientific impulse that saturated early Soviet artistic culture.

Nikolai Istselenov delivered the first statement of SINSKUL'PTARKh's principles in a lecture on 'the rebirth of the pure meaning of architectural structure – as the temple of a new cult'. Istselenov argued that 'utilitarianism was foreign' to the temples of the past and that in the modern age 'the pure meaning of the architectural art had been lost'. He echoed Taut's concept of the *Stadtkrone* (city-crown) in his call for the construction of a new, non-utilitarian building that

George Grosz and John Heartfield, First International Dada Fair, Berlin, 1920

would be a collaborative work of painters, sculptors and architects. This structure was to be a work of architectural art which would loom over the city as a new cult building.[10] Members of SINSKUL'PTARKh tested this proposal in theoretical projects for a 'temple of the communication of peoples' – the first of many paper projects in which radical new ideas would be articulated. Istselenov's temple resembled a mountain of crystalline forms. Its fractured geometric planes towered above a broad, variegated base, evoking a dynamic monumentality.

Istselenov curiously vanished from the Soviet scene soon after his inaugural address to SINSKUL'PTARKh. He reappeared a few years later in the pages of *Frühlicht*, the journal edited by Taut between 1920 and 1922 during his tenure as city building director for Magdeburg. Istselenov published a description of the architecture of Soviet Russia in the spring 1922 issue. In one of the first accounts of post-revolutionary architecture to appear in Germany, he described the 'dynamic impressions' and 'towering effects' of the projects produced by his former collaborators in Moscow.[11] Some of these designs won critical acclaim at the First Russian Art Exhibition at the von Diemen gallery in Berlin in fall 1922.

Cultural contacts between Germany and Soviet Russia were given a new economic and political foundation with the signing in 1922 of the Treaty of Rapallo, which normalised diplomatic relations between the two countries. This followed the 'New Economic Policy' (NEP) that Lenin instituted the previous year in order to boost the production of agriculture and manufactured goods and open markets to international investment. The Berlin-based, trilingual journal *Veshch'/Objet/Gegenstand* applauded the cultural effects of the new situation, proclaiming that 'the blockade of Russia is coming to an end'.[12]

El Lissitzky and Il'ia Ehrenburg, the journal's editors, wrote of a new internationalism in the arts, noting that all of Europe and America had entered a new 'creative period'. Through growing networks of communication – journals, exhibitions, conferences, personal contacts – Russian architects and institutions participated in the international world of modernism. These were mutual exchanges: both Russia and the West sought to create new forms and new practices for a 'new, collective, international style'.[13]

Foreign Relations

'The revolutionary pursuits of the avant-gardes of modern architecture of all countries overlap. They forge a new international language, which is clear and comprehensible despite border posts and barriers.'[14] These lines from Moisei Ginzburg's programmatic essay of 1926, 'The International Front of Contemporary Architecture', convey the boundless territorial ambition at the heart of architectural constructivism – its aim to reconstruct one sixth of the world, or more, depending on the success of the socialist revolution. Revolutionary visions aside, running through Ginzburg's text is an unmistakable enthusiasm for international recognition, for the arrival of Soviet modernism on the world stage. Through the mediation of El Lissitzky, the Hungarian critic Alfréd Kemény and others, constructivism had become a driving force in Central Europe. Konstantin Melnikov's USSR Pavilion at the Exposition Internationale held in Paris in 1925 was, like Le Corbusier's *L'Esprit Nouveau* pavilion, a breath of fresh air. Soviet architecture was featured in the foreign press, displayed in exhibitions abroad, and published in such influential books as Walter Gropius's *Internationale Architektur* and Adolf Behne's *Der moderne Zweckbau*. Conversely, the work of architects in Western Europe and the United States of America was closely monitored in the Soviet professional press. The founding in 1925 of VOKS, the All-Union Organisation of Cultural Ties Abroad, facilitated the travel of foreign architects and critics to the USSR. Ginzburg's vision for an international front seemed to be gaining force and cohesion.

But not everyone was happy with the balance of foreign relations. Scandal erupted in 1925 after it was revealed that a major commission had been awarded to a foreign architect without so much as a proper competition. At the centre of this controversy was Erich Mendelsohn, who had been approached by the Leningrad Textile Trust earlier that year. They were impressed by his factory in Luckenwalde and asked him to design the physical plant of the Krasnaia znamia (Red Banner) bleaching and dyeing works. As contract negotiations dragged on for the better part of a year, Mendelsohn complained about the Russian tolerance for bureaucracy in a letter home from Leningrad: 'They make a basic revolution but they are bogged down by even more basic administration.'[15] Meanwhile, several factions within Moscow's architectural community made their grievances public in what

Hinnerk Sheper, interior perspective, Narkomfin building, Moscow, 1929

First exhibition of modern architecture, Moscow, 1927

became known as the 'foreign problem'. Aleksei Shchusev, chairman of the Moscow Architectural Society, noted that 'our social structure and local economic conditions place us closer to the solution of such a task than Westerners.' The leaders of ASNOVA, the group of rationalist architects that had been founded by Ladovskii in 1923, conceded that the USSR needed to adopt the advanced technologies available in the capitalist West but disputed the textile trust's reliance on foreign design expertise. 'The art and architecture of the USSR is valued quite highly in the West', ASNOVA wrote, 'and we are justified in asking for this recognition at home as well'.[16] Such commissions as the Krasnaia znamia plant were rare in 1925, and Soviet architects evidently wanted a fair shot at winning them. Mendelsohn, for his part, would ultimately be cut out of the project by the engineers of the textile trust, whose less than ethical opportunism would be reported in the pages of *Bauwelt* in 1926.[17] Only the power house of Krasnaia znamia would ultimately be constructed in a form faithful to Mendelsohn's design.

Throughout the Krasnaia znamia affair, Mendelsohn was consistently supported by OSA, the Union of Contemporary Architects. Led by Ginzburg and the Vesnin brothers (Aleksandr, Viktor and Leonid), OSA promoted constructivist principles and the integration of the international architectural vanguard. They disseminated their ideas through multiple channels: through *Sovremennaia arkhitektura* (*SA*, Contemporary Architecture), the journal OSA published between 1926 and 1930; through leadership in Moscow's architectural schools; and through dialogue with protagonists from abroad. Their definition of an international front materialised in the First Exhibition of Contemporary Architecture, held in Moscow in summer 1927. This was a landmark event. It presented work from leading constructivists, student projects from VKhUTEMAS (the Higher Artistic and Technical Workshops), and designs from France, Germany, Poland, Czechoslovakia and the Bauhaus.

Gropius's recently completed Bauhaus building in Dessau featured prominently in the exhibition, reflecting OSA's special interest in the international school of design. In the following years *SA* presented Gropius's project for Erwin Piscator's Totaltheater, without, however, indicating Sebök's contribution to the design. The journal announced Hannes Meyer's takeover after Gropius's departure by publishing a translation of Ernő Kállai's essay celebrating of the new productive orientation of the school: 'The Bauhaus lives!'[18] In 1928 a delegation of students from Moscow's architectural schools undertook a month-long excursion to Germany to meet the architects and see the sights that had been so prominently featured in the Soviet press. Ginzburg, too, visited the Bauhaus in person. He was so impressed by the use of colour as a device for orientation in the Bauhaus building's interior that he invited Hinnerk Scheper, the director of the wall painting workshop, to Moscow. There he would produce, among other projects, colour designs for the interior of the Narkomfin Communal House designed by Ginzburg and Ignatii Milinis. Ginzburg was reinforcing his international front in both word and deed.

Both ASNOVA and Le Corbusier were palpably absent from OSA's exhibition. ASNOVA's exclusion points to the increasing tension between Soviet architectural factions and suggests that the vanguard envisioned by Ginzburg was not all-inclusive. Le Corbusier, on the other hand, was a celebrity to Soviet architects. His buildings and theories were widely published and discussed in Moscow and Leningrad. This popularity helped him prevail in the 1928 competition for the Tsentrosoyuz Headquarters. His Soviet colleagues were so impressed with his work that many of them forfeited their chance at the commission and lobbied the jury on Le Corbusier's behalf.[19] Designed with his cousin, Pierre Jeanneret, and in collaboration with Nikolai Kolli, the Tsentrosoyuz building was both Le Corbusier's largest institutional commission to date and the most significant project awarded to a foreigner. Raised on a forest of *pilotis* and connected to the ground by undulating ramps, the project served as a crucial testing ground for Le Corbusier's approach to architecture as circulation and inspired Soviet imitations.

While architects celebrated the growing integration of the Soviet scene with international modernism, a group of young communist architects objected to a trend they interpreted as the slavish imitation of bourgeois forms. Consolidated as VOPRA, the All-Union Union of Proletarian Architects, this group rejected the theories of both OSA and ASNOVA. VOPRA proclaimed that 'in the age of the dictatorship of the proletariat and the fight for the socialist reconstruction of the world, architecture must have class-form and class-content'.[20] Their emphasis on class warfare was symptomatic of the broader cultural revolution of the late 1920s and early 1930s which sought to establish distinctly anti- capitalist modes of cultural production.

Brigades of Architects

Despite VOPRA's rhetoric, architects from the capitalist West would play a significant role in the reconstruction of the USSR during the First Five-Year Plan. The financial crash of 1929 shook the economic foundations of the United States and Western Europe and lent credibility to the Soviet Union's programme of forced industrialisation. As building industries faltered, foreign architects flocked to the USSR in search of work. Hannes Meyer, after his dismissal from the Bauhaus for alleged 'communist activity,' settled in Moscow with a 'Red Brigade' of former students. Ernst May, director of urban planning for Frankfurt am Main, accepted a contract from the Soviet government to assist in the design of cities. They both landed in Moscow with prestigious appointments: Meyer was given a professorship at the Institute of Architecture and Construction (VASI) and made the director of a trust in charge of school construction (GIPROVTUS); May, as recent research has shown, would take over the institute *Standartgorproekt* (the Standard City Design Office), which had a 'brigade' of 800, 150 of whom were foreign specialists.[21] May was charged with the design of numerous industrial cities, including Magnitogorsk, ex nihilo. While he always maintained his political neutrality, he marvelled at the opportunity to construct socialist cities without the impediments of private land ownership. Meyer couldn't suppress his envy for May's position when he told a Berlin audience in 1931 that 'the construction of entire new cities, as May has described it, is so to speak the cake', noting that 'the renovation of existing cities is our daily bread'.[22]

Despite the sobering work required to modernise the Soviet Union's urban fabric, the atmosphere of the First Five-Year Plan encouraged big thinking. In 1930 Le Corbusier proposed the complete reorganisation of the Soviet capital in his famous 'response to Moscow'. Arguing that Moscow was 'in reality a provisional city', he called for the demolition of all but the most significant historical structures and the creation of a new city based on a grid of functional zones, a field of expansive redent blocks, and diagonal connecting streets. Although his Soviet audience gave the project a mixed reception, Le Corbusier would make it the basis of his major urban statement of the 1930s: the *ville radieuse*.[23] Le Corbusier's proposal was one of a flurry of projects for Moscow produced by an international array of architects. The intense debate on Moscow's urban form prompted the *Congrès internationaux d'architecture moderne* (CIAM) to select the city as the initial site for its conference on the 'functional city' in 1931–32. Moscow, in Le Corbusier's opinion, had become 'the focus of architecture and city planning in the world'.[24]

The plan's principal architectural front, however, was industrial. The Soviet Union's great leap forward was accomplished with American technical assistance. Through the American-Russian Trade Association (Amtorg), the Soviet government purchased entire production lines from the Ford Motor Company. Albert Kahn Inc, which designed Ford's River Rouge plant, expanded automobile factories in 'Soviet Detroit' – Nizhniy Novgorod. Kahn's firm provided designs for plants at sites across the USSR: tractor factories in Stalingrad, Cheliabinsk and Kharkov; steel works in Nizhniy Tagil and Kuznetsk; airplane factories in Kramatorsk and Tomsk, and many others.[25] American know-how also helped complete the metallurgical complex at Magnitogorsk and the hydro-electric station on the Dniepr River.

The cultural revolution materialised in highly publicised competitions for workers' clubs, palaces of culture and mass theatres. At this time Kharkov, the capital of the Ukrainian SSR, became an epicentre of architectural creativity. This city had already shaped the international image of Soviet architecture significantly. The vast semicircular mass of the Gosprom Building, which Henri Barbusse described as 'half a street of great grey palaces of dizzy [sic] height', had circulated throughout the world in magazines and photographs.[26] In 1930, Kharkov attracted the attention of architects in both the USSR and the West with an international competition for a 'theatre for musical mass-productions' with capacity for 4,000 spectators. The number of projects submitted indicates how little architectural work there was to be had in Europe: of 142 entries, 91 came from outside the Soviet Union. Gropius was among the competitors and, although he rarely gets the credit he is due, Sebök contributed significant features to the design. Drawing on the concept of the Totaltheater they had created for Piscator, Gropius and Sebök foresaw a network of projectors that would 'flood' interior surfaces with films, enliven the space, and thereby activate the audience. Although the jury applauded the 'cinematisation' of theatrical space, the team was awarded eighth prize. The Vesnin brothers won first prize, but their design was never executed.

The Kharkov theatre competition was the starting point of Sebök's most innovative independent project:

his design for a monument to Taras Shevchenko, the Ukrainian national poet. Also a competition entry for a site in Kharkov, Sebök's was no ordinary monument. Synthesising the concepts underpinning Tatlin's Monument to the Third International, Gustav Klucis's diagrams of multimedia constructions and El Lissitzky's speaker's tribune, Sebök offered a radical reworking of the form and function of the monument. Its basic structure – a platform supported by a central mast and reached by a spiral stair – was present in renderings of the Kharkov theatre project. Using projectors, screens and loudspeakers, Sebök sought to replace the static equestrian monument with a dynamic media machine. It was an ambitious attempt to transpose the 'cinematisation' of theatrical space into urban space and thereby activate the urban mass. Although Sebök's project resonated with influential critics, including Alfred Kurella and Alfréd Kemény, the closest it came to realisation was its display in model form at the exhibition of the work of 'October', the Soviet association of artists, that took place in Berlin in 1930.[27]

At the nadir of the depression, Berlin and Prague became centres for anti-capitalist architectural thought. Models and theories developed in the Soviet Union migrated west, where they entered the critical arsenal of socialist architectural factions. In 1930 architects from the Czech group Levá Fronta drew on Soviet models of collectivised housing for their so-called 'L-project', which included individual 'dwelling cells' for adults, separate dwellings for children and communal facilities. Karel Teige, a long-time supporter of Soviet architectural culture, applauded the project and declared that 'the architectural avant-garde, led by constructivism', had a duty to 'further the struggle of the proletariat actively, and not through utopian-political tracts'.[28] A group of communist students organised a 'Collective for Socialist Building' in Berlin in 1931, declaring that 'architecture must become a weapon in class war'.[29] In response to the 'Great German Building Exhibition' of that year, they organised a 'Proletarian Building Exhibition' which displayed recent advances in Soviet city planning.[30] The Swiss publicist Alexander von Senger decried these undertakings in his incendiary book *Moscow's Torch*, which painted the entire modern movement in architecture as a product of *Baubolschewismus* – Bolshevist building.[31] The spirit of Soviet architecture haunted Europe. The Soviet Union appeared as either a land of architectural possibility or a collectivist spectre, depending on one's vantage point.

Tensions on the Popular Front

After the second round of the competition for the Palace of the Soviets, the French journal *L'Architecture d'Aujourd'hui* announced, in May 1933, that several of the USSR's most influential modern architects had been stripped of their professional credentials and 'given time to rethink' their approaches to design. Ginzburg, Ladovskii and the Vesnin brothers had allegedly disregarded the Communist Party's call for the incorporation of classical architectural motifs in projects submitted to the competition. The French journal called their dismissal an 'aesthetic reaction in the USSR'.[32]

The news shocked the international architectural community. Architects in Western Europe and America were still reeling from the dramatic conclusion of the first round of the competition for the Palace of the Soviets in early 1932. Le Corbusier declared that the outcome of this event had caused the 'mystique' of the USSR to evaporate.[33] CIAM cancelled plans to hold its meeting on the functional city in Moscow. Protesting the competition results, Sigfried Giedion, CIAM's secretary, sent Stalin a photomontage that compared one of the winning designs with 'pseudo-modern department store and church architecture'. The ties between Moscow and CIAM and, by extension, the international modern movement, were becoming tenuous.

Although Ginzburg, Ladovskii and the Vesnin brothers dismissed the claims made by *L'Architecture d'Aujourd'hui*, Soviet architecture had been irrevocably altered. Compounding the disappointments of the Palace of the Soviets competition there was a consolidation of artistic and literary organisations, which in 1933 produced the Union of Soviet Architects (*Soiuz sovetskikh arkhitektorov,* SSA). The structure of the union enabled communist architects, who represented only a small fraction of the profession, to exert greater influence over the politics of architectural affairs.[34] The SSA soon criticised the alleged excesses of constructivism and rationalism and directed architects toward the 'critical assimilation of architectural heritage', the theoretical elaboration of which was a principal aim of the newly created Academy of Architecture.

In reply to a request to provide 'friendly words' to the inaugural issue of the SSA's newspaper, JJP Oud reacted to the changes taking place in the Soviet Union with sentiments shared by many outside observers. While he praised the initial phase of Soviet architecture's development, he wrote: 'I've come to understand from Russian journals that columns, capitals, cornices and so forth more often than not find goodwill. Why is that?' Did this mean that Soviet architects had become convinced that only 'old forms' were artistically expressive? 'I object to this – now and forever – most strenuously!' Oud exclaimed. Clearly troubled by the situation, he revealed the reason for his deep disappointment at the new direction in Soviet architecture: 'Early on you yourselves demonstrated in perhaps the most convincing fashion the great possibilities for artistic expression of "New Objectivity"!'[35] For the architects of the capitalist West to see the Soviet Union reject the conventions of modernism provoked disillusion precisely because the Soviet vanguard had been such forceful modern pioneers.

Foreign architects living in the USSR either left, as Ernst May did in 1933, or came to terms with the new directive. Hannes Meyer now argued that the 'artless' architecture of functionalism was fundamentally rooted in capitalism's desire to push down building costs. Conceding the value of art in Soviet architecture he wrote: 'I have learned that it is self-evident to the masses of workers that socialist construction should include the creation of a great proletarian art that synthesises murals, sculpture and architecture in order to shape the lives of socialist people in an uplifting artistic form.'[36] Hans Schmidt employed a similar logic in accommodating himself to the use of historical precedents in architecture and urban design. Such rationalisations exacerbated tensions between foreign architects working in the USSR and architects abroad.

Although links between Soviet architects and the international front of modern architecture were all but severed by the mid-1930s, Soviet architectural culture retained a commitment to internationalism. But this internationalism was supported by a new view of foreign relations and a new architectural geography. Through the Academy of Architecture, a new generation of architectural students was able to travel to Western Europe on a grand tour of monuments, both ancient and modern. The academy also published a variety of translations, ranging from Andrea Palladio to Lewis Mumford. Many foreign architects who remained in the USSR during the 1930s worked for the academy's journal *Arkhitektura za rubezhom* (Architecture Abroad), a publication devoted entirely to architecture and design news from beyond the Soviet Union's borders. In a 1935 issue, one finds Sebök reporting on the furniture of Marcel Breuer and others.[37] There were also technical study tours, such as the trip to the USA undertaken by Boris Iofan in 1934–35 to study the art and engineering of the American skyscraper. Many foreign architects would attend the First Congress of Soviet Architects in 1937. Frank Lloyd Wright was a notable guest but, with few exceptions, the foreigners made little impact on the event. As the decade progressed, Soviet architects reached out beyond their borders less to establish relationships with foreign colleagues than to assimilate the knowledge, technical and otherwise, that could be gained from the outside world.

The standing of many foreign architects working in the USSR was threatened by the outcome of the show trial of August 1936, where it was revealed that 'Trotskyist enemies of the people' had allegedly been conspiring to overthrow the Soviet government. One of the defendants identified a pair of German architects as spies for the National Socialist Party working in the Soviet Union.[38] At a closed meeting of party-member architects held soon after the trial, suspicions of all things German were voiced. Some claimed that Hannes Meyer had collaborated with the spies. Others questioned the loyalty of such long-time residents as Hans Schmidt and Grete Schütte-Lihotzky. The trial initiated the 'Great Terror', the campaign of state-sponsored violence in which countless individuals were imprisoned or executed.

Given the dangerous political atmosphere in Moscow and the rising xenophobia of the bureaucracy, it is remarkable that Sebök was able to continue working at such a high level through the end of the 1930s. In 1936 he contributed to a project by S Liashchenko and Viktor Vesnin for the pavilions of the Industries of Socialism exhibition. At the end of the decade he worked closely with Viktor and Aleksandr Vesnin on projects for stations on Moscow's third metro line and suburban rail stations.[39] These designs were characteristic of the 'enriched' architectural language that had been developing in Moscow throughout the decade. They nevertheless sought innovative technical and spatial effects. With a depth of 70m, Paveletskaya Metro Station was to be one of the deepest of Moscow's system. The typical layout of a deep station separated the central hall by massive piers, leaving only small openings for communication between them. The project submitted by the Vesnin brothers, Sebök and Liashchenko, however, was a broad, open space divided only by a screen of pillars. Mosaics on the barrel vault depicted scenes of industry and everyday life in the Donbass.[40] Other projects on which Sebök worked include the Vesnin brothers' design for the Second Building of the Council of National Commissars (SNK) in Moscow, which won first place in a competition of 1940. Unfortunately none of these projects were realised; some, like the SNK building, were casualties of World War II, while others were awarded to different brigades of architects. Although it is difficult to find built records of Sebök's work in Moscow, it is worth noting the value Viktor Vesnin placed on the former Bauhäusler. In September 1939, Vesnin intervened on Sebök's behalf in a letter to Lazar Kaganovich with a request that Sebök and his family be allowed to remain in the apartment they had occupied for nearly five years. As chairman of the National Commissariat of Thoroughfares, Kaganovich was technically Sebök's boss; but he was also the chairman of Moscow Soviet and one of the most feared members of Stalin's political elite. Vesnin, in seeking patronage from Kaganovich, was putting a great deal on the line for Sebök.

Soviet architects undertook one final international adventure before the outbreak of war, this time in New York City at the World's Fair of 1939. The Soviet Pavilion, designed by Boris Iofan, was among the largest at the event. The Soviet *chargé d'affaires* described it as a manifestation of 'a will for peace and progress at a time when in various parts of the world forces of war and regression are unleashed.'[41] The Soviet government could not maintain this rhetoric of peace for long. The USSR and Nazi Germany soon concluded the Molotov-Ribbentrop Pact – the non-aggression agreement that facilitated Hitler's invasion of Poland in that year. As Soviet and German statesmen divided Central Europe into spheres of influence, the Red Army moved into western Ukraine, Belarus and the Baltic States. Diplomats and cultural emissaries tried to assure the international community of the USSR's peaceful intentions through the union's participation in the New York World's Fair of 1939. But the Red Army's invasion of Finland during the Winter War of late 1939 exposed the USSR's aggressive territorial ambitions. The USA and Europe were outraged; the Soviets demolished their New York Pavilion, refusing to participate in the fair's second season; images of the Soviet invasion were installed on the undulating walls of Alvar Aalto's Finnish Pavilion.[42] The Second World War had begun, and the lines of Soviet architecture's international front would have to be redrawn.[43]

1
István Sebök, Letter to Walter Gropius, 6 January 1936, Bauhaus Archiv, Berlin.
2
Erich Mendelsohn, *Eric Mendelsohn: Letters of an Architect*, edited by Oskar Beyer, trans. Geoffrey Strachan (London: Abelard-Schuman, 1967), p 97.
3
Ibid, p 125.
4
Anatole Kopp, *Quand le Moderne n'était pas un style mais une cause* (Paris: École nationale supérieure des Beaux-Arts, 1988).
5
Richard Huelsenbeck, *En avant Dada: eine Geschichte des Dadaismus, Poetische Aktion* (Hamburg: MaD, 1976), p 43.
6
David Shterenberg, *Aufruf der russischen fortschrittlichen bildenden Künstler an die deutsche Kollegen* (1919), reproduced in Christian Schädlich, 'Das deutsche Echo aus die russisch-sowjetische Avantgarde der Kunst und Architektur', in Margarita Iosifovna Astafeva-Dlugach et al (eds), *Avantgarde 1900–1923: Russisch-sowjetische Architektur* (Stuttgart: Deutsche Verlags-Anstalt, 1991), p 131.
7
Manfred Schlösser (ed), *Arbeitsrat für Kunst, Berlin 1918–1921: Ausstellung mit Dokumentation*, Akademie der Künste 129 (Berlin: Akademie der Künste, 1980), p 112.
8
Bruno Taut, 'Der Sozialismus des Künstlers', *Sozialistische Monatshefte* 25 (1919), p 261.
9
Bruno Taut, 'A Necessity' (1914), in Timothy O Benson and Edward Dimendberg (eds), *Expressionist Utopias: Paradise, Metropolis, Architectural Fantasy* (Berkeley, CA: University of California Press, 2001), p 175.
10
Istselenov's text is reproduced in S O Khan-Magomedov, *Ratsionalizm: ratsio-arkhitektura: 'formalizm'* (Moscow: 'Arkhitektura-S', 2007), pp 59–62.
11
N I Istselenov, 'Die Architektur in Russland', *Frühlicht* Spring (1922), p 91.
12
El Lissitzky and Il'ia Ehrenburg, 'Blokada Rossii konchaetsia', *Veshch'/Objet/Gegenstand* 1–2 (1922), p 1.
13
Ibid, p 4.
14
Moisei Ginzburg, 'Mezhdunarodnyi front sovremennoi arkhitektury', *Sovremennaia arkhitektura* 1:2 (1926), p 41.
15
Eric Mendelsohn, *op cit*, p 92.
16
'O privlechenii inostrannykh spetsialistov k stroitel'stvu SSSR', *Stroitel'naia promyshlennost'* 3:12 (1925), p 823.
17.
See Irina Grigoreva, 'Erich Mendelsohns Wirken als Architekt in der Sowjetunion' (Ludwig-Maximillians-Universität, Thesis, 2003).
18
Ernö Kállai, 'Bauhaus zhivet!', *Sovremennaia arkhitektura* 3:5 (1928), p 148.
19
Jean-Louis Cohen, *Le Corbusier and the Mystique of the USSR: Theories and Projects for Moscow, 1928–1936* (Princeton, NJ: Princeton University Press, 1992), p 79.
20
VOPRA, 'Deklaratsiia ob"edineniia proletarskikh arkhitektorov', *Pechat' i revoliutsiia* 6 (1929), p 127.
21
See Thomas Flierl, '"Possibly the greatest task an architect ever faced": Ernst May in the Soviet Union (1930–1933)', in *Ernst May 1886–1970* (Munich: Prestel, 2011), pp 157–95.
22
Hannes Meyer, 'Bauen, Bauarbeiter und Techniker in der Sowjetunion', *Das neue Russland* 8/9 (1931), p 47.
23
Le Corbusier, *La ville radieuse, éléments d'une doctrine d'urbanisme pour l'équipement de la civilisation machiniste* (Boulogne (Seine): Éditions de l'architecture d'aujourd'hui, 1935).
24
Cited in Jean-Louis Cohen, op cit, p 90.
25
Anatole Senkevitch, 'Albert Kahn in Russland', *Bauwelt* 86:48 (1995), pp 2808–17.
26
Henri Barbusse, *One Looks at Russia*, trans. Warre B Wells (London: J M Dent & Sons, 1931), p 54.
27
Hubertus Gassner (ed), *Medienturm von István Sebök* (Munich: Haus der Kunst, 2002), p 39.
28
Karel Teige, 'Architektura a třídní boj', *ReD* III, 10 (1929–31), pp 309–10.
29
'Arbeitsgemeinschaft proletarischer Architekten', *Bauwelt* 4 (1931), p 128.
30
Kollektiv für sozialistisches Bauen, *Proletarische Bauausstellung* (Berlin: Kollektiv für sozialistisches Bauen, 1931).
31
Alexander von Senger, *Die Brandfackel Moskaus* (Zurzach-Schweiz: Verlag Kaufhaus, 1931).
32
'La Réaction esthétique en URSS', *L'Architecture d'Aujourd'hui* 5 (1933), p 106.
33
See Jean-Louis Cohen, *op cit*, pp 193–95.
34
See Hugh D Hudson, *Blueprints and Blood: The Stalinisation of Soviet Architecture, 1917–1937* (Princeton, NJ: Princeton University Press, 1993), pp 136–46.
35
J J P Oud, Letter to the editors of the *Arkhitekturnaia gazeta*, 7 December 1934, RGALI, f 674, op 1, d 14, l 27–28.
36
Hannes Meyer, 'Flucht ins Leben', in Lena Meyer-Bergner and Klaus-Jürgen Winkler (eds), *Bauen und Gesellschaft: Schriften, Briefe, Projekte*, Fundus-Bücher 64/65 (Dresden: Verlag der Kunst, 1980), p 187.
37
Zebek, 'Novye tipy mebeli', *Arkhitektura za rubezhom* 2:1 (1935), pp 30–34.
38
People's Commissariat of Justice of the USSR, *Report of Court Proceedings: The Case of the Trotskyite-Zinovievite Terrorist Centre* (Moscow: People's Commisariat of Justice of the USSR, 1936), p 102.
39
Viktor Vesnin, 'Lecture on the design for the 'Paveletskii vokzal' Metro Station to a meeting of workers', 27 July 1939, RGALI, f 2772, op 1, d 22, l 14–19.
40
Viktor Vesnin, Letter to L M Kaganovich, 4 September 1939, RGALI, f 2772, op 1, d 97, l 14.
41
'Russia Lays Stone for Fair Building', *New York Times*, 7 November 1938, p 21.
42
See 'Russia Quits Fair; Finns to Stay; Reds to Raze $4,000,000 Pavilion', *New York Times*, 2 December 1939, p 1. Anthony Swift, 'The Soviet World of Tomorrow at the New York World's Fair, 1939,' *The Russian Review* 57 (July 1998), pp 364–79.
43
Richard Anderson, 'USA/USSR: Architecture and War', *Grey Room* 34 (2009), pp 80–103.

Acknowledgements

My serious interest in Stefan Sebök began when my youngest son, Daniel, studying architecture, wanted to know more about his great uncle. Thus started my quest and journey. I would like to take this opportunity to express my thanks to those whose help has been absolutely vital in making this book a reality.

It would have been impossible to get started without two people in particular, the late architectural historian and expert on constructivism, Catherine Cooke, and Erwin Nagy, László Moholy-Nagy's nephew. By uncovering Sebök's name as it would have been spelt in Russian – Zebek – Catherine made it possible to search for traces of him in the Soviet Union. This daunting task was taken up by Erwin, who wrote the required and onerously bureaucratic letters to the Soviet authorities, and thus managed to secure the interrogation archives from the FSB, which in turn helped me trace the steps Sebök had taken from his early days in Hungary to his death in Moscow. I am also especially grateful to Catherine for instructing me in the demands of architectural research and on the importance of recording each of my finds, and to Erwin for subsequently putting me in touch with other Russian authorities, to say nothing of his valuable hints and tips as to how to deal with them.

Peter Hahn, director of the Bauhaus, took a personal interest in this subject from my very first visit and gave me free access to all the archives, allowing me to take photographic records of the Sebök works in their collection and to build up a base from which I could start my further research. Realising my emotional attachment to these works, I am also very grateful for the way he negotiated the release of two Sebök portraits of my grandparents and one of my mother. The presence of these drawings in my home has been a continual delight, and I like to think that they have also spurred me on.

A large number of historians and curators have been very supportive, supplying me with valuable information as I continued my search. I am indebted to Éva Forgács, an authority on Hungarians in the Bauhaus, not only for putting me in direct touch with the Nagy family, but also for her many valuable suggestions over the years, for looking critically at the material I have collected and recorded, and for her contribution to this volume. Karin Wilhelm and Hubertus Gassner in Germany and Eva Bajkay in Hungary were the first to show an interest in Sebök, some 30 years ago, and I have benefited greatly from their expertise. In Hungary, Levente Nagy put me in touch with his cousins, Erwin and Hattula, and my good friend Zsuzsa Denes helped secure contact in Budapest with the art historians Lenke Pap, Kristina Passuth and the late Julia Szabó, who all openly shared their insights with me.

In the US, Nan Rosenthal, then curator of the modern collection at the Metropolitan Museum of Art, made a special study of the Light-Space Modulator when she was a post-graduate student at Harvard University and she gave me free access to her research material and also put me in touch with Woodie Flowers from MIT, who recounted to me the problems he had found when constructing a copy of the Light-Space Modulator for the 1972 Venice Biennale. Richard Anderson, from Columbia University, shared information relating to Sebök's work with the Vesnin brothers and like Éva Forgács, contributed a wonderfully informative essay to this book. The architect Peter Yeadon, who produced a virtual reconstruction of the Kinetic Constructive System, also freely shared his findings with me. At the Busch-Reisinger museum in Boston, the curator Peter Nisbet provided access to the material and permission to record it. Emilie Norris, the former curator of their Gropius archives, gave me permission to use the material from her thesis on the Totaltheater and also provided me with copies of very valuable reprint material which I would otherwise have had great difficulty in accessing.

In London I got a lot of help and advice from the curators of two recent exhibitions that displayed some of the Sebök material: Achim Borchardt-Hume, curator of the Albers and Moholy-Nagy exhibition at Tate Modern in 2006, and David Crowley from the RCA, who worked on the Modernism exhibition at the Victoria & Albert Museum in 2006.

In Germany, at the Bauhaus-Archiv in Berlin, Annemarie Jaeggi, the current director, and their archivists Sabine Hartmann and Elke Eckhart enthusiastically helped me in searching through the archival material and supplying me with a large number of superb scans from their collections. At the Akademie der Künste in Berlin, which holds many of Sebök's drawings from his student days which they got through the Hoffmann legacy, both Matthias Schirren, the previous director of the architectural section, and the more recent director, Eva-Maria Barkoven, together with their staff, gave me valuable material and advice. Their former and recent curators, Karin Golke and Petra Albrecht, spent considerable time in deciphering and identifying a large number of Sebök's sketches. Helga Moritz, Hoffmann's stepdaughter in Graz, was later able to give me further background information on the Hoffmann and Sebök connection. At the Theatre Museum in Cologne, Gerald Köhler gave me access to all archives relating to the theatre productions in which Sebök was involved with Moholy-Nagy, including both *The Merchant of Berlin* and *The Tales of Hoffmann*. He also provided scans for the illustrations held by the museum of Sebök's work with Moholy-Nagy and also some of the Totaltheater. Matthias Lienert, chief archivist at the Technische Hochschule in Dresden, tracked all the archival material from Sebök's university days and also provided extremely valuable information on the background of the school and its curriculum and teaching in the 1920s.

In Szolnok, Hungary, Kathalin Gulyas of the Damjanics Museum verified Sebök's exact birth date, found some school archives and helped to identify various drawings in Sebök's sketchbooks of his hometown.

In Russia, at the Shchusev Museum, I got support from the late director David Sarkisyan, the deputy director Igor Kauzus and from the archivist Arkadi Krasheninnikov. Arkadi was not only our guide in the museum but took personal efforts to accompany us to Sebök's old apartment, also acting as our translator. With the recent help of deputy directors Igor Kauzus and Pavel Kuznetsov the museum also supplied the illustrations of the metro project in this book. Also in Moscow, Sergei Lar'kov at the Memorial Foundation advised me on the key questions to be asked of the FSB and also offered advice as to how to search for Sebök's family.

The translation of archival material was helped by many friends: Douglas Bowden, Miklos Muller, Vera Murray, Kati Vamos, Nikolay Zavadenko and Sasha Zavadenko.

Two personal friends also played a key role in accessing the Russian archives: Tiina Talvik from Estonia accompanied my husband and myself to Russia. Her persistent and imaginative efforts were able to secure multiple visits to the archives of the FSB. Nikolay Zavadenko in Moscow helped smooth our way to the Shchusev Museum through his personal meeting with David Sarkisyan.

The illustrations in this book would never have reached the standard required without the help of Pat Clough, who taught me the basics of Photoshop, and initial designs by Neil Eakapong. My sister-in-law Jean Dubowitz was responsible for finding out the fate of Sebök's wife and daughter through the Yad Vashem files and also the name of the relative who notified them. Through this information, our friends Jack and Gila Abrahamson were able to track down Sebök's wife's nephew, Alex Levin, in Israel, from whom I received copies of many family photos. Alex also put me in contact with his sister-in-law Irena in Moscow, who recently presented me with an original photo of Stefan and his Russian family.

In terms of the book itself, Sybil Banks, Jane Duncan, Penny Lewis, Debbie Nyman, Kati Vamos and Gerta Vrbova provided critical comments on drafts of the manuscript and offered helpful guidance on its presentation. I am also very grateful to my son Dan Dubowitz, who not only took a number of photographs of the illustrations for this book, but also encouraged me to keep going. I owe a special debt of gratitude to Yasmin and the late Dennis Sharp for encouraging me to publish this material, and to Malcolm Frost who prepared a superb *blad* which helped get it off the ground. However, the final push in bringing it all together and helping me to reach my final goal was achieved by my superb editor at the AA School of Architecture, Thomas Weaver. I am extremely grateful to him for the enthusiastic way in which he took this project on from the very beginning and the excellent input, vision and expert guidance he has provided, assisted by Pamela Johnston and Mollie Claypool. I also appreciate his coping with my volatile central European temperament and dyslexic spelling. Thanks also to Brett Steele, director of the Architectural Association School of Architecture, for generously agreeing to publish this material. My final bouquet is for the enthusiastic and very talented young designer Grégory Ambos for bringing it to final fruition against all the odds.

Last, but not least, my greatest thanks goes to my husband, Victor, who learned fast how to multi-task, being my photo-archivist, subeditor and moral supporter. Without his tolerance and patient reassurance I think I would have lost this book, to say nothing of my mind.

Credits

Akademie der Künste archive, Berlin © Lilly Dubowitz
10–11 (HHof-103), 12 (top) (HHof-103), 13 (top) (HHof-103), 61(HHof-103), 64–65 (HHof-103), 88 (HHof-104), 90–95, 92–97 (HHof-103), 96 (HHof-102), 98 (HHof-102), 136–37 (HHof-118)

Courtesy Bauhaus-Archiv, Berlin
20 (BA6241_1), 25 (BA6444), 27: gelatin silver reprint (BA6218/1), original at the Busch-Reisinger Museum, 34, 42 (top) (BA2563), 42 (bottom) (BA6446), 44 (BA2576), Leporello insert (BA5388), 86–87 (BA6380), 101 (BA6398/1), 102 (BA6398/5), 103 (BA6398/2), 104–13 are silver gelatin reprints: 104–05 (BA6765/7), 106–07 (BA6756/5), 108–09 (BA6756/1), 110–11 (BA6756/3), 112–13 (BA6756/8), 116–17 (BA2410), 120 (BA3531), 121, 122 (BA2561/1), 123 (BA2561/2), 124 (BA2560), 125, 138–39, 171, 189, 202

Courtesy Bauhaus-Archiv, Berlin © Lilly Dubowitz
12 (bottom) (BA6406/13), 13 (bottom) (BA6406/1), 45 (BA6422), 48 (BA2568), 49 (BA2573), 50 (BA2567), 51 (BA2575), 52 (BA2571), 54 (BA2572), 55 (BA6415/2), 56 (BA2574), 57 (BA2570), 58 (BA2573), 62 (BA6407/3), 63 (BA6407/3), 66–71 (GS19, Signature 613), 76–77 (BA6417), 78–79 (BA2559), 80–81 (BA2553), 82–83 (BA2558), 84 (BA7057)

Courtesy Busch-Reisinger Museum, Cambridge, MA
30–31 (GA24.19), 32–33 (BRM24.100), 36, 37 (BA2726/11), 39 (GA 48.223), 40–41 (GA48.11)

Courtesy Dresden Technische Hochschule Archiv: Student archives, Sebök Files, Inv No 9548
132–35

Courtesy © Haulis Lenke
22

© Hungarian National Museum
181 (1697–1954), 182 (1711–1954), 185 (66–156), 186 (66–2137)

Courtesy Petöfi Library, Budapest
46–47

Courtesy RGALI archives, Moscow
166, 168, 194–95

Courtesy Shchusev Museum, Moscow
159, 160–61 (PLA5073), 162 (PLA6598–6), 163 (PLA6598–5), 164–65 (PLA5073), 166–67 (PLA6598–1)

Courtesy Theatre Museum, Cologne
24 (TMK30807), 26–27 (TMK30807), 57, 115 (TMK5261), 118 (TMK5262b), 121 (TMK5262a), 126, 128–29

Family archives © Lilly Dubowitz
8, 14–15, 16–17, 19, 24, 74, 78, 91, 100, 130, 143, 158, 212

FSB Archives, Moscow
145, 148, 150–52, 154–56

Yad Vashem Archives, Jerusalem
168

Stefan Sebök with his Russian family, *c* 1936
(clockwise from top left) Alex, Israel, Mariya, Stefan, his mother-in-law and father-in-law